A Culture
of Corruption

Institute of Criminology Monograph Series

Series Editor: Professor John Braithwaite
Research School of Social Sciences, ANU

Aboriginal Perspectives on Criminal Justice, Chris Cunneen (ed) op

Doing Less Time: Penal Reform in Crisis, Janet Chan

The Man in White is Always Right: Cricket and the Law, David Fraser

The Prison and the Home, Ann Aungles

Women, Male Violence and the Law, Julie Stubbs (ed)

Psychiatry in Court, 2nd edition, Peter Shea

Gender, Race and International Relations: Violence against Filipino Women in Australia, Chris Cunneen & Julie Stubbs

Anatomy of a French Murder Case, Bron McKillop

Reform in Policing: Lessons from the Whitrod Era, Jill Bolen

A Culture of Corruption: Changing an Australian Police Service, David Dixon (ed)

Defining Madness, Peter Shea

The Institute of Criminology Monograph Series

A Culture of Corruption

Changing an Australian Police Service

Editor

David Dixon

Hawkins Press
1999

Published in Sydney by

Hawkins Press
A division of The Federation Press
71 John St, Leichhardt, NSW, 2040
PO Box 45, Annandale, NSW, 2038
Ph: (02) 9552 2200 Fax: (02) 9552 1681
E-mail: info@fedpress.aust.com
Website: http://www.fedpress.aust.com

National Library of Australia Cataloguing-in-Publication data:
    A culture of corruption: changing an Australian Police Service.

    Bibliography.
    Includes index.
    ISBN 1 876067 10 1

    1. New South Wales. Royal Commission into the New South Wales Police Service. 2.
    Police corruption. 3. Police corruption – Australia. 4. Police administration. 5. Police
    administration – Australia. I. Dixon, David. II. Title. (Series: Institute of Criminology
    monograph series).

364.13230994

Typeset by The Federation Press, Leichhardt, NSW.
        Printed by Ligare Pty Ltd, Riverwood , NSW.

Contents

Contributors   vii

1   Corruption and Reform: An Introduction   1
David Dixon

2   From Police Force to Police Service? Aspects of the Recent History of the New South Wales Police   6
Mark Finnane

3   Issues in the Legal Regulation of Policing   36
David Dixon

4   The Normative Structure of Policing   69
David Dixon

5   Police Culture   98
Janet Chan

6   Reform, Regression and the Royal Commission into the NSW Police Service   138
David Dixon

Bibliography   180

Index   197

Contributors

Janet Chan PhD is an Associate Professor in the School of Social Science and Policy, University of New South Wales. Her research interest has been in reforms and innovations in criminal trials, sentencing, penal policy and policing. Her publications include three monographs on media and deviance (with Richard Ericson and Patricia Baranek): *Visualizing Deviance* (1987), *Negotiating Control* (1989) and *Representing Order* (1991); *Doing Less Time: Penal Reform in Crisis* (1992); *The Price of Justice? Lengthy Criminal Trials in Australia* (with Lyn Barnes 1995); and *Changing Police Culture: Policing in a Multicultural Society* (1997). Her current research includes projects on the socialisation of police recruits, the impact of information technology on police organisations and managing the impact of media publicity on criminal jury trials.

David Dixon PhD is an Associate Professor in the Faculty of Law, University of New South Wales. He has published widely on policing and crime control. His publications include *From Prohibition to Regulation* (1991), *Law in Policing: Legal Regulation and Police Practices* (1997), and (with Dr Lisa Maher) *Anh Hai: Young Indo-Chinese People's Perceptions and Experiences of Policing* (1997), and *Running the Risks: Heroin, Health and Harm in South West Sydney* (1998). His current research includes projects on drug policing, 'zero tolerance' and new policing strategies, and police interviewing of suspects and video-recording of such interviews.

Mark Finnane PhD is Professor of History and Head of the School of Humanities at Griffith University, Brisbane. His major research interests include criminal justice history, especially the history of policing, punishment and the criminal law. His books include *Police and Government: Histories of Policing in Australia* (1994) and *Punishment in Australian Society* (1997). He is preparing a history of police unions and politics in Australia.

1

Corruption and Reform: An Introduction

David Dixon

History, regulation, and culture are key aspects of policing for those who would understand and reform it. This book presents essays on them that are based on research papers which were prepared at the request of the Royal Commission into the NSW Police Service. It concludes with a reassessment of the Royal Commission and of the fate of the reform process in the period since its Final Report. Despite its specific origins, this is not a book just about policing in New South Wales, or even in Australia. The issues and themes discussed here are of much more general interest and relevance. In providing critical analyses of history, regulation, culture and reform, it is hoped that this book will contribute to the Australian and international policing literature at a time when the impact and longevity of reform processes are once again in question in several jurisdictions.

As a result of a parliamentary motion by an Independent MP, John Hatton, the Royal Commission into the NSW Police Service was established in May 1994.[1] The conservative Coalition Government opposed the motion, but it was passed by an alliance of Labor and Independent members. To some extent, this division reflected a broader dichotomy in attitudes to police. On one hand, allegations against some well-known serving and ex-police officers were widespread: 'who bribed whom for what' had long been 'a commonplace of cynical Sydney conversation' (Clark et al 1978: 18). Hatton's speech in Parliament was constructed around a series of specific allegations of corruption. On the other hand, the New South Wales Police Service held itself out as a reformed organisation. Following a Royal Commission which had reported in 1981

---

1   Parliamentary Assembly, 11 May 1994, pp 2286-97 (J Hatton).

(Lusher 1981), the Service had been undergoing a process of reform, which included civilian oversight by a Police Board, strengthening the powers of the Ombudsman, redevelopment of police training, and commitments to decentralisation and community policing. At the centre of these efforts was a highly respected Commissioner, John Avery, who held office from 1984 to 1991.

The NSW Police Service presented a complacent face in the early 1990s and enjoyed some international recognition (Sparrow et al 1990: 72-7). An application for an Australian Quality Award (itself some indication of self-confidence) reported on a 10-year program of developing 'professional, accountable, responsible and innovative police officers' (NSW Police 1994: 3). The Police Service sought to 'perform as a "good corporate citizen"' providing 'leadership in the community', and considered itself to be 'at the fore-front of implementing Community-based policing world-wide and so are trail blazing' (ibid: 5, 7). John Hatton's motion to establish the Royal Commission was described by the then Minister of Police as 'an attack on the very institutions of our State that have achieved direct results in cleaning up the Police Service ... which ... may ultimately jeopardise the future of policing in New South Wales'.[2] The Deputy Premier said that, instead of 'launching this unwarranted attack on the NSW Police Service', John Hatton 'should be acclaiming the service as one of the finest in the world. He should be thankful for the law and order it provides to him and to the community'.[3] Police Commissioner Lauer told the Royal Commission that 'in today's Police Service, institutionalised corruption does not exist'.[4] This was a Police Service not in a trough of scandal, but at a height of self-confidence.

The Royal Commission's terms of reference were detailed and extensive, but most important was the first: the Commission was to inquire into 'the nature and extent of corruption within the Police Service, particularly of an entrenched or systemic kind'.[5] Unlike a typical English Royal Commission, this was not inquiry by committee. A single Royal Commissioner, the Hon JRT Wood was appointed.[6] The Commission

---

2   Ibid, p 2308 (T Griffiths)

3   Ibid, p 2316 (I Armstrong).

4   In evidence to the Royal Commission, quoted *Sydney Morning Herald*, 22 October 1996. Lauer resigned in February 1996.

5   Subsequently, the Commission's terms of reference were broadened to include both police corruption specifically associated with paedophilia and a general review of the law relating to paedophilia and pederasty, the criminal justice processes for handling allegations of paedophilia, and the protection from sexual abuse of children in the care of or under the supervision of Government agencies. This largely separate stream of inquiry produced two additional volumes of the Final Report (cf Wood 1997d; Cossins 1999). For the consolidated terms of reference, see Wood 1997c: App 4.

6   In 1996, a second commissioner, another judge, His Honour PD Urquhart, was appointed to help deal with the mass of specific inquiries.

collected written and oral evidence in the usual ways: but in addition, as discussed in Chapter 6 below, it undertook intensive investigative activity. The Commission produced two interim reports (Wood 1996a, 1996b) and a three-volume Final Report on corruption and reform in 1997 (Wood 1997a,b,c).

Tony Lauer's denial of institutionalised corruption came back to haunt him. As will be detailed in Chapter 6, the Royal Commission's investigation found a 'state of systemic and entrenched corruption' (Wood 1997a: 84), which extended throughout certain squads, across whole areas, and reached very senior officers. The two most notable features of the Royal Commission's approach were that, first, it defined corruption as including 'process corruption'[7] and, secondly, that it regarded the treatment of corruption as inevitably requiring a comprehensive analysis of the Police Service's structure, activity, and culture. This insistence on a broad approach has significantly influenced consideration of police corruption in England and Wales (Newburn 1999).

Since 1994, the NSW Police Service has been subject to searching investigation and critique. Public attention has focused upon dramatic revelations by the Royal Commission into the NSW Police Service of corruption and misconduct. However, it is clear that the success of the Royal Commission will depend upon the durability of the reforms which it recommended. In turn, this will depend upon the depth of its understanding of policing. It was in this context that the Royal Commission invited us to write research papers on key aspects on policing: history, culture, and regulation.

The book has a dual purpose (and audience). It is intended as a resource for policy makers and professionals by providing a convenient and critical introduction to the policing literature in Australia and overseas. We also hope that, by also making a significant contribution to that literature, it will be of interest to Australian and international academics, researchers, and students in policing and criminal justice, and public administration more generally. In addition, the final chapter's review of the Royal Commission's Report and of the subsequent reform process contributes to the continuing debate about the future of the NSW Police Service.

---

7   Defined as the 'male fide exercise of police powers' (Wood 1997b: 25), including mistreatment of suspects, unlawful searches and interrogations, planting of evidence, fabrications of confessions, and institutionalised perjury. Such corruption was 'routine' in some stations: 'the "police verbal" and "loading" of accused' had 'become an art form within certain sections of the NSW Police Service' (Wood 1996a: 39, 40). There was 'a widely held perception that the NSW Police Service is . . . a law unto itself' (Wood 1996a: 116).

While particular authors take full responsibility for specific chapters, the book is intended to constitute an integrated whole. The Royal Commission originally asked me to work full time in its research section. When this proved to be impracticable, I suggested that a research program could be best carried out by combining Mark Finnane's, Janet Chan's and my work. While the authors prepared individual chapters, we worked together in designing a package of research papers for the Royal Commission which complemented each other, and continued to exchange drafts, comments and ideas in putting this book together.

The second chapter is a critical study of the recent history of the NSW Police Service in the three decades leading up to the Royal Commission. Written by Australia's pre-eminent police historian, Mark Finnane, this chapter highlights the historical formation of policing, seen as a changing set of relations between police and the various communities and public interests which they seek, in recent parlance, 'to serve'. In Chapter 3, I discuss the legal regulation of policing through general analysis of the place of law in policing, and through specific examination of particular issues such as investigative practices, corruption and accountability. In Chapter 4, methods of regulation are addressed though my critical discussion of using codes of ethics, codes of practice, and other normative devices. Chapter 5 addresses the crucial issue of police culture. Written by Janet Chan, a leading international scholar in this area, this chapter subjects a concept (which has often been little more than a cliché in debates on Australian policing) to rigorous analysis and critique. Drawing on her extensive theoretical and empirical work, Chan provides a significant reformulation of the concept of police culture, and discusses the policy implications of this. In Chapter 6, I examine the Royal Commission's Reports critically and consider how the reform process has developed subsequently. The Royal Commission was given extensive, but largely distinct, terms of reference to investigate and report on matters relating to paedophilia, including police investigations, law, trial procedures, and child protection processes. This book excludes almost entirely consideration of the paedophile reference (see Cossins 1999, Wood 1997d).

Chapters 2 to 5 are presented without major change from the research papers which were prepared from the Royal Commission. There has been some editing and updating, particularly to deal with what now would be anachronisms. The original papers were designed according to briefs negotiated with the Royal Commission. Chapter 2 was commissioned to help fill a major gap in historical work on the New South Wales police. Chapters 3 and 4 met the Commission's request for specific treatment of a wide range of particular topics in the general field of regulation. This accounts for the relatively brief treatment of topics (such as the relations between drug prohibition and police corruption) which could, of course, have been investigated in much more depth. Here, as in the final chapter, the emphases are also dictated by my interests and expertise: notably, each of my chapters looks, from differing angles, at the issues of investigative detention and custodial interrogation. Chapter 5 provides an authoritative review of a topic which, it was clear from the beginning, was to be of great significance for the inquiry. It draws together material, some previously published elsewhere, in a presentation which was informative for the Royal Commission and should be of interest and assistance to current readers.

The Royal Commission graciously acknowledged the assistance provided by the research papers (Wood 1997c: A11). In turn, we express our gratitude to the Hon JRT Wood both for inviting us to contribute to the Royal Commission's work and for granting us permission to publish them.[8] Their appearance in this form has been delayed by various factors. Frustrating as it has been, this delay appears in retrospect to give some advantage. As the final chapter suggests, the reform process is experiencing considerable difficulties. Understanding of these may, we hope, be assisted by our papers.

---

8   Other research carried out for or by the Royal Commission included Chris Cunneen's paper on Aboriginal and police relations in NSW and a questionnaire survey of all serving officers and a selection of officers who had resigned from the Service within their first five years of service (see Wood 1997c: A30-4, 102-86).

2

From Police Force to Police Service? Aspects of the Recent History of the New South Wales Police

Mark Finnane

This chapter outlines some of the principal developments in the organisation of policing in New South Wales in the post-war years leading up to the establishment of the Royal Commission into the NSW Police Service. The approach taken here seeks to highlight the historical formation of policing, seen as a changing set of relations between police and the various communities and public interests which they seek, in recent parlance, 'to serve'. It focuses on some of the principal changes affecting the organisation of the NSW Police Service since its inception in 1862. In particular, my intention is to emphasise those ways in which policing has changed in recent decades and to provide a description of those changes.

It is important to note that this chapter cannot purport to offer much more than an account prepared on the basis of publicly available documentation, including published reports of government departments and inquiries, including Royal Commissions, the records of the NSW Parliament, newspapers, journal articles and some published books. The archives of the NSW police, excepting some personnel records, are closed to public access for 100 years, a policy which was adopted in the early 1980s and makes the record of this department one of the most closely guarded in Australia. Indeed it is easier these days to get access to the KGB archives than to investigate the 20th-century history of the New South Wales police. One result is that there has been only limited historical inquiry into the recent history of the New South Wales police, especially of the kind which can inform a chapter of this kind. The one exception is in an area of special concern to the Wood Commission, that of corruption, which has been the subject of a number of books, continuing journalistic commentary, and official inquiries.

1. Police and policing in New South Wales before 1960

The NSW Police Service has an organisational history extending back to 1862, when the Government of the day integrated a number of police forces into a single body under the control of an Inspector-General. Its functions in the 19th century were broadranging, including tasks of prevention and detection of crime, keeping the peace in the cities, towns and rural areas of the then colony and acting as an agency of government for a range of purposes, including the conduct of elections, the management of petty sessions in many areas and the collection of government statistics of population and production.[1]

The police of the day were recruited from farming and labouring backgrounds, with many also having migrated from earlier careers in policing in other countries, especially Ireland and England. Police were required to be literate, to commit themselves to almost continuous service and be moved at the Inspector-General's will from one end of the colony to the other. There is some evidence that turnover was high and that drunkenness and other offences, including occasional corruption, were the cause of dismissal in a large number of cases. Strict discipline, training, and more screening at recruitment may have reduced the volume of offending by the end of the century (Finnane 1990; Walker 1984).

Police in colonial Australia and after were in an ambiguous position. Indubitably they were agents of government. Their role in the management of industrial disputes in the 1880s and 1890s tagged them as such, although there is evidence that police leaders sought to play a more neutral role than the representatives of labour or employers may have wished (Walker 1986). On the other hand their tasks also included the much more mundane ones of watching out for truant children, arresting drunks (a major part of police business for many decades), controlling street brawls and occasionally (but reluctantly) attending to domestic and neighbourly conflict (Golder and Hogg 1987). Public attitudes towards the police have continued to reflect the conflict between the different

---

1   There is no substantial history of the New South Wales police. Major sources to date include Walker (1984), Moore (1991), a number of essays in Finnane ed (1987), Finnane (1994), and Seggie (1988).

kinds of roles police are expected to perform. As might be expected of an occupation that daily places its agents in situations of conflict (whether between individuals or groups, or between legal proscription of certain behaviours and popular condonation of the same behaviour), police have been the objects of fluctuating levels of public esteem.

The shaping of a police role in 20th-century New South Wales was affected by the reorganisation of Australian government and politics around the turn of the century. The prospect of being governed by those whom police had once been intended to control sharpened the sensitivity of senior police administrators to the vulnerability of their own office and of the future role and functions of police generally. Labour in government would require police who were not viewed as apologists and protectors of employer interests. Some police commissioners found the challenge difficult to accept. Most faced within their own ranks of subordinates an emerging solidarity of interests in wages and conditions, which found expression in the emergent police unions (Finnane 1994: ch 2).

A different kind of change was evident in the effective role played by police at this same time in seeking statutory change affecting areas of their work and responsibility. The policing of vice, for example, was decisively affected in New South Wales by changes to police offences laws in 1908, changes which were significantly informed by police advice. The changes enabled police to have a more direct control over the management of prostitution and gambling, in ways which have been argued to underlie subsequent corruption (Allen 1984; Golder and Allen 1979).

Social and industrial conflict from the 1910s to the 1940s saw police repeatedly embroiled in political controversy, at the same time as the leadership of the force became committed to following some of the changes which were being adopted in other countries under the objective of 'professionalisation'. In the inter-war years, a growing sophistication in the organisation of detection and surveillance placed New South Wales at the front of Australian police forces: fingerprint records for example became centralised in New South Wales, reflecting also some achievements in inter-agency cooperation signalled by the annual interstate conferences of police commissioners from early in the century.

During the inter-war years New South Wales police were twice at the centre of public attention in relation to the policing of vice. In the 1920s the outbreak of conflict between competing gangs of sly-grog and gambling rings led to sustained attention by crime detectives to the activities of those involved in the vice rackets. Such attention was facilitated by statutory reform which enhanced police powers for the control of criminal elements, through 'consorting' legislation. In spite of the evident success of police in reducing the incidence of open gang warfare and street violence, in the 1930s police involvement in the maintenance of illegal gambling was the subject of a lengthy inquiry over a number of years by Judge Markell (McCoy 1980; O'Hara 1988).

During these decades most Australian police became members of police unions, which succeeded in improving police pay and conditions in most states. While relations between police commissioners and unions were not always cordial, the police unions were active players in formulating political demands for resources and other matters affecting the fundamentals of policing, such as enhanced police powers. By the 1930s the police unions had joined the police commissioners, judiciary and executive government, as well as the print media, in the arena where matters of law and justice were fought out.

Although the NSW Police Association did not win registration as an industrial union of employees until 1946, the influence of the unions was evident before this, being felt over time not just in terms of claims for improved pay and hours of work, but also in respect of employee rights. From 1923 the police in New South Wales won the right to appeal against decisions of the Inspector-General in promotion or disciplinary matters. Attempts by the Inspector-General (retitled from 1935 the Commissioner of Police) to amend staffing policies, such as the principles governing promotion and transfer, were potentially the cause of conflict between union and police leaders, with the outcome sometimes influenced by the readiness of government to intervene. In 1941-2 relations between the Commissioner and the union executive deteriorated to such an extent that the New South Wales Premier, WJ McKell, assumed ministerial control of the police from the Chief Secretary and directed the transfer back to Sydney of police union officials who had been disciplined by the Commissioner, WJ MacKay (MacCormaic 1988; Brien 1996).

Much of the tension between the Commissioner and the police union at this time appears to have stemmed from the union's success in having the government approve the introduction of promotion by seniority in place of a system which was seen by many in the police to favour favouritism and nepotism. The disposition of the police unions on this matter is understandable in terms of their defence of the pay and service conditions of their members. It was not a position of unqualified faith in the seniority system, as is evident from the reported remarks of the president of the NSW Police Association in 1941:

> I am not holding with the seniority system as an ideal one. It probably is an evil system to a certain extent, but the system we now have [ie decisions by

the Commissioner which took account of ability as well as length of service] is more evil. (MacCormaic 1988: 30)

Nevertheless the strength of union resistance on such a crucial matter of police administration was such as to send a strong signal to future Commissioners wishing to assert the need for promotion by merit or more closely linked to the specific needs of the service.

The leadership of Commissioner WJ MacKay constituted a significant break between an organisation of policing which was strictly hierarchical, with little division of labour, and one which became from the 1930s for the next half century more internally differentiated. MacKay was an innovative administrator who sought to put in place methods of monitoring of police activity and effectiveness, such as 'crime maps' and 'crime graphs'. Up to the 1920s police administration was organised vertically, with small branches of detectives, water police and traffic police the only areas of specialisation. The enhancement of the Criminal Investigation Bureau from about 1929, under MacKay's leadership as Detective Superintendent, was marked by an expansion of detective numbers and a division of responsibilities according to the putative targets of police work: vice, pillage, homicide, arson, companies, etc. MacKay completed the expansion on becoming Commissioner in 1935. The changing composition of the police work force is indicated in the following table.

Table 2.1: Composition of NSW Police Workforce, 1925-88

Year	Total Police	Detectives	Traffic	% Detective/Total
1925	2997	52	208	2%
1935	3510	330	233	9%
1945	3468	453	145	13%
1955	4607	841	492	18%
1965	6051	913	861	15%
1970	7144	1176	1072	16%
1975	8382	1249	1088	15%
1980	9225	1401	1150	15%

Source: New South Wales Police Department, Annual Reports (1970, 1975, 1980 figures do not include scientific and technical staff – their allocation is unclear in the earlier published statistics)

One consequence of this specialisation of police functions was the emergence by the 1960s of police leaders and managers who had detailed knowledge of only one area of police work, a matter which was the subject of comment for example at the time of appointment of Commissioner Norman Allan in 1962. Another consequence was a high degree of corporate identity in particular elements of the police force, especially in the CIB. When Commissioner Avery and the NSW Police Board came to regionalise the police in 1988 and devolve specialised functions to the regions, much of the resistance of course stemmed from the long history and solid culture of work in such units. Reacting to the change, one time Superintendent at the CIB, Ray Blissett, wrote of the prospect that from 'whatever point of view, aesthetic, effective, practical, operational', the New South Wales police without a 'Criminal Investigation Branch will be like a ship without a rudder' (Blissett 1987).

In the post-war period the New South Wales police, like those of other states, benefited from a substantial expansion of personnel, a consequence in part of changing working conditions which reduced the average working week, and hence added to the planned personnel needs of services such as police. The changing demands of police work were reflected in different rates of expansion of the police workforce according to specialisation of function. Much of the expansion in numbers of police, for example, was taken up by the traffic branch in the two decades after 1945 (see Table 2.1 above).

By the beginning of the 1960s, the New South Wales police was a very large organisation of over 5200 officers as well as nearly 800 ancillary staff, including women police, who were not admitted as rank and file police until after 1965 (and not fully integrated in the force until 1978). Its tasks were focused on the processing of large numbers of minor offenders against good order and traffic regulations, the combination of which accounted for almost 80 per cent of total police activity in arrests and summons processed through petty sessions courts (NSW Police Department Annual Report 1960: 35). The public self-image of police was however preoccupied with the small number of incidents each year which gained wide media attention, such as the Graeme Thorne kidnapping in 1960 (the lead item in the 1960 Annual Report).

Yet for some time the police had been shaping a greater involvement with the community, for example in their role as educators of young people seen as potential citizens. This was evident in the Police Boys Club movement (initiated in Australia by Commissioner MacKay in the 1930s) and more recently by police involvement in road safety education in schools. A converse of this concern with the safety and interests of future citizens was the particular preoccupation with the policing of homosexual offences, which was a matter of regular comment by Commissioner Delaney (1952-62) and the origin regularly of over 400 charges a year around this time. The Commissioner noted as cause for concern in 1960 the 'incidence of offences denoting homosexuality and other forms of perversion' which among other threats posed 'possible serious threats to younger members of the community' (NSW Police Department Annual Report 1960: 13; Wotherspoon 1989).

Yet for the most part police activity appeared targeted at serious crime and the annual reports spend a disproportionate amount of space in describing the features of major crime, a phenomenon of police journals, including at some periods the police union literature, throughout the past fifty years. The relatively mundane world of much police work is consequently devalued and its particular challenges failed to receive attention during these decades. The mass processing of relatively trivial offences would only become a matter for concern when some of their adverse consequences (such as rates of death in police custody) were made visible in the 1980s.

While police had to meet a minimal standard of literacy and numeracy on recruitment there was a substantial emphasis on physical attributes. 'All appointees to the police force', parliament was advised in 1964, 'are accepted on the understanding that they will be able to perform general police duty, which necessarily requires a high standard of physical fitness'. There was a preference for those having at least an intermediate certificate (obtainable at about age 15 in New South Wales at that time). Yet beyond that the only admission examination consisted of a dictation test ('taken from the leading article of a daily newspaper') and simple arithmetic, 'together with two problems involving speed, cost or proportion' (Mr Renshaw, NSW Parliamentary Debates, 13 October 1964: 1131-2). Researching recruiting standards in the late 1960s Duncan Chappell and Paul Wilson found these standards to be common in Australasian jurisdictions, although the physical minima in New South Wales were higher than for other forces. Notably they reported that most police associations with whom they had discussed the height requirement were 'bitterly opposed to any reduction', usually on the basis 'that a policeman of good physique and height had a psychological advantage in his dealings with the public' (Chappell and Wilson 1969: 143).

The consensual profile of New South Wales policing during the Delaney years and into the 1960s did not wholly disguise an undercurrent of dissatisfaction with the performance and standards of police. Post hoc accounts of some police in recent years have suggested that there was a good deal of concern about various practices of policing in the 1950s. Ex-Superintendent Blissett claims that he was transferred back to uniform work in the 1950s after he objected to the practice of crime recording known as 'Paddy's Book', which served to disguise the real incidence of offences known to police and highlight only those cases 'cleared up' – a practice finally exposed during the Arantz case in 1970-71 (Arantz 1993: 11-12, 18-20; Blissett 1987: 16). Public inquiries during the 1950s had also exposed to public scrutiny the potential abuse of police power in interrogations, and evidence of police corruption in the licensing arena (Dovey 1954; Maxwell 1954). In neither case was there much public evidence of subsequent remediation of the problems that underlay such policing practices.

2. Policing New South Wales since 1960

During the 1960s the organisation and effectiveness of policing in New South Wales became a topic of increasing public comment and political disputation. Symptomatic of the change was the success of one of Australia's first law and order elections in which the Liberal Party's Robin Askin won the 1965 election against a longstanding incumbent Labor Government, on a platform which included a promise to employ more police to meet a rising threat of crime (Gardiner 1973: 38-40). Increasing political conflict in the following years centred on extra-parliamentary protest during the years of the Vietnam War, protests which involved the police in continuous political controversy. At the same time the Askin Government's commitment to supporting increased police numbers seemed confirmed by the outbreaks of crime gangland warfare which resulted in a number of shootings on Sydney streets in the late 1960s (McCoy 1980: 187-98).

This period was one marked also by the idiosyncratic leadership of Commissioner Norman Allan. Like Delaney before him, Allan presided over the police for some 10 years, although his departure in 1972 in the wake of the Arantz affair did little to salvage a waning reputation. Allan's style of leadership continued the emphasis on the pre-eminent and somewhat solitary office of Commissioner. One of the earliest amendments to police legislation during his office was that in 1964 which abolished the office of Deputy Commissioner, while adding a number of Assistant Commissioners (NSW Police Department Annual Report 1964: 26; *Police Regulation Amendment Act* 1964). Allan's tendency to take all control into his own hands was evident in his extraordinary personal involvement in the Wally Mellish affair in 1967 as well as in a persistent reluctance to delegate to others, even during a long period of absence on sick leave in 1964 (Gardiner 1973: 44, 84).

Allan became the target of severe public criticism as his tenure extended into the 1970s. Apart from matters of personal style, such as his procrastination in decision-making and delays in producing reports for a government which had helped to create a law and order agenda for itself, there was increasing media attention to evidence of rising crime on the one hand and police misconduct (including allegations of corruption and assault) on the other. The police control of crime statistics became itself a matter for public controversy. When in 1970 the *Sydney Morning Herald* obtained leaked crime figures from a police source, which suggested that crime was rising at a much faster rate than the Commissioner had reported to government, and that police effectiveness in solving it was minimal, the political consequences for the New South Wales police became unpredictable. Responding initially by supporting Commissioner Allan's attempt to have the 'whistleblower', Detective Sergeant Philip Arantz, certified and detained in a mental hospital, the government later started to withdraw support from Allan, eventually appearing to force his resignation. It also responded by initiating steps to establish a non-police agency for the collection of crime statistics and associated research, subsequently the Bureau of Crime Statistics and Research within the Department of the Attorney-General and of Justice (Arantz 1993; NSW Police Department Annual Report 1971: 5).

The public reputation of police by the early 1970s was therefore at a low ebb. This was in spite of the very substantial increases in police numbers and resources during the Askin period: in his 1970 Budget statement the Premier boasted that the addition of 200 more police would accumulate to an increase of 2127 in police numbers since his election in 1965, an increase of 31 per cent compared with population growth of 12 per cent in the same period (NSW Parliamentary Debates, 17 September 1970: 6075-5). Police ineffectiveness in responding to what was seen as increasing crime had been questioned by elements within the force itself. Continuing conflict between police and protesters had diminished public confidence in the management of the police and raised questions about its partiality. At the same time police conditions of service had been improved. Increased salaries in the December 1970 award supplemented an agreement in 1969 to pay overtime, in place of the previous system of working off overtime in lieu (NSW Parliamentary Debates, 2 August 1969: 125; NSW Police Department Annual Report 1970: 24), total police budget had expanded three fold during Allan's time and police strength had increased from 5500 in 1962 to 7700 in 1972.

Media commentary and political pressure in parliament raised concerns consistently during the Allan years about the standards of police administration, as well as abuse of police powers. These matters were typically raised in reference to particular incidents of police malpractice or allegations of corruption. In 1968 a Chinese restaurant owner, Mr Ng Biu Kuen, had been fined over possession of opium in circumstances which, he subsequently alleged, suggested that some police had planted it on his Dee Why premises. Ng had made allegations that senior police had been seen gambling in Dixon Street; he believed that police had targeted and threatened him as a consequence. His conviction had been overturned on appeal. Two of the police involved had been subject to departmental action after Customs police had questioned them over possession of two radios which they had taken from Ng's premises. A lengthy report by Commissioner Allan was tabled in the NSW Parliament in February 1969, refuting the need for a royal commission into the affair. It is noteworthy that the Premier of the day, Mr Askin, appeared less confident and sought further legal advice before announcing that there would not be a royal commission.[2]

Attempts to bring police administration and malpractice under more public scrutiny continued during the last few years of Allan's term as Commissioner. There was a recurring theme of questions being raised about the management of police misconduct throughout his term – the hospitalisation with severe internal injuries of a prisoner direct from Sydney Central Police Station in 1965 provoked parliamentary questioning of the investigation of police misconduct by internal police inquiry (NSW Parliamentary Debates, 16 November 1965, 1964). An assault by police on one Geoffrey Rixon in 1968, which resulted in a successful civil action against the police involved was another such occasion inspiring calls for judicial inquiry (NSW Parliamentary Debates, 7 October 1970: 6448-9). A further attempt followed in December 1971 when the Leader of the Opposition moved to establish a Select Committee to 'inquire into all aspects of police administration'. The precipitating occasion was the suspension of Detective Sergeant Arantz following his release of crime statistics to the *Sydney Morning Herald*. More generally it was noted that there appeared to be a crisis in morale in the force, with 111 police having been dismissed since January 1969 and other reports of dissatisfaction and unrest in the ranks. The report which informed this parliamentary comment had noted that there had also been 360 resignations in the same period, many of them to 'avoid charges of dismissal' (*National Times*, 5-10 March 1973, p 6). Reference was made to 'widespread public criticism and cynicism' which placed in jeopardy 'the good

---

2   NSW Parliamentary Debates, 18 February 1969, 3686; 19 February 1969, 3749; 26 March 1969, 5128; 27 March 1969, 5244; *Sydney Morning Herald*, 27 March 1969.

reputation of the police force'. Predictably the government was not moved to support the initiative (NSW Parliamentary Debates, 8 December 1971: 4091-4). In the wake of this parliamentary rebuttal of moves for an inquiry, however, the government's support for Commissioner Allan appears to have evaporated, and he announced his impending retirement early the following year (Gardiner 1973: 209-10).

The parliamentary reference to dismissals appears to have been well founded – by the end of Allan's time the rate of dismissal of errant police appears to have increased, particularly in proportion to some decline in departmental disciplinary charges (see Table 2.2). The published annual

Table 2.2 Police Disciplinary Charges, NSW 1960-85

Year	Departmental action	Criminal charge	Number of police dismissed
1960	106	6	18
1961	111	10	12
1962	109	12	11
1963	141	6	19
1964	122	17	23
1965	92	17	24
1966	162	30	46
1967	150	18	30
1968	172	20	25
1969	136	27	32
1970	158	38	41
1971	108	27	52
1972	116	16	72
1973	64	17	27
1974	45	10	13
1975	35	9	10
1976	40	22	17
1977	41	17	20
1978	28	22	22
1979	60	27	19
1980	23	21	14
1981	30	26	4
1982	72	26	23

Source: New South Wales Police Department, Annual Reports (1982 figure is for 18 months to June 1983); evidence for later years is not available in the Annual Reports (although some evidence is available in the annual *Report of the Internal Affairs Branch* during the 1980s)

reports do not usually indicate the nature of charges leading to dismissal, beyond a solitary reference to 'charges ranging from withdrawing from duty to stealing'. However, information tabled in response to a parliamentary question in 1972 suggests that 44 police were dismissed between 1965 and August 1982 for 'soliciting or accepting a bribe' (NSW Parliamentary Debates, 6 September 1972: 763-4 (qn of Mr Mallam)). While much of Allan's leadership was focused on the cultivation of a highly defensive public posture which sought to minimise damage to police image rather than provide answers to legitimate queries and concerns, it is evident that behind the scenes other responses to police behaviour may have been in play. Further, to the extent that the annual reports present a public profile of police priorities, there was change over time in the presentation of police business. In place of the emphasis on police crime work which had characterised Delaney's reports, the later years of Allan's leadership saw an emphasis on the range of police functions, with little attention to the 'crime stories' of earlier years. The change is evident in the 1969 Annual Report with its (rather overblown) preamble pointing towards a 'servicing the community' objective:

> The New South Wales Police Force is in touch with almost every aspect of the lives of the 4½ million inhabitants of the State. The duties of its members are varied, onerous and often dangerous. As well as carrying out their primary responsibility of preventing and detecting crime, they save life, protect property, aid those in difficulty or distress, and instruct and guide the young in the ways of good citizenship.

Management rhetoric also informed the 1969 report, with a formal division into areas of 'operations, administration and training' (NSW Police Department Annual Report 1969: 4).

This is consistent with another aspect of Allan's leadership, which was somewhat at odds with conventional policing in Australia. In a period where police shootings were attracting national attention (Harding 1968), Allan's unusual management of the Wally Mellish siege emphasised a non-violent outcome. The extent to which he was prepared to put his own reputation in the line in this way (the prolonged siege during which Allan arranged and attended Mellish's wedding in the siege house attracted much media attention and mirth as well as dismay in police ranks) suggests at the very least a readiness to assert a different view of policing at this time (Gardiner 1973: 218). But if this was part of a larger vision of a new style of policing, it was not one which he or anyone else in the New South Wales police at this time seemed ready to articulate. There was through the 1960s some sense in Australian police circles of the need to attend to the relations between police and public, reflected to a degree in Allan's attention to 'public relations'. But there was also disagreement among police as to what this would mean in relation to fundamental issues of citizen rights and police powers (see Hawkins 1963) – the formal commitment to community policing as an overriding philosophy was some way off.

During the 1970s public debate and dispute about the role of police in New South Wales increased. Increasing evidence of an organised drug trade had already prompted calls in 1969 by community leader Reverend Ted Noffs for stronger action against drug trafficking (NSW Parliamentary Debates, 19 February 1969: 3750). In the early 1970s concerns about the management of licensed premises and the poker machine industry focused attention on the involvement of criminal elements in New South Wales clubs. When Mr Justice Moffitt was appointed to inquire into 'allegations of organised crime in clubs' in 1973-4, the police responded defensively. In an extraordinary move by the police department it was submitted to the inquiry that Moffitt not voice publicly in his report any adverse findings that he might draw against the police. It was a submission he dismissed since 'to criticise and correct will in the end enhance rather than diminish the respect for the Police Force' (Moffitt 1974: 11, para 39).

Such police responses were symptomatic of a mentality that found it difficult to accept public criticism. Questioning of the performance and effectiveness of police nevertheless continued to characterise public debate about crime and policing, especially in the period leading up to the 1976 return of the Labor Party to government, under the leadership of Neville Wran. In contrast to the generally supportive disposition of the Labor Party towards police during their previous term in government, a new approach was evident, especially in the readiness of the government to address civil liberties concerns in relation to policing. Wran (in whose portfolio as Premier the police were located) intervened early to direct the police vice squad not to vet art exhibitions and called for a report from the Commissioner on a police raid on a commune in northern New South Wales (NSW Parliamentary Debates, 1 September 1976: 414-5). Labor policy to extend the powers of the Ombudsman to investigate citizen complaints against the police was a subject of early discussion between the Premier, the Police Force and the Police Association (NSW Parliamentary Debates, 7 October 1976: 1579). The government was also preparing a significant reform of statutory powers of police in relation to a wide range of street and other summary offences, which resulted in 1979 in the repeal of the Askin Government's *Summary Offences Act* 1970, decriminalising some offences and redefining others. The response of the police, especially through their vocal Police Association, was hostile. It has been argued that police in some districts engaged in selected policing of street offences in an effort to embarrass the government (Egger and Findlay 1988).

Another concern of the new government was the leadership and administration of the police force. There was not only ongoing criticism of policing practices by civil liberties groups and other bodies (including professionals whose work acquainted them with police abuse of power, such as lawyers criticising policing of Aborigines (NSW Parliamentary Debates, 16 September 1978, 1264; 18 September 1978, 1975)). Early in Wran's period of office, a commission of inquiry was being canvassed as a way of exposing police administration to public scrutiny, to address the reorganisation of the force which was seen as being 'top heavy, over-centralised, and ... not getting the right recruits'.[3] The difficulties of achieving reform were compounded by a contrast which was evident between their position under a critical Wran Government and what many police viewed as the supportive attitude of the Askin Government. According to a former Liberal Government minister Askin had known the 'political value' of the police, cultivating them 'as part of his electoral policy':

> He always said that despite what the intellectuals say there are seven or eight thousand police out there trusted by the community. They're wanted on P & C committees, on the cubs and scouts. Their influence in the community was important for the Liberal vote electorally. (P Coleman, quoted in Marr 1976)

The Police Association concurred in this view of the Askin years (Marr 1976: 23). The contrast was seen in 1976 as one which required Wran to proceed not too hastily.

An indication of the depth of problems which formed the background to the Lusher Inquiry was evident in the very matter of police leadership, which became over time a matter of real difficulty for the Wran Government. Allan's successor Commissioner Fred Hanson was undistinguished in his leadership (and later subject to allegations of corruption)[4] and when he retired in 1976 he recommended to the government the appointment of Assistant Commissioner Mervyn Wood. During a decade in which there was constant criticism of police inaction on gambling and prostitution, Wood's early statements to the media on his

---

3   M Cass, quoted in *The Bulletin*, 6 November, 1976, p 25.
4   An unappreciative biographical commentary (by Bruce Swanton and Lance Hoban) in the *New South Wales Police News* notes that 'Hanson served as Commissioner for a brief four colourful, controversial years, generally an unproductive, cavalier and intemperate regime which contributed minutely to the welfare, reputation and progress of the Police Service' (1990: 33).

priorities reflected a complacency that was disarmingly frank. Interviewed in the *Sydney Morning Herald* after six months in office as Commissioner, Wood avowed that:

> Police are a product of their own environment. I'll work with complaints. I'll honestly turn a blind eye to something that's technically wrong so long as other people are not being inconvenienced.... It's a big city and you can't drive everything underground. You're foolish to try.

Hence it was better, he suggested, to tolerate 'social offences' by which he meant prostitution, SP betting 'and so forth'. On the 'crime solution rate' which he put 'in the 30s – 30 percent' he elaborated that 'you invariably find that the man invariably gets caught'. Readers concerned about police corruption would not have been reassured by Wood's response to a question on whether police corruption 'is inevitable':

> Of course, you must remember that some police get a lot of temptations that you wouldn't get in other vocations. Are we any more corrupt than any other section of society? No. Definitely not. There's an old expression: 'We're all thieves at heart'. We'll all steal from the income tax department. You don't see too many extremely wealthy police. (*Sydney Morning Herald*, 1 July 1977, p 7)

Directions by the government to close gaming casinos were publicly resisted by Wood, who was also subject to political criticism for associating with club and casino operators. The legalisation of gaming casinos was early the subject of an inquiry by EA Lusher QC, appointed to the task by the Wran Government soon after its election (Lusher 1977). But this did not address continuing maladministration of the force. Further allegations of corruption led eventually to Wood's resignation in 1979.[5]

Around this time it was evident that relations between police and government were exceedingly poor. The Government had a low regard for the capacity of the police force to reform its administration and to address the constant stream of allegations of misconduct and corruption, especially in relation to the regulation of drugs, gambling and prostitution. The police faced a government that by 1979 had broadened the powers of the Ombudsman to review complaints against police, and instituted a repeal of the *Summary Offences Act*. In marked contrast to the experience of the Askin-Allan years, police-government relations were continually in tension and the Wran Labor Government had shown it was prepared to direct police to take a different approach to law enforcement than in the past.

---

5   NSW Parliamentary Debates, 16 August 1979: 311-17 (speech by Mr John Hatton) canvasses some of the context of Wood's resignation. See also Wilkinson (1979: 10).

3. The Lusher Inquiry

This background informed the framing of the terms of reference of the Lusher Inquiry into Police Administration, appointed in June 1979. Mr Justice Lusher, who had previously inquired into the legalisation of gaming, was appointed by the Wran Government to inquire into the 'structure of the administration of the New South Wales police force', a task which the government had committed itself to on the day of Wood's resignation (NSW Parliamentary Debates, 14 August 1979: 49). While initially Lusher was asked to report by the end of 1979, the magnitude of the task was such that he was given a Commission in November 1979 to inquire into not only the structure of police administration, both of the police force and the police department (the public service arm), but also into 'the structure of the relationship between the Police Force and the Executive Government'. In the latter task, Lusher was being asked to look at territory which had been explored in other states during the 1970s, especially in South Australia, as well as in academic and political commentary on that relationship (Plehwe and Wettenhall 1979).

The Lusher Inquiry lasted 18 months, with an exhaustive scrutiny of police administration in particular. The recommendations informed subsequent restructuring of the New South Wales police in such a substantial manner that they bear some outlining.

Conscious of developments in management theory over recent decades, Lusher described an organisation in which long-established patterns of hierarchy had stifled the capacity for innovation and responsiveness. Commencing with a discussion of police functions, he found a lack of definition of police objectives in the statutes and rules of New South Wales police administration, which contributed to confusion over the police's appropriate role. Clarifying the definition of police services would help the Force to set objectives that were realistic and also subject to performance assessment over time. He entered numerous cautions against the police assuming an inflated sense of their powers and duties, recommending that the formation of 'special squads' for the control of civilian disorder should require ministerial approval and surveillance (Lusher 1981: 55). Further, Lusher appealed rhetorically to what is commonly known as the 'Peelite' vision of police and community as one and the same thing:

> it is by the maintenance of the relationship and balance between the community and the police that an acceptable degree of law and order can be maintained with the least stress, that rights and duties can be sustained and a peaceful and safe community be maintained. (Lusher 1981: 46)

This idealised view of the interdependence of police and community in a democratic society was subsequently to shape the organisational rhetoric of police restructuring in New South Wales.

Lusher's investigations to some extent took place in an action-learning context. Already there were elements of change in the police force as he observed it, and these proceeded while his inquiry moved to its conclusion. Nevertheless, the Report's major recommendations required government direction and resourcing. The changes recommended were of two kinds, one being concerned with the macro-organisational structures, while the other addressed matters of administration within the force, especially concerning personnel management.

In addressing the macro-organisational issues, Lusher had been asked to attend to the relations between government and the Commissioner. His view was that police were independent of government, with a duty to enforce the law, which meant they must operate free of the direction of government. The Minister's responsibility was to provide the resources and to ensure that 'police act efficiently and responsibly and according to law'. It was a position with substantial legal authority behind it, but somewhat at odds with that adopted in another recent inquiry in South Australia, where Mr Justice Bright had acknowledged the reality of political direction of some policing decisions in recommending their formalisation as Ministerial directives to the Commissioner (Plehwe 1973). Moreover, Lusher's view of the accountability of police to law and of the availability to ordinary citizens of legal remedies for abuse of police powers was sanguine:

> The protection against excess or abuse by police of their powers, by and large, is to be found in the Courts and it is to be expected that the citizen is not likely to suffer such abuse lightly. The wrongful arrest, the unauthorised assault, the unlawful detention or imprisonment, the unauthorised search and the general misuse of power and authority, are readily subject to remedies at law. (Lusher 1981: 720)

Lusher's regard for the notion of constabulary independence influenced significantly his recommendations for the structural reform of police management and relations to government. In considering the options, he canvassed the idea of an Advisory Board which might serve as a means of advising both the Police Force and the Minister. It is telling that one of his reasons for rejecting this idea was that it would be likely to be ignored by the police. The possibility of such a Board persuading a Minister of the wisdom of particular policies might be:

> difficult, given the long standing position of power enjoyed by the Police Force and the fact that the police could argue that the Board's advice was

> theoretical and remote from the practical difficulties of police operations. (Lusher 1981: 787)

In considering the merits of an 'Executive Board' Lusher cautioned against a model which might ignore 'the continued independence of the Police Commissioner and the Police Force in their duties relating to law enforcement and the discretions related thereto'. At the 'operational level it is considered that the chain of command and ultimate responsibility should be left in the hands of the Police themselves' (Lusher 1981: 788).[6]

Consequently Lusher proposed a Police Board, comprising three members, including the Police Commissioner, which would be responsible to the Minister and have functions and responsibilities including formulation of advice to the Minister on police matters, including law enforcement, and development of policy on personnel matters especially (Lusher 1981: 791-3). The proposal was an innovative one in Australia where the solitary position of the Commissioner as the source of advice to the government on police policies had been in place since the 1860s.

The Inquiry provided extensive guidance for subsequent reform in matters of internal administration, including especially policies and practices affecting personnel recruitment, promotion, transfer and discipline. Lusher concluded that the relationship between the rank system and the job classification system displayed 'anomalies, double standards and inefficiencies which underlay 'many of the other problems in the overall Police administration'. The ultimate solution was to be found 'in a total revision of the relationship between ranks, jobs and promotion' (Lusher 1981: 413). The reforms recommended had the objective of producing a Police Force which was more flexible, more professional in its personnel management and notably more focused on its primary responsibilities, however these might be defined.

In this last respect Lusher's recommendations for a clearer statement of the mission of the NSW Police Force can be seen as having provided a strong sense of direction of the police over the following decade in which the Force became a 'Service' and sought at the management level to clarify functions and responsibilities and establish performance targets. At the same time, Lusher did not disguise his view that achieving change from within would be difficult, especially in the areas of training of police personnel for management functions rather than looking always to operational performance as the core of police work. The rationale for a Police Board was in part to establish a means of

---

6   Hogg and Hawker (1983) take issue with Lusher's views on the implications of a notion of the constable's sole and disinterested accountability to law.

producing some outside advice to police administration. If reform focused only on change from within it 'runs the risk of perpetuating the insularity which now pervades the Police Force' (Lusher 1981: 61).

4. From police force to police service after the Lusher Inquiry

Many of the changes introduced to New South Wales policing after the Lusher Inquiry were completed under the leadership of Commissioner John Avery. Almost simultaneous with the Lusher Report was the publication of Avery's influential book, *Police – Force or Service?* in which then Inspector Avery argued the case for a review of the fundamentals of policing in Australia. As he put it:

> powerful social forces have produced a state of affairs where social control no longer resides in the body of citizens and . . . some effort should be made to reverse that process.

What was needed was a 'closer relationship between the police and the citizens involving a responsibility to assist each other to maintain the peace in the community' (Avery 1981: 73, 77). Drawing on surveys of police work in a number of Sydney police stations, Avery confirmed other international police research which showed that 'law enforcement' provided only about a fifth of the public calls for police assistance with the majority of calls relating to 'service'. Police were little trained for their role of 'providers of service to the community' as opposed to law enforcement or peacekeeping (Avery 1981: 50-7). The analysis provided an empirical as well as theoretical justification for refocusing policing as a task shared by police and citizens. The later development under Commissioner Avery of a commitment to 'community policing' was an important change in the police mandate in New South Wales as elsewhere. Predictably it was also a change that provoked resistance in the ranks of police who had been recruited and trained in a quite different environment, one which presumed police 'ownership' of the policing domain.

The emergence of a mandate for community policing was only one aspect of the changes which affected New South Wales policing after Lusher. But the principal matters affecting police organisation were as follows.

The establishment of the Police Board in 1983 provided a vehicle for instituting change in police administration, especially in reviewing the system of promotion by seniority, in the area of education and training (with the establishment of the new Police Academy in Goulburn) and in reforming the modes of centralisation and inflexibility that had characterised administration (Jackson 1988). In that task the Board was assisted by the new perspectives on policing introduced by the first Commissioner appointed by recommendation of the Board, John Avery.

The focus of the NSW Police Board on matters of appointment and leadership in the organisation was understandable following the problems identified by Lusher. These concerns were given extra weight by the continuing undercurrent of controversy over allegations of police corruption and misconduct during the period 1981 to 1983, years in which a Deputy Commissioner, Bill Allen, was allowed to resign following an investigation over his links with gambling interests, and during which there was continuing conflict between the police and the Ombudsman over the adequacy of police internal investigation of complaints. A result of the latter tension was the enactment in 1983 of a new system for investigation of complaints against police, in which the Ombudsman was allowed to conduct an independent investigation as well as continue to review police internal affairs inquiries into such matters.

The enhanced powers of the Ombudsman, together with the non-police majority membership of the Police Board constituted a new environment for New South Wales policing. External oversight or monitoring had been resisted by police in New South Wales as elsewhere. Its future impact on policing practices was uncertain, in a context in which the legitimacy of a role for non-police agencies did not appear to have the consent of significant elements of police (Page and Swanton 1983).

This changing organisational environment was complemented from 1987 by a major restructuring of the New South Wales police. The central element of this change was the establishment of four police regions along with the progressive devolution of centralised functional police agencies and squads (including CIB, Traffic, Internal Affairs, etc). As Commissioner Avery explained it, this change followed from the adoption by government of 'Community Based Policing as the principal operational strategy'. The emphasis of the new approach to policing was said to lie in the delivery by each police officer of 'service', according to a Statement of Values placing an emphasis on 'integrity above all', and working with the community (NSW Police Department Annual Report 1987: 6, 24). Regionalisation, which proceeded in the following year, involved a flatter organisational structure, thus addressing a longstanding criticism of the Police Force as overcentralised with too many levels of command. The regions were to be 'microcosms' of the whole organisation, sharing all functions equally – the geographical design involved regions which extended from Sydney to the State borders in four directions, thus encompassing approximately equal populations, each with a mix of urban and rural communities.[7]

The reasons for the change were administrative as well as policy-led. The major problem, it was said in 1987, was that 'functional groups, for example CIB, Traffic, overlay a geographical management structure'. Regionalisation of police functions would help to clear lines of 'authority, responsibility, accountability and communication' and assist the development of greater district autonomy, strategic planning and program budgeting (NSW Police Department Annual Report 1987: 28).

These changes were strongly endorsed during the 1980s by the Labor Government of New South Wales, which had established the Lusher Inquiry and sought to implement its recommendations, including meeting significant budget implications that involved an expansion of police numbers (see Table 2.3).

Table 2.3: Police Strength and Expenditure, 1960-90

Year	Strength	Strength per 100,000	Expenditure	$ per cap
1960	5260	137.2	130689	34.08
1965	6120	146.6	161913	38.79
1970	7144	158.0	245101	54.20
1975	8411	172.2	356071	72.90
1980	9091	179.0	360855	71.06
1985	10608	193.7	393906	74.40
1990	12593	na	na	na

Source: SK Mukherjee et al, *Source Book of Australian Criminal and Social Statistics, 1804-1988*, Canberra: AIC, 1988: 139-40; NSW Police Annual Report, 1991-2: 114

However, the important changes in leadership and direction under Commissioner Avery did not reduce the political temper surrounding policing in New South Wales. The Commissioner's annual reports registered a continuing struggle to address corruption, with a strengthened activity in Internal Affairs and a constant stress on the importance of integrity as a value in personnel recruitment, training and promotion decisions. In spite of the changes there were repetitive charges in Parliament and the media throughout the 1980s of the incidence of corruption, even while politicians and other observers recognised that major reform was under way. State and Federal inquiries into matters of policing in areas such as drugs, prostitution, and organised crime all provided some evidence and many allegations regarding corruption in policing.

---

7   On 'microcosm' see evidence of Asst Commissioner Jarratt, RCNSWPS, 13 December 1994: 538 (29-34).

Corruption of this kind was not however the only issue on the public agenda affecting New South Wales policing. The role of police in the arrest, prosecution and incarceration of Aboriginal people in New South Wales became the focus of political agitation and then a major Commonwealth and State Royal Commission from 1987 to 1991. The role and practices of police crime investigators and prosecutors were similarly placed under intense scrutiny in the inquiries into the conviction of the Ananda Marga sect members in 1986, and into the arrest and charging of ex-police officer Harold Blackburn in 1989. And the activities and role of police special squads, such as the TRG and SWOT teams became the focus of further controversy in the inquiries into the fatal shooting of David Gundy in 1989 and the shooting of Darren Brennan in 1990.

Other changes in the political environment affecting the New South Wales police (eg the changing and expanding roles of non-police agencies) are discussed in more detail later in this chapter. The enactment of a new *Police Act* in 1990 may serve here as the conclusion to this overview of the history of the NSW Police Force since 1960.

As outlined by the Minister in Parliament the Police Service Bill aimed to replace the bifurcated Police Force-Police Department with an 'integrated Police Service' with the following 'main purposes':

> reinforcement of the successful policy of community based policing by stressing the concept of service to the community; overcoming the problems associated with a bifurcated work force and related outmoded internal working arrangements by a fully integrated staff while retaining the special role of operational police; reflecting the Government's initiatives in modernising the management of the public sector; upgrading the role of the Police Board in relation to the Police Service; and replacing over-regulatory constraints on police with a modern values-orientated approach. (NSW Parliamentary Debates, 2 May 1990, 2121)[8]

Taking up Lusher's recommendation for a clearer statement of the role and functions of police, the legislation identified the 'mission' of the Police Service – 'to have the police and the community working together to establish a safer environment by reducing violence, crime and fear' (*Police Service Act* 1990, no 47, s 6(1)). The *Police Service Act* thus sought to consolidate in a new statute the changes in police organisation which had taken place since the Lusher Inquiry. In endorsing the change of name from Force to Service the new law aspired to a different

---

8   Hon EP Pickering, Minister for Police and Emergency Services; cf comments by David Dixon in Chapter 3, below, on the significance of the shift from law as the 'prime legitimator of policing' to a values, problem-solving and community-oriented approach.

conception of policing to that which had prevailed thirty years before. The conscious commitment to a notion that the police role was one of service to a community rather than a function of government in the control of crime and disorder was perhaps more symbolic of a longer term ambition than descriptive of a completely altered police organisation. Certainly there remains a contradiction between a rhetorical commitment to service and both the reality of a significant proportion of everyday police work in law enforcement, on the one hand, and the agendas of 'law and order' politics on the other. This is not to deny the value of an aspiration to 'serve the community' with a new style of policing. But we need to remember that this aspiration is subject to competing pressures arising both within the police organisation itself (from those committed to a law enforcement style of policing) and from outside forces, including politicians and the media.

5. Corruption and reform in New South Wales policing – some historical comments

Corruption has been a constant feature of public debates as they affect the organisation of Australian policing since the decades preceding the formation of centralised police in the middle of the 19th century. We have noted already the continuity of allegations of corruption as they have impinged on 20th-century New South Wales policing. What was unique in the Wood Commission's inquiry was the focus on police corruption as itself the problem. The reasons for this focus may be examined historically through documenting the way in which corruption has previously been addressed.

It has been argued in the main historical account of organised crime in New South Wales that prior to the Second World War such crime was of limited significance, and easily addressed through rigorous policing. Police corruption was an element in sustaining criminal activity but not on a scale which emerged in the post-war period (McCoy 1980). It is likely, however, that such a view underestimates the incidence of police corruption seen in broader terms as misconduct, whether for immediate personal gain or in fulfilment of other objectives such as facilitation of police work. It has to be said that there has simply been too little historical investigation of such conduct for us to be confident in making judgments about the extent of misconduct or gross corruption. Such investigation would be possible to a limited degree through closer scrutiny of available police personnel files – though it should be noted that such inquiry by independent researchers would not presently be possible in New South Wales owing to restrictions on access to police records. The impression of this writer from a scan of personnel records in Queensland up the 1920s suggests a relatively high frequency of incidents of misconduct leading to internal investigation. These would be handled, as they were in New South Wales up to the 1960s, strictly by line supervisors with reports going up the Commissioner of Police for determination of finding and punishment (Finnane 1994: ch 9).

The incidence of charges under the 'disciplinary' heading, which have been noted earlier (see Table 2.2), signifies the breadth of definition of misconduct, including corruption. Some charges were brought under the head of breaches of rules and instructions; others might involve criminal conduct leading to prosecution. The result of a charge might range from admonishment, through fines and demotion, to dismissal. In the absence of further investigation it is impossible to determine the proportion of incidents which were investigated by the police on the basis respectively of external or internal information. Both sources were certainly present, and the few public inquiries into the behaviour of police prior to the 1960s show the capacity of citizens to draw attention to abuse of police powers and evidence of misconduct (eg, Dovey 1954).

The difficulties faced by individual complainants in the absence of the right kinds of political and institutional contexts, however, cannot be underestimated. The case of Ng Biu Kuen in 1969 (as discussed above) in which allegations of police corruption were handled internally and unconvincingly by the police was an indication of the barriers in the face of credible address to possible corruption issues. Nevertheless such incidents constituted a public airing of matters which had a chronic presence in popular knowledge of policing from at least the 1930s in Sydney. And it contributed to a political climate which can be seen to have resulted eventually in a succession of commissions of inquiry and the establishment of internal and external reviews of police conduct in the 1970s and 1980s, as reviewed earlier.

In respect of corruption, what characterised the approach of public inquiries prior to Wood? There has been no shortage of inquiries raising such issues, from the Moffitt Commission in 1974 through a spate of inquiries into drug trafficking and organised crime in the late 1970s and early 1980s to more recent investigations by the Independent Commission Against Corruption (ICAC).

An examination of these inquiries suggests that there have been two ways in which allegations of corruption have arisen. In one, there has been a focus on an area of regulation or of criminal offending in which corruption or misconduct of police was simply one symptom among others of the dysfunctional state of legislation or regulation. For example:

- The Moffitt Commission of Inquiry into 'Allegations of Organised Crime in Clubs' was highly critical of police procedure in investigations related to organised crime, including inter-agency cooperation and training matters. The object of the recommendations as they related to the police identified the need in establishing a reliable 'special squad of police' to 'minimise the chance of corruption of members of this squad or its standing being lessened by practices leaving members open to suspicion of corruption. It should be appreciated that they are likely to be the target for corrupt approaches' (Moffitt 1974: 136-7).

- The Royal Commission of Inquiry into Drug Trafficking (Stewart Commission) with its reference deriving from a number of governments (the Australian and New Zealand, New South Wales, Victorian and Queensland governments) provided almost unlimited capacity to make recommendations regarding the enforcement of the criminal law and the role of relevant agencies, arising out of its enquires into drug trafficking and associated corruption. More so than any other inquiry preceding the Wood Commission, the Stewart Commission explored the links between evidence of particular instances of corruption and the management of police. In considering 'corruption and complaints against police' it canvassed the recent record of Australian inquiries touching on police corruption and misconduct, and reviewed international strategies (especially in the USA, England and Hong Kong) to address the same. Its recommendations included one that 'The Commissioners of Police forces ... should be directed to insist strictly on command responsibility and accountability within their forces' (Stewart 1983: Rec 35, p 839). In also endorsing the direction of Lusher recommendations on the administration of the New South Wales police, the Stewart Commission helped to legitimise subsequent changes in police administration in New South Wales.

- The Select Committee on Prostitution (1986) was a parliamentary inquiry into the organisation of the industry and its regulation which identified the incidence of police corruption related to prostitution as one of the elements which required attention in any systematic review of the law. It considered there was evidence of a change in the nature of corruption involving street prostitution following decriminalisation of street soliciting, and that a further change in the law affecting brothels would 'significantly decrease problems of corruption'. In addition to law reform, the Committee recommended attention to organisational reform of police, including the Vice Squad and local stations (Rogan 1986: 226-8).

In the second kind of approach the matter of corruption has arisen as primarily an organisational matter, one which was capable of touching many areas of work in the police domain. The significant examples in New South Wales include:

- The Lusher Inquiry, in which corruption was briefly addressed as a symptom of the organisational culture of the New South Wales police, and a matter which would be best addressed through organisational change. Lusher was critical of the limited way in which police approached corruption on an individualised and legalistic basis, governed by the 'rotten apple theory'. Consistent with the emphasis of his Report on managerial reform, he drew attention to the failure of such an approach 'to deal with the matter in any sense as an institutional problem or managerial function'. He recommended instead a commitment to 'positive protective and vigilant management objectives and procedures' to address 'institutional corruption'. Such an approach would necessarily involve 'strict responsibility and accountability ... fixed in the officers and supervisors in the area where the activity is operating' (Lusher 1981: 643, 639). The Report was however somewhat vague in its calculations of what kinds of supervision and accountability would actually work. For example, would the following scenario painted by Lusher (1981: 639) address the problem of compliance with supervisory responsibility as a guard against corruption: 'officers and supervisors can be asked to certify in written periodic reports the state of their knowledge and belief with reasons as to the continuance or otherwise of the activity in their area'? Such a mechanism of supervision has in fact existed in policing, one of the most bureaucratised public services, for over a century, but without avoiding the very real likelihood that such procedures become routinised and purely formal. This is only to say of course that any administrative solution to the problem of corruption must be multifaceted and embedded in a deep knowledge of work practices.

- ICAC's Milloo Inquiry: A second example of a systemic treatment of misconduct and corruption issues was provided more recently in the ICAC investigation (known as Milloo) into the use of informants (ICAC 1994). This investigation involved a two part strategy, involving in the first place an inquiry into a number of case histories of the relationship between informers, police and others involved in criminal justice process. The second report outlined the process by which ICAC and the Police Service had jointly developed an 'Informant Management Plan', one which involved discussion with working police as well as calling on expertise in other areas. Although the longer term impact of such a process must await evaluation, the attention of this investigation to a management process taking account of the complex inter-play of law, police-work and administrative capacities of the Police Service, such as the quality and modes of supervision and training, was innovative and arguably provides a constructive model for future approaches to such inquiries.

The model of inquiry, review and policy development deployed in the ICAC Milloo investigation is consistent with the changing approach to the role of external agencies in monitoring police administration in recent years (eg the somewhat similar approach adopted by the Criminal Justice Commission in Queensland). This has been evident in the tendency to move from a *post hoc* legalistic inquiry with a punishment outcome towards a more pro-active and policy sensitive approach to dealing with the conditions under which misconduct, corruption and other abuses of process arise. (The changing relationship between the Ombudsman's Office in New South Wales and the Police Department – from a combative approach in the early 1980s to a more cooperative approach a decade later – might be another example.) The consequences of the Wood Commission's investigation and reports should enable some assessment of the effectiveness of such a structural approach to police misconduct. What is evident from past experience is that the process of public exposure of corruption and misconduct, followed by some policy recommendations without attention to the processes of implementation, has failed to guarantee a longer term remedy to the problems identified. In this respect it is notable that the Commission flagged its intention to work closely with the Police Service in seeking remedies to current problems[9] and such cooperation was evident in the Final Report.

6. Conclusion

This overview has described a transformation of police organisation and policing over the last three decades. If the Royal Commission unveiled a depth of corruption in significant elements of the New South Wales police, it is possible that this in part was made possible by the very magnitude of the changes which have occurred in the organisation of police during recent years. In summary, those changes have produced an organisation which is characterised by the following differences from 1960.

There has been a fundamental change in the police definition of their role and functions, from one focused on law enforcement and peacekeeping (above all rhetorically on crime fighting) to one focused on service to and cooperation with 'the community'. This change is now registered in both the organisation of police under statutory authority, and in the strategic planning and directions of police administration and operations.

There has been a significant alteration in the policing domain in respect of issues of accountability and monitoring. The institution of the Ombudsman's office in New South Wales in the 1970s together with a multitude of public inquiries into aspects of policing during the last two decades has placed policing in New South Wales under unprecedented scrutiny. The departure from a model in which the Commissioner had autocratic control and oversight of policing to one in which a Police Board with non-police membership had a significant role to play in policy preparation and advice constituted an important foundation for implementing change, even if experience proved this arrangement incapable of eradicating corruption.

There has been a gradual, if not yet decisive, change in the composition of the New South Wales police. Changed requirements in recruiting together with the institution of new expectations of education and training, as well as reform of promotion and personnel management generally, has altered the social composition of the police, including integration of women especially, dating from 1978.

---

9   RCNSWPS, 2 February 1995: 1419, re comments of Commissioner Wood. Note also the comment here by Asst Commissioner Schuberg that the most useful work in the ICAC Milloo investigation was 'when the Commission [ie ICAC] started to work with the Police Service to improve systems and methods'; and see also similar views of Asst Commissioner Jeff Jarratt, in evidence to RCNSWPS, 1 February 1995: 1375.

While major change is thus evident in terms of 'mission', accountability and personnel, all pre-conditions for an effective change in performance and direction, there remain other features of the policing environment which are more longstanding. They include the following.

The primary responsibility of the Commissioner for 'operational' matters remains in place, unchallenged by Lusher or subsequent changes. While it might be argued that the capacity of the Minister and the Board to give directions in policing matters generally was enhanced by statute in the wake of the Pickering-Lauer affair in 1992,[10] the Wood Commission reasserts police dominance of a widely if uncertainly defined 'operational' domain.[11] It has been demonstrated elsewhere that there is a considerable capacity in a police organisation to resist change in operational matters, even when this might be expected following adverse legal judgement (eg, Dixon 1997: ch 5).

Second, the industrial environment of policing has remained one which is characterised by the strong presence of police unionism. The NSW Police Association has played an important role in changing the conditions of employment of police since its establishment in 1921. The union is influential in representing police views to the media and in public fora. The regular appearance at its Annual General Meetings of both the Minister responsible for police and the shadow Minister epitomises the union's standing. In common with other Australian police unions the New South Wales body has in recent decades been very ready to take a public stand on issues of law reform and policing policies.

Third, in spite of the policy of community-based policing there appears to be still a deeply entrenched commitment to crime fighting and peacekeeping through coercion as the essence of police work. This tradition surfaces in conflicts between the development of a 'problem-based' approach to policing which has been seen as integral to the new strategies of community policing and the reactive and coercive response style which has led elements of the New South Wales police into repeated public controversy in recent years (eg in the instances of the killing of David Gundy, the shooting of Darren Brennan, and the Redfern 'raid' involving police and Aborigines in 1990). As a rhetoric of policing,

---

10 The amendment of the *Police Service Act* in 1993 removed the proviso of s 19(2) in the 1990 Act which provided that 'nothing in this Part affects the responsibility of the Commissioner for the operational command and day-to-day management of the Police Service' – this deletion would appear to involve some writing down of the Commissioner's 'independence' at least in so far as this had been given statutory recognition in 1990.

11 See Dixon, Chapter 6, below.

commitment to the latter style emerges in the police union literature as well as in the media more generally.

Fourth, the repeated public controversies over corruption in policing since the 1960s have shown no sign of diminishing. An important change in the political and organisational environment of policing has been the relatively greater success of opponents of corruption in bringing allegations to the point of public inquiry. A police organisational focus on corruption issues has been another innovation distinguishing the most recent decade from earlier ones. At the same time, in the absence of sustained research into the history of corruption and misconduct in Australian policing, it is almost impossible to determine whether the incidence of such practices is now greater or less than in earlier decades. The Wood Inquiry offered an unprecedented opportunity to assess this issue as a central concern rather than ancillary to other matters as has usually been the case in earlier public inquiries.

In sum, the recent history of the New South Wales police has been far from one of continuity of longstanding traditions and bureaucratic inertia. The rate of organisational change has been intense, at least at a senior management level. What remains to be assessed is how deep such change runs in the organisation.[12]

---

12   For evidence of limitations on change in the police 'culture' at operational level, especially in relation to 'community policing', see Chan (1997).

3

Issues in the
Legal Regulation of Policing

David Dixon

1. Introduction

This chapter seeks to explore some implications of a criminological truism. Deviance can be understood only in relation to normality: it is a relative concept. If we are to understand police corruption and misconduct, the starting-point has to be the designation of 'good' policing. This is not (or not only) to be found in formal statements (such as the *Police Service Act* 1990 s 6), but rather in the organisational practices and cultures of the police. As Punch suggests:

> when policemen[1] are accused of deviance, their riposte is frequently in terms of 'We were only doing our job'. This requires us to look at the nature of police work and at what policeman are asked to do as a routine and accepted part of the job. (1985: 202)

It is argued here that a fundamental problem in New South Wales policing has been a failure to clearly demarcate expectations of good and bad policing.[2] Too often, scandalised attention is devoted to specific instances of alleged corruption and partiality without first properly

---

[1] The choice of word is justified by Punch on the grounds that he had 'not found a single reference to corrupt policewomen' (1985: x). While the Wood Commission 'found relatively few women involved in corrupt practices' (1997a: 42), the 'previously clean reputation of Australian police women was sullied' by evidence collected by the Royal Commission (Prenzler et al 1996: 47). The Commission commented usefully on this issue (1997a: 42-3).

[2] See McConkey et al 1996. The NSW Police Service is not unusual in this respect: a common theme in much recent literature on policing has been identification of the need to reward good work, rather than (as has been the dominant tradition) to punish failings. For an influential statement, see Braithwaite 1992.

considering the normality from which they deviate. This chapter comments on the problematic designation of 'good' policing by examining specific areas of procedural and substantive law which were central to the Royal Commission's inquiry: respectively, the legal regulation of aspects of police investigative activity, elements of police accountability, and the prohibition of certain substances and services, often called 'victimless crimes'.

2. Law in Australian policing

It is important to situate police attitudes to law in the context of long-term trends in policing. The central mandate of police forces which were introduced or reorganised in the early and mid-19th century (in Australia, as well as in Britain and the USA) was the control and deterrence of public disorder and crime by means of preventative patrol. To this was added a diverse range of regulatory duties: the police were a convenient (and often the only) resource available to perform administrative tasks.

In the late 19th century, police forces sought to negotiate a monopoly over an area of state activity which would eventually allow them to be accredited as specialists or 'professionals'. This area was criminal law enforcement by means of detection and investigation. By identifying itself with the law, policing was able to benefit from the ideology of law's political autonomy. This was of particular significance in the USA, where self-presentation as law officers assisted police in attempting to distance themselves from the political influence and corruption of urban politics. A concrete expression of this movement was the emergence of 'full enforcement' statutes which, declaring it to be the duty of police to enforce fully the criminal law,[3] equated the exercise of discretion with abuse and partiality. The relationship between law and policing in the USA was strongly affected by a series of decisions by the Supreme Court which sought to control police investigative practices and to protect and develop suspects' rights. However limited the instrumental effect of these decisions may have been (Leo and Thomas (eds) 1998; Milner 1974), they had a vital symbolic impact, notably producing endless complaints from police about legal 'technicalities' obstructing police work. It is important to appreciate that the ideological impact of these developments extended far beyond the USA. (The limited effect of law on policing in New South Wales is discussed below.)

---

3   In the late 1990s, full enforcement enjoyed an unfortunate resurrection in the enthusiasm for 'zero tolerance' (Dixon 1999b).

In Britain, a specific inflexion was provided by the attempt in the years following the Second World War to foster and maintain a view of police as governed by law and as having a peculiar relationship of trust and affection with the public. The police officer, quintessentially but quite inaccurately presented as a 'citizen in uniform', was accountable to a concept of the 'rule of law' which was distinguished largely by its imprecision. In Australia, 'professional' policing developed as a more straightforward enterprise of crime-fighting (Finnane 1994: ch 4), with the ideological connection to the law having less significance. The limited effect of legal regulation on policing in New South Wales is discussed below. None the less, law has been important both as justificatory resort when policing is criticised ('we're just enforcing the law'), and also (in rather contradictory, even hypocritical fashion) as a target of complaint – 'legal technicalities make the job impossible'. So professional law enforcement has had a profoundly ambivalent attitude towards the law.[4]

By the 1960s in each of these jurisdictions, an image of professional policing in slightly varied form had been firmly established. However, what had been seen as the path to acceptance as professionals then took unexpected turns. Civil disorder in the USA in the 1960s and in England in the 1970s and 1980s indicated serious problems between police and sections of the public. The research into policing practices which began in earnest in this period showed that the promises of policing as law enforcement were largely unfulfilled, and indeed unfulfillable by conventional means (Bayley 1994; Manning 1997; Clarke and Hough, eds 1980). It became clear that police had a very limited ability to affect crime either by random preventative patrol or by reactive detective investigation. Their ability to 'clear up' offences relied less on speed of response and detective ability than on the provision of information by the public (Bittner 1990: chs 4 and 5; Reiner 1992: 138-46).

Recognition of these problems was to seed a paradigm shift in policing which was as great as that associated with the rise of policing as professional law enforcement. The new policing is usually called 'community policing' (Moore 1992; Greene and Mastrofski, eds 1988). The limitation of this label is that it encourages too limited a focus on specific tactics or programs (such as geographic 'area' policing or Neighbourhood Watch). However, community policing is much more than such specific components: it entails a new ethos, philosophy or ideology. Its implications have not yet been worked out: policing may be

---

4   See, eg, Morris and Hawkins: 1970: 88-9; such attitudes form part of the 'occupational paranoia' described by Punch 1985: 188-9; see also Chan 1997 and Chapter 5, below.

in the early stages of a fundamental reconstitution which may (if the previous example of professional policing is an indicator) continue for decades. There are already signs that community policing and its partner, problem-oriented policing, are being colonised by new crime and disorder control strategies, of which 'zero tolerance' is merely a rhetorical excess (Dixon 1998a, 1999b).

An aspect of these developments which has attracted little attention is its implications for the place of law in policing. A notable feature of recent developments in policing has been the reaction against the detailed legal and administrative regulations which proliferated in the era of law enforcement policing. Such rule-based models have been challenged by arguments both from within and outside the police that true professionalism requires broad discretion rather than rule-based direction (NSW Police 1988; Sparrow et al 1990). Drawing managerialist lessons from corporate practice, '[p]olice executives are ... relying less on rules and constant supervision and more on selection, training and the articulation of values to create a culture that can properly guide officer conduct' (Moore and Stephens 1991: 5; see also Cordner 1989). This form of response reflects a much deeper change in theories and rationales of policing. The new policing associated with problem solving and community-oriented strategies (Moore 1992) distances itself from law and 'enthusiasm for these reforms grows precisely because of the perceived failures of the rule of law' (Mastrofski and Uchida 1993: 353). Once law enforcement is no more than one part of the police function, law may lose its place as the prime legitimator of policing. Meanwhile, the new crime control policing uses law much more flexibly and pragmatically than previous modes (Dixon 1999b). For the time being however, appeals to law or the 'rule of law' as central to policing continue to be made (eg Lauer 1994: 65), but their substance is questionable.

What this suggests is that the place of law in New South Wales policing is uncertain. It has been affected by ideological interpretations with little relevance to Australian conditions and is currently being influenced by potentially profound shifts in the nature of policing. In this context of uncertainty and change, it is important to articulate a clear conception of how policing should be related to and be regulated by law.

3. Legal regulation of investigative detention

Police practices in detaining and questioning suspects provide an excellent example of deficiencies in the current model of legal regulation and of the difficulties in identifying 'good' policing (and of the problems of not doing so). A brief background to legal developments in the area is required.

In the mid-19th century, the respective roles of police and magistrates in criminal procedure changed substantially, as each began to develop a distinctive 'professionalism'. The police (whose job had previously been simply to introduce arrested suspects to the judicial system by taking them to a magistrate who would then question the suspect or direct further inquiries) began to take on responsibility for the investigation of crime. Magistrates withdrew from active involvement in investigations to a narrower judicial role (Stephen 1883: 221). The fact that this was a gradual process contributed to the crucial failure of the law to recognise it. Throughout the first two-thirds of this century, the law did not acknowledge that a central feature of crime investigation was the questioning of suspects at police stations before they were taken to magistrates. (The only legal recognition came in bail provisions allowing police to charge and bail suspects from police stations, so that they did not need to be taken to magistrates.) English common law began to accept detention for questioning in the 1960s (*Dallison v Caffery* [1964] 2 All ER 61), a trend formalised by the House of Lords in 1984 (*Holgate-Mohammed v Duke* [1984] 1 All ER 1054) and, soon after, in the *Police and Criminal Evidence Act* 1984 (Dixon 1997: ch 4).

Police practice in Australia was similar to that in England: suspects were routinely taken to police stations for questioning before charge. However, when the issue came before the High Court in 1986 (*Williams v R* (1986) 66 ALR 385), the court rejected the English development of the common law and insisted that Australian common law required officers to take arrested suspects to magistrates as soon as practicable. The desire to question a suspect (or to carry out other investigative activity) did not justify any delay. If detention for investigative purposes was to be permitted, this should be done by legislatures rather than by judges.

Twelve years after *Williams* and eight years after the NSW Law Reform Commission (NSW LRC 1990) recommended legislative provision of power to detain between arrest and charge, New South Wales finally implemented such legislation in 1998.[5] Between 1986 and 1998, police practice was little affected by the *Williams* decision (Dixon 1997: ch 5). Officers continued to investigate offences between arresting

---

5   *Crimes Amendment (Detention After Arrest) Act* 1997. See Chapter 6, below. For other Australian jurisdictions, see 'Comparative analysis of police powers throughout Australia and New Zealand', paper prepared for the Police Commissioners' Policy Advisory Group 1998.

suspects and taking them to magistrates by three means. First, the fiction of 'voluntary attendance at stations' was used, so that suspects were not formally arrested, but were merely 'helping with inquiries'. Secondly, police arrested suspects at times when magistrates were not immediately available (eg in the late afternoon, making questioning possible until the suspect was taken to court the next morning). Thirdly, officers took the chance either that a confession would lead to a guilty plea (thereby avoiding judicial scrutiny) or that, if a case went to trial, that the judge would not exercise the discretion to exclude evidence of confessions obtained during unlawful detention.

The last of these methods is of most interest here: officers (both before and after *Williams*) relied on the courts not to apply the law strictly.[6] If judges consistently refuse to exclude evidence obtained in some unlawful way (which they have done almost as a matter of routine in New South Wales: see Dixon 1997: ch 5), then that practice has a judicial imprimatur which is hard to distinguish from authorisation. (While it is true to say that the practice is not fully legalised in the sense that it may provide the basis for a civil claim, this possibility is usually not significant.) If judges (and other actors, notably prosecutors[7] and defence lawyers[8]) condone legal fictions about police practices, they are substantially if not formally legalised. Officers were encouraged to act in this way by their superiors.[9] Concern about the implications of *Williams* was allayed by amending the Commissioner's Instructions. Rather than reflecting the High Court's decision, the new Instruction was modelled on Chief Justice Gibbs' dissenting judgment (itself modelled on *Dallison v Caffery*) which argued that officers could delay taking suspects to magistrates for a reasonable period, during which questioning and other investigative activity would be legitimate. Concurrently, officers were reminded of the Crown's vicarious liability for 'police acting in accordance with the directions of the Commissioner of Police' and were informed that the Commissioner would 'accept responsibility for the actions of police, performing their duties in good faith and in accordance

---

6   This may not have been ended by the *Detention After Arrest Act*: see Chapter 6, below.

7   See, eg, the advice given by prosecutors to police on the arrest of Harold Blackburn (Lee 1990: 360).

8   By encouraging guilty pleas and by failing to object vigorously to the admission of unlawfully obtained evidence.

9   This has a long and murky history: see, eg, Philip Arantz's account of being ordered by the head of the Criminal Investigation Bureau to verbal a suspect (Arantz 1993: 39).

with the statement of values'.[10] In short, the police effectively refused to accept the authority of the High Court's decision, and were encouraged and enabled to do so by other sectors of the justice system. It is an episode which puts in question the substance of rhetorical statements of devotion to the rule of law.

The significance of the example of investigatory detention is that it illustrates the difficulty of identifying 'good policing' in an area of investigative practice of the greatest significance. The law, as expressed by the High Court in *Williams*, was clear enough. But normative police practice was quite different: detention for questioning was informally authorised by judicial practice, Commissioner's instructions, prosecutors' advice, and the 'gimmickry' of arranging arrests out of hours. In 1991, the then chair of the Police Board commented cynically on calls for legislative reform of police powers: 'I confess that I sometimes wonder if it matters very much. With the present powers, our police manage to keep the criminal courts quite busy and the prisons full' (Jackson 1991: 25).

It is hardly surprising that officers were routinely found to be ignorant of the law.[11] Practices may be illustrated by a quotation from a police officer in which he explained how arrest and detention were used in dealing with suspects in the early 1990s:

> You might grab them with reasonable cause or suspicion or whatever, but they're not actually under arrest, if you know what I mean. They are brought back here [to the station] to clear it all up... You might go to a scene and he's there, he's got a knife in his hand and witnesses saying, 'That's him'. That's enough for me to arrest him. You might go to a scene and he hasn't got a knife. There's no witnesses saying anything, but the victim says, 'Yeah, that's him.' I suppose you've got enough to arrest him there and then, but you prefer to say 'Would you come back to [the station] where we can clear this up?' And most of the time they will. If they want to kick up a barney, you just arrest them anyway.

Similarly, another officer explained how he would deal with a person who objected to a stop/search for which there was insufficient specific suspicion to legally authorise a search:

> As the law says, there's not much you can do. But what you actually do is a bit different... Ninety percent of it is common sense and baffle them with bullshit. You know, 'There's been a bust up the road. We just want to clear you from getting in the shit.' More times than not they will come around and just let you search them.

---

10 'Instructions to police as to the effects of Williams case on police investigation of criminal offences', Commissioner's circular 88/98, 15 June 1988. For fuller discussion of the Williams case and its consequences, see Dixon 1997: ch 5.

11 See, eg, *Foster* (1993) 113 ALR 1 and *McKinney and Judge* (1990) 49 A Crim R 7, discussed in Dixon 1997: ch 5.

If consent is refused, 'the main thing I do is just lob them back into the station and have a chat to them here'.

4. Attitudes to law in other specific contexts

Investigative detention provides an example of the obscure relationship between 'good policing' and 'bad policing'. By conforming with institutional practice and senior officers' directions, operational officers would be led to act unlawfully. Their failures to understand and follow the law in this area could hardly be surprising or be thought particularly blameworthy. However, in other areas which have attracted public scrutiny, legal requirements have been clearer and officers' attitudes to them less condonable.

David Gundy was an Aboriginal man who was shot and killed in his home by police who were searching for another Aboriginal man, John Porter, who had killed a police officer. The Report of the Royal Commission into Aboriginal Deaths in Custody's inquiry into the shooting included scathing criticism of police attitudes towards legal requirements. Senior detectives and Special Weapons and Operations Section officers treated 'the law and its processes disdainfully' (Wootten 1990: 2). Search warrants were obtained by 'the making of patently untrue statements' in an attempt to get a 'general warrant' (Wootten 1990: 3, 53). Even if the warrants had been obtained properly, the house in which Gundy was shot was entered unlawfully, before the time specified in the warrant: this was one of several ways in which officers:

> demonstrated their lack of respect for the law. . . One detects an assumption that the law will look after police acting to catch a serious criminal, and inconvenient legal rules can safely be ignored. . . Police felt entitled to make their own law. . . [I]n the whole operation, the extent of their legal powers does not seem to have been considered. (Wootten 1990: 4, 17, 18, 130-1)

The attitudes and practices of the officers in this operation were subsequently supported and defended by senior officers (Wootten 1990: 17-18). This was not a case where the police could legitimately feel constrained by the law:

> Their problem was not that the law gave them insufficient powers – their problem was that they had insufficient information about Porter's whereabouts to justify action and were not prepared to wait for further information. (Wootten 1990: 92)

This was a damning indictment, not just of the officers involved in this operation, but also of an organisation's purported commitment to the rule of law.

A second major recent inquiry was the Royal Commission on the Blackburn case. Its Report (Lee 1990) shows that the investigation of Blackburn's suspected involvement in two series of sexual assaults included the improper obtaining of a listening device authorisation (Lee 1990: 224-31), abuse of search powers (Lee 1990: 232-90), and two unlawful arrests (Lee 1990: ch 19, 313).[12] Such examples suggest the pervasive nature of inappropriate attitudes towards law and basic misunderstandings of legality and of its proper relationship to policing practices.

5. Attitudes to law and 'good cause' or 'process' corruption

Most importantly for present purposes, the examples in Sections 3 and 4 (above) illustrate the problem of derisory police attitudes towards law. Police officers are presented with, and themselves relay, contradictory messages: law is both the fundamental structure of society and the object of their activities, and yet simultaneously an irrelevant, outdated obstacle to the achievement of socially mandated tasks of crime control and order maintenance. In resolving this contradiction, it is hardly surprising if officers justify unlawful or questionable activities by pointing to the desirability of their objective: in the traditional formulation, the ends justify the means.[13] They are encouraged to do so by accounts of crime control being strangled by due process in statements by senior officers (eg Drew 1989), by public commentators, and, routinely, in fictional representations.

As ends come to justify means, then the road to 'good cause' or (Justice Wood's preferred term) 'process' corruption becomes clear. Perhaps the clearest expressions of this have been by senior English officers in arguing for reform of criminal procedure. Metropolitan Police Commissioners Mark and McNee unashamedly stated that their officers had to cut legal corners in order to work effectively:

> In the past, the police . . . have been dealing with a population which, in the main, was ignorant of its civil rights. Because Parliament had become very reluctant to face up to the necessity of giving the police adequate powers to deal with crime, officers have been expected to rely upon this ignorance when making the necessary inquiries and tests for the solving of crime. . . [M]any police officers have, early in their career, learned to use methods

---

12　For a summary of the 'faults and misconduct' of police in the case, see Lee 1990: 311-15.

13　See, for a particularly relevant example, 'Haken fingers the Cross' *Sydney Morning Herald*, 26 August 1998.

> bordering on trickery or stealth in their investigations... One fears that sometimes so-called pious perjury of this nature from junior officers can lead to even more serious perjury later in their careers. I consider it quite wrong that police officers ... should be expected by stealth or by force ... to exercise necessary powers in the investigations of crime. (McNee 1983: 180-1; see also Mark 1978)

This statement includes some key themes: the decay and irrelevance of the law, Parliament's irresponsibility, the ability (indeed duty) of police to do 'what has to be done', and the legal and political system's culpability for providing the conditions from which corruption can grow.[14] McNee sought authority for his claims in judicial dicta (notably from Lord Denning).

Does process (or 'good cause') corruption lead to other forms of corruption? Suggestions that it does rely on a very familiar account of individuals and institutions alike being set on a slippery slope by minor infractions (Kleinig 1996: 174-81). Such commonsense metaphors are inadequate for at least two reasons. First, the literature of police corruption consistently points to distinctions which many officers make between acceptable and non-acceptable deviance (eg, accepting services, but not money; taking bookmakers' but not drug-dealers' bribes; 'embellishing', but not concocting suspects' statements). While it is clear that what was unacceptable may become acceptable, this is not a natural process, and that the step to a previously unacceptable activity may be as great as the initial step into deviance. Second, the causal sequence is oversimplified: different types of deviant activity may co-exist, but may do so because they are produced by similar factors, rather than because one causes another. It is perhaps more important to examine a general atmosphere or culture in which deviance is encouraged than to seek causal connections between types of deviance.

It should however be noted that knowledge or belief about process corruption can be very influential, especially when senior officers' reputations are involved. If some senior officers have reputations (deserved or not) for having used illegitimate means to achieve desirable ends, then the ideological effect on junior officers may be significant (cf ICAC 1989).

Measures to deal with the problems illustrated in Sections 3-5 must go beyond legal reform or clarification of police powers (although the need for this will be stressed in Section 7, below). What is required is a

---

14 McNee ended the relevant chapter of his book by moralising, without apparent appreciation of its irony in the context of what went before: 'We cannot expect others to lead honest lives and then indulge in small dishonesties ourselves. We cannot expect others to speak the truth while we tell lies' (1983: 186).

fundamental shift in police cultural attitudes towards legal regulation. The starting point for this must be a re-evaluation of the way in which law is taught to police trainees. While knowledge of powers and procedures is of course vital, this must be presented in a way which teaches legal values and principles, making invocations of the 'rule of law' more than merely rhetorical. It must be acknowledged that this is not an easy task, particularly in the context of currently fashionable critiques of rules and emphasis on the professional use of discretion which was noted above. Officers have to be taught that discretion means choosing one of possibly a number of ways of using legal authority: it means taking choices within what the law provides. Law is not just a rhetorical backdrop to policing activities: it provides their structure (in legal powers and duties) and their substance (in legal values and principles). Police officers have to be taught that the law applies to them, not just to others, that being a law officer carries special responsibilities, rather than that it provides exemptions.

Of course, training does not finish when officers leave the Academy. The approach outlined above must permeate subsequent in-service and advanced training. It should also inform the neglected process by which officers are informed about legal developments and the impact of case-law on their powers and duties.

6. 'Case theories' and strategy in criminal investigation

The Blackburn case illustrates another important issue: strategy in investigative activity. Many crime investigations are characterised by the use of 'case theories', a strategy which is produced from the ambivalent position of police in the adversarial process as both investigators and preliminary prosecutors (Hogg 1991: 243-4):

> Once the police form suspicions against an individual, they quickly develop a case theory which for them makes sense of what probably occurred. . . [T]he police attempt to make the evidence fit a plausible theory; that which is consistent with their case theory may be accepted at face value; that which is inconsistent explained away as mistaken or ignored. (McConville 1989)

Such practices draw on cultural beliefs in the reliability of good investigators' 'hunches'. Indeed, in many investigations where, for example, police are directed to a suspect by witnesses or reliable informants, the strategy is effective. However, problems can arise in cases where initial suspicion does not justify focusing exclusively on a particular suspect, where this leads to other lines of inquiry being ignored or abandoned, and where officers become too committed to proving the guilt of 'their' suspect. In the worst cases, evidence contrary to the 'case theory' is distorted or suppressed.

The Blackburn investigation was almost a caricature of police improperly operating on a case theory. One officer's hunch that Blackburn resembled descriptions of a suspect in a sexual assault case led to 'the falsification and distortion of virtually all the evidence brought against him and complete suppression of the evidence pointing to his innocence' (Lee 1990: 473). The Blackburn case also shows how case theories can spread beyond the investigating officers: senior officers (including Tony Lauer, then head of the Professional Responsibility Section and subsequently Commissioner) publicly committed themselves to the theory. Ironically, this was, at least in part, produced by a desire to show that the Police Service was prepared to take vigorous action against its own officers.[15] The officer who took over the Blackburn case when the senior investigator was injured in a road accident exposed the deficiencies in the case, only to suffer accusations that he had 'gutted the brief' in a corrupt attempt to embarrass the force leadership. The Lee Report found that 'the police officers of all ranks involved in the investigation into Mr Blackburn's guilt [sic], from the Commissioner down, failed lamentably to exercise the supervision which their rank demanded of them' (Lee 1990: 19; see also ibid 472).

A second, perhaps even more notorious case, is the charging, conviction, and ultimate acquittal of Tim Anderson on three counts of murder arising from the Hilton bombing in 1978.[16] The most charitable explanation (for this and others, see Carrington et al (eds) 1991) of this episode is that the authorities convinced themselves of a suspect's guilt, and pursued a conviction relentlessly. The result was the construction of a case by the provision of information from police to witnesses, which was then re-presented as evidence. As the defence demonstrated its flaws, the prosecution's case was reconstructed during the trial. The case is a complex one, with many facets which will not be considered here, where there is space to deal with only three points (see Carrington et al (eds) 1991).

Anderson was arrested (according to the Crown) in response to the highly unreliable (and subsequently discredited) claims of a man

---

15   See Lee 1990 and *Blackburn v New South Wales* (unreported, SC NSW, 13944/1990, 31 January 1991, Hunt J) at 24.

16   *Anderson* (1991) 53 A Crim R 421.

described by the Court as 'a notorious prisoner'.[17] The senior investigator (then New South Wales police's most renowned detective) explained that:

> he was working on this principle: 'One old detective used to say, "When you haven't got much, pull them in. The brief will only get better". This was certainly true in our case.'

This was a remarkably honest admission about how powers supposedly dependent on 'reasonable' suspicion are used.

Prosecution counsel apparently became equally committed to the case theory and presented argument in a way which earned the disapproval of the Court of Criminal Appeal. This illustrates again that it is wrong to focus just on the police: their attitudes towards prosecutions and the law can be shared and shaped by others, including their senior officers, officials in other parts of the criminal justice process, and the media. The Court of Criminal Appeal quoted, with apparent approval, defence counsel's comment that:

> from time to time it was necessary to make a positive effort to remind oneself that this had been a criminal prosecution in which the Crown carried the onus of proof beyond reasonable doubt. . . [O]n occasion, it was easy to get the impression that the relevant search was for some hypothesis consistent with guilt.[18]

Anderson's conviction was quashed, with the court refusing to order a retrial on the ground that the prosecution should not be given 'a further opportunity to patch up its case. . . It has already made one attempt too many to do that'.[19] Such prejudice had also been a notable feature of media reporting of the trial (Carrington et al (eds) 1991: ch 6).

It is vital here to reiterate a point made earlier. The Blackburn and Anderson investigations are examples of case theories which led officers spectacularly astray. However, they are not isolated incidents of abuse or misconduct: rather, they are extremes on a continuum which runs back to everyday, often reliable hunches felt and assumptions made by officers in the course of their investigations.

---

17   Ibid. On the use of prison informants, and their development as an alternative to confessions (genuine or otherwise) during police questioning, see Brown and Duffy 1991.

18   *Anderson* (1991) 53 A Crim R 421 at 426.

19   Ibid at 453.

7. Reforming criminal investigation

Here there are two issues for consideration: first, the limits and possibilities of using legal regulation; secondly, the need for broader change in investigative practice. Together, these provide valuable lessons for the consideration of change in policing.

i. Legal regulation of policing practice

To what extent can policing practices be effectively changed and regulated by law? In considering the example of investigative detention, the impact of the *Police and Criminal Evidence Act* 1984 (PACE) on policing in England and Wales provides a useful comparison.

In the very extensive research literature on this legislation, three general positions can be identified. The first suggests that PACE brought about a 'seachange' in English policing, shifting towards a supposedly American model of due process and successfully changing officers' practices in and attitudes towards criminal investigation. Such research has mainly been by police officers, although some research by the Police Foundation provided a degree of support to this position. (For a review, see Dixon 1992: 518-21.) The second, in extreme contrast, argued that nothing (or, at least, nothing for the better) was changed by PACE. In accounts by McConville and colleagues (1991), policing is dominated by an impermeable police culture; rules are subverted, avoided and broken; legal reform, at best, legitimates police practices.

The third, not surprisingly, takes a middle position, arguing that the first position is overoptimistic, influenced by police interests and methodologically suspect, while the second is excessively pessimistic and deterministic (Dixon 1997: 42-8; Brown 1997). It argues that PACE has had some success in clarifying police powers and suspects' rights: both police and suspects have benefited from removing much of the legal obscurity which characterised these areas. Indeed, the experience of PACE suggests the inadequacy of the conventional 'balance' model of criminal justice, in which the interests of police and of suspects are inherently antagonistic, and in which powers and rights can only be increased at the expense of each other (Ashworth 1994; Dixon 1997: 283-5). While problems have not been removed, there is certainly evidence that a significant number of officers now view working within the law as professional conduct, and treat with disdain the older traditions of detective misconduct. PACE has, in other words, contributed to a shift in police cultures. While difficulties in the key area of providing effective legal advice continue, PACE was significant in giving some real substance to suspects' rights. An important tool used in PACE is the codes of practice.[20] As well as clarifying police powers and suspects' rights, PACE relies on managerial supervision as a key element of reform. This has two major features: significant recording requirements (particularly of a suspect's treatment during detention in custody records and of interrogations on audiotapes); and allocating personal responsibility to custody officers for the treatment of detained suspects, so signifying an important division between the roles and interests of investigating officers and custody officers (Dixon 1992; 1997: ch 4).

The more general implications of the third position are that legal reform can contribute to change in policing. The nature of the subject matter is, naturally, significant. If it is an area such as criminal investigation which is both ideologically and instrumentally important to police, and about which there are strong cultural beliefs, it is unlikely that legal change in itself will be effective if change is in a direction resisted by a significant number of officers. Legal reform is most likely to be effective if it contributes to a flow of other changes. In the case of PACE, legal reform had some effect because it was consistent with contextual changes in policing, which included growing dissatisfaction (within and outside the police) about the inefficiencies of investigative practices and, more generally, a reorientation of policing towards a new model of police 'professionalism'.

ii.   From case theories to strategic investigating

The position adopted here implies a need for a fundamental review of investigative practice, not just an attempt to eliminate deviance. This need has been recognised in other jurisdictions (eg Audit Commission 1993; Maguire et al 1991; Maguire and Norris 1992). In New South Wales, some work has already been done (eg ICAC/NSW Police 1993; NSW Police 1995) and reviews of investigative practices and strategies continue. The challenge of such reviews must be to build investigators' skills (including the use of hunches) into a more reliable strategy. This involves, inter alia, greater supervision of crime investigation, the structuring of the scrutiny of case theories and self-review into investigators' practices, and a clear legal regime for investigative activity (including the detention of suspects).

It is perhaps worth concluding by stressing the importance of such reviews. If investigations are led astray by inaccurate case theories, the result may be improper arrest, prosecution and conviction of innocent

---

20   See Chapter 4, Section 2iii, below.

people. But a corollary too often ignored is that the people who are really guilty are not brought to justice: the failure to detect and convict those responsible, for example, for the Bulli sexual assaults, the Hilton bombing, and several notorious homicides is attributable, to no small degree, to the deflection of investigators by inaccurate case theories (Hogg 1991: 251-2).

iii. The use of informants

A specific and important investigative tactic is the use of informants. This has attracted considerable recent scrutiny (ICAC 1993; Wood 1997b: 431-41; HMIC 1999; see also Finnane 1994: 77-9 on the history of police using informants), and comments here are limited to some general observations about problems in using informants. Informants are linked to corruption by their use in areas of police work where corruption is endemic (see below): crucially, as Manning and Redlinger point out, informants 'are the heart of the enforcement of narcotics laws' (1991: 405).

Manning and Redlinger have argued that the use of informants can produce 'pressures to obstruct justice':

> insofar as to be successful one must: (1) protect informants who constitute the [officer's] vital link to the underworld; (2) create informants through threats of prosecution on pending cases if cooperation is not forthcoming, and when they do cooperate persuade officials to drop charges against them; and (3) suppress information on cases pursued by other officers (for example where one's informant is also responsible for a burglary). The last category of obstruction also occurs when there is interagency competition. (Manning and Redlinger 1991: 402)

The fact that some informants have incentives to provide inaccurate information with potentially very serious effects on the administration of criminal justice has been exemplified by concern about a special category of informer which has apparently been something of a speciality of the NSW Police Service – the prison informer. Recent experience has illustrated the potential for abuse of and by prison informers (Brown and Duffy 1991).

8. Reforming police accountability

This section begins with a general overview of aspects of police accountability, before moving on to comment on issues of effectiveness and possible development in specific contexts.

i. Accountabilities: an overview

What are the meanings of accountability? Confusion begins in debates about accountability when, for example, people do not make clear whether they refer to an obligation of some kind to give a retrospective account by explaining an organisation's activities (eg a company's annual report to its shareholders) or to accountability in the sense of *a priori* control (eg the determination of strategy and tactics). The crucial variable is that of power: does accountability mean real external direction and control, or merely a concession of consultation or explanation?

Some other dimensions of accountability include:

- individual/organisational: to what extent can mechanisms primarily designed to respond to individual grievances (notably, complaints procedures) deal with broader organisational issues and concerns?

- policy/operations: at what point does direction by outside agencies become inappropriate? In policing, can a distinction be made between broad policy and specific operational decisions? At what point (if at all – cf Grimshaw and Jefferson 1987) can we isolate 'policies' which are appropriately set or supervised by external bodies?

- public/private: what are the implications for accountability of the trend towards privatisation of criminal justice agencies? In the shorter term, what are the implications for accountability of tendencies such as professionalisation and managerialism in policing? If police services are increasingly presenting themselves in the guise of commercial companies (with 'stakeholders', 'customers', etc) does a model of public accountability designed for *state* institutions become problematic?

The problems of an essentialist definition of accountability are illustrated by a partial listing of the very different types of accountability which can be found in policing. Formal modes of accountability include:

- political: to parliament via the government – the Rigg affair brought antagonism between the Police Commissioner and the Minister to a head, resulting in the *Police Service (Management) Amendment Act* 1993 (Joint Select Committee Upon Police Administration 1993). Political accountability may be to local rather than central government: this is notionally the case in England and Wales (outside London), although the last decade has seen a significant centralisation of effective control over provincial policing, exemplified by the reform of provincial police authorities in 1994 (Jones and Newburn 1997);

- complaints procedures via the Police Service and the NSW Ombudsman;[21]

- to Royal Commissions, judicial inquiries and other ad hoc investigative bodies;

- to specialist state agencies, such as the Police Board (Wood 1997: 373-81) and ICAC (until 1997) and now the Police Integrity Commission;

- to law: this takes various forms: 'constabulary independence'; criminal law; courts' power to sanction misdemeanours in police investigations by excluding evidence: civil actions against police for torts; use of legal regulation to specify police powers and suspects' rights (as in the *Police and Criminal Evidence Act* in England – see above); administrative law; freedom of information legislation;

- internal police controls: supervision, management and disciplinary practices within the police organisation;

- financial and budgetary controls, both of and within the police organisation; efficiency audits; performance indicators and other managerialist measures;

- community policing structures, such as police-community liaison committees, neighbourhood watch, and lay visitors to police station.

There are also a range of informal modes of accountability which perhaps should also be included, eg:

- the Press and other media;

- civil liberties and other pressure groups;

- monitoring groups, for example those set up by some English local councils which have no legal status.

Finally, it is important to consider how accountability changes as its contexts change. For example, political accountability has changed as the state has been transformed by democratisation and by more recent trends of corporatism and centralisation. Legal accountability has changed as (some) judges reassess their role as watchdogs within the state: notably the High Court has recently become much more active in criminal justice matters. Traditional political accountability appears to be losing ground to

---

21 See the *Police Service Amendment (Complaints and Management Reform) Act* 1998.

more incisive modes of accountability such as specialist audits such as the work of the Audit Commission in England and Wales (eg Audit Commission 1993).

ii. Accountability and organisational reality

The catalogue of modes of accountability provided above can be taken to indicate a high level of accountability: in surveying the field (then Commissioner) Lauer claimed that the 'profession of policing has never been more accountable' (1994: 61). It is necessary to go beyond the promise of accountability to assess performance. Lauer put great weight on legal accountability: 'For many officers this is the chief and single most important form of accountability' (1994: 65). However, as has been suggested above, legal accountability in practice is often weak: it seems that in 'talk of policing operating under the rule of law, of the police being answerable to the law, of police officers being officers of the law' (Lauer 1994: 65), there is more rhetoric than substance. Similarly, political accountability is apparently crucial, but is in practice limited by the lack of clarity in allocating responsibility between Commissioner and Minister. It has been argued convincingly that such confusions are functional, allowing a choice of interpretations of particular problem and so insisting that disputes about police accountability will be settled politically rather than by the application of a legal formula (Hogg and Hawker 1983). Consequently, it is not surprising that the Royal Commission's recommendation that the relationship between Police Minister and Commissioner should be clarified by statute was rejected by the government.[22]

In a variety of accounts, police organisations are presented as if they conform to a model of legal-bureaucratic rationality in which law is the major determinant of police activity and police institutions operate as efficient bureaucracies (Dixon 1997: 1-8). Punch is scathing about such accounts:

> one could generalize that the police organisation appears to be a semi-military bureaucracy with high levels of command and control but is rather characterised in practice by considerable autonomy for the lower ranks, the alienation of senior staff from street work, training unrelated to practice, considerable rivalry between units, a cynical and secretive occupational culture, and poor performance in terms of cultivating leaders and managers, setting coherent policy, and achieving efficiency and effectiveness. (Punch 1985: 195; see also Manning 1997)

---

22 See 'Reform rejected as too esoteric' *Sydney Morning Herald*, 15 May 1998 and Chapter 6, below.

It has become almost a cliché in academic police literature to cite Wilson's observation that 'the police department has the special property . . . that within it discretion increases as one moves down the hierarchy' (1968: 109). Legal accountability appears often as a device for avoiding real accountability: the strange history of the invented tradition of the 'office of constable' bears testimony to this. Police powers are sometimes distinguished from those of other state officials by the supposed nature of the 'office of constable': '[t]he essential feature which distinguishes Police organisations from most other organised bodies is that the Police-man's powers are not delegated to him by superior authority' (RCPPP 1929: 15). Powers are said to be given to an officer as a constable, not as a member of a police force: 'in essence a police force is neither more nor less than a number of individual constables, whose status derives from the common law, organised together in the interests of efficiency' (Hailsham 1981: 107). The doctrine of the constable's office has been the subject of (and confused by) considerable controversy in British debates about police accountability (see eg Brogden 1982; Jefferson and Grimshaw 1984; Lustgarten 1986).

While it is true that officers must make their own decisions about, for example, whether they have reasonable suspicion necessary to exercise a power and in this sense cannot be ordered to exercise powers, this is not distinct from a general administrative law requirement that officials should exercise discretion given to them by law and must not act under dictation. There is nothing special about police or police powers in this regard. Concentration on this legal requirement largely serves to ignore the reality of police organisation and command, which does assign officers to tasks, including the exercising of powers. An administrative law requirement that a public official should make her/his own decision and not act under dictation is not inconsistent with the operation of a bureaucratic structure of this kind. It certainly does not provide the basis for the assertion of some unique constabulary independence. As Lustgarten suggests, the exceptional cases of officers persevering with prosecutions against orders in fact prove the rule rather than subvert it: subsequent prosecutions are brought by the officer as an individual, not as a member of a police force (1986: 11-13, 171).

iii. Complaints procedures and corruption investigations

Evaluation of institutional mechanisms for dealing with complaints and corruption must go beyond abstract discussion of what may seem to be bureaucratically or administratively rational for two reasons. First, the specific political context, and how any new or reformed institution would fit into it, must be considered. For example, there would little point in recommending that the institution should be accountable to the parliament via a select committee if, in the jurisdiction under consideration, parliamentary committees were ineffective and the parliament was weak.[23]

Secondly, account must be taken of subjective factors. In this area, public perceptions of the complaints process are significant. If the public lacks confidence in investigations which are only conducted internally by police (and '[p]ublic scepticism is amply justified by the findings of numerous official commissions of inquiry' – Goldsmith 1991b: 20), then external bodies must be introduced into the supervision or processing of complaints: David Bayley argues bluntly that 'civilian review is critical to the legitimacy of the police' (1991: ix; see also Goldsmith 1991b: 14). Equally, account has to be taken of police attitudes to such procedures and investigations. Given the effective political power of police institutions, external involvement in such procedures may be difficult to provide and may be strongly resisted (Bayley 1991: v-vi; Goldsmith 1991b: 32). The history of the Victorian Police Complaints Authority provides a good case study (Freckelton 1991). In contrast to the usual police opposition to external involvement, the NSW Police Service and the NSW Police Association favour external handling of complaints. The NSW Ombudsman and the Police Integrity Commission oversees complaints against police.[24] In 1998, the NSW Parliament reformed complaint and disciplinary procedures as recommended by the Royal Commission, inter alia simplifying the system, increasing the Police Commissioner's managerial power, and allowing local commanders to deal with minor complaints.[25]

To this point, complaints procedures and corruption investigations have been considered together. However, it is important that they should be distinguished institutionally. A persistent threat to bodies dealing with complaints is that they become bogged down in dealing retrospectively with individual instances which are brought to them, and have little time or energy left for proactive investigations, for attempts to examine

---

23 See, for example, the Fitzgerald Report's emphasis on the need 'to revive parliament as a more effective forum for scrutinising executive power' (Prenzler 1997: 14). The fate of such recommendations has been crucial to the stalling of the reform process in Queensland.

24 See *Police Service Act* 1990; *Police Integrity Commission Act* 1996; on agreements between the Ombudsman and the PIC on complaint handling, see PIC 1998: 5-8.

25 See Wood 1997b: ch 4; *Police Service Amendment (Complaints and Management Reform) Act* 1998.

patterns and structures, or for prospective, preventative strategies.[26] These are necessary because complaints simply do not provide an adequate measure of problems in policing: reasons for this include the notorious underreporting of complaints (Mollen 1994: 101) and the fact that, in many cases of more serious wrongdoing, there is no conventional victim to act as complainant. For example, when police officers steal drugs and money from drug dealers and users, the latter are unlikely to complain. Being the victim of police misconduct is, often realistically, interpreted as a better outcome than being arrested or charged (Maher et al 1997: 42-5). Such problems are not peculiar to policing: more generally, a key concern of modern public law is the need to develop practices, procedures and institutions which use legal techniques, but are able to see beyond retrospective consideration of the individual instance (Birkinshaw 1994; Goldsmith 1991b; 1991c). So the institutions for dealing with complaints and for corruption investigation need to be separate – although, of course, they need to work closely together, with the complaints body bringing apparent patterns of corrupt conduct to the other body's attention.

A crucial question in this area concerns whether such institutions should be internal or external to the police. As noted above, the conflicting demands of public perception and police interest must be considered here. They are best resolved by challenging the somewhat simplistic internal/ external dichotomy which has tended to stultify debate in this area. It is increasingly accepted that a combination of internal and external institutions is the best option. Reflecting the arguments of academic and public policy analysts (eg Sherman 1978; for a good overview, see Goldsmith 1991b), the Mollen Commission's Report provides an eloquent case for combination, a 'double-track strategy' (1994: 152, cf 109). The record of internal investigations is poor: they 'have been the target of sustained criticism across a range of forces in different jurisdictions' (Goldsmith 1991b: 27). Notably, the Internal Investigations Section of the Queensland Police attracted scathing criticism in the Fitzgerald Report (Fitzgerald 1989: 289).

Such criticism may lead to significant internal reform. However, external involvement is indispensable because experience makes clear that, without it, police commitment to tackling corruption and misconduct decays as scandal dissipates and other priorities come to the front (Mollen 1994; Goldsmith 1991a: 1). The concern to avoid damaging publicity and the protection of personal and institutional reputations were responsible

---

26   On the significance of 'premonitory' preventative and detective measures, see Sherman 1978: 247-8. Contrast the comment on the NSW Ombudsman's use of powers to examine systemic issues in Goldsmith 1991b: 45.

for the collapse of real commitment and achievements of the New York City Police Department in the years after the Knapp Commission (Mollen 1994: ch 4). While acknowledging the dangers of drawing lessons from a very different context, a matter deserving close attention is whether similar processes have operated in the NSW Police Service in recent years. This is certainly a plausible explanation of assertions by senior officers that structural corruption had been eradicated and the apparent unwillingness to acknowledge the blatant signs of serious problems in Kings Cross and elsewhere.

A dedicated, external body is necessary to prevent police departments from slipping away from commitment to the minimisation of corruption. The Mollen Commission provides useful terms of reference for such an independent body – it should:

> (i) perform continuous assessments and audits of the Department's systems for preventing, detecting and investigating corruption;
> (ii) assist the Department in implementing programs and policies to eliminate the values and attitudes that nurture corruption;
> (iii) insure a successful system of command accountability; and
> (iv) conduct, where necessary, its own corruption investigations to examine the state of police corruption. (1994: 152)

Mollen's discussion – and the effects in New York of the failure to construct such a body – provided significant impetus to the development of the Police Integrity Commission in New South Wales.

Creation of an external body (whatever its specific configuration) is likely to be politically attractive. However, close attention needs to be paid to arguments against relieving police organisations of duties to deal with corruption and misconduct. Mollen argued convincingly that it is wrong to strip a police service of:

> its capacity – and, most important, its responsibility – to investigate itself. We believe that the Police Department is the entity best able to prevent and investigate corruption amongst its members. It is the Department that bests understands the corruption hazards facing cops, the culture that protects it, and the methods that can most effectively uncover it. The challenge is to devise a structure that compels the Department to do just that. (1994: 152)

The Mollen Commission expressed the 'firm belief that the Department must remain chiefly responsible for policing itself if lasting reform is ever to be achieved. The fundamental principle . . . is that the Department must deliver itself from the scourge of corruption' (1994: 149; cf Sherman 1978: 263).

There are several good reasons for insisting on police retaining responsibility in this area. First, there is the applicability of a truism in social control theory: an institution (like a person) which internalises norms and learns self-discipline will behave better than one conforming under the threat of external sanction. This is particularly important given that the conditions which produce opportunities and incentives for corruption are unlikely to be removed: 'the most we can expect is a cycle of deviance, scandal, reform and repression, gradual relaxation and relapse into former patterns of deviance, followed by a new scandal'. Consequently, 'control is continually problematic' (Punch 1985: 200, 19; see also Sherman 1978).

Secondly, allocating all responsibility to an external body would be to invite the antagonism and scapegoating encountered elsewhere (eg Freckelton 1991). Thirdly, if police services are to achieve their ambition of being recognised as a profession, they must take on the responsibilities of self-regulation which the established professions claim (and, of course, to carry them out more effectively than the latter have sometimes done). As argued above, police organisations may be beginning to change fundamentally: new agendas and opinions provide room for significant change, breaking away from the restrictive dichotomies and antagonisms of the past (Bayley 1991). If approached appropriately, complaints may be seen not merely negatively, as an indication of failure, but positively, as a resource for guiding institutional self-improvement:

> complaints need to be seen not simply as *threats* to existing policies and procedures or individual officers but more importantly, as *opportunities* for re-examination of organizational policies and practices ... of immense potential benefit to the police as well as to the public. (Goldsmith 1991b: 19, original emphases; see also Moss 1998)

It hardly needs to be added that such a change entails a much broader change in police attitudes, in which all too often their work is seen as a kind of police private property. External bodies can play a crucial role in such adaptation (Goldsmith 1991b: 15).

If some responsibility for dealing with corruption and misconduct is to retained by police, where specifically should it be allocated? Internal investigation units face difficult pressures of antagonism from other officers and dangers of becoming compromised and inactive. Again, Mollen provides useful advice, despite contextual differences. Investigation of allegations of corruption and misconduct should be carried out by a special unit. But responsibility for dealing with corruption and misconduct should be spread through police supervisory ranks: local commanders should be made responsible 'for undertaking consistent efforts to prevent, detect and report' corruption and misconduct to the special unit, thereby spreading 'the values and incentives necessary to combat corruption successfully' (Mollen 1994: 77).

Responsibility in this context is similar to that discussed in (i) above. Supervisors should have personal responsibility for what happens in their commands. This does not mean that their heads roll if corruption is found: this simply encourages supervisors to be more interested in their officers being 'discreet than honest' (Mollen 1994: 78). Rather, when corruption is discovered, 'the Department must conduct inquiries into whether corruption disclosures are evidence of commanders' poor performance in maintaining integrity or good performance in uprooting it' (Mollen 1994: 79). Finally, there are practical matters of 'front-line' supervision: measures must be taken to ensure that shift supervisors are realistically able to carry out supervisory duties (Punch 1985: 196).

This interest in good performance must be linked to a more general change: police organisations must become as adept at identifying good practice and rewarding officers for carrying it out as they are at creating disciplinary rules and punishing officers for breaking them. As Punch argues, 'a programme of "positive discipline" stressing and rewarding integrity is crucial' (1985: 196). Police organisations notoriously rely on negative discipline. It is conventional to include them in Gouldner's category of 'punishment centred bureaucracies'. However, it is less often appreciated that the punishment in such bureaucracies is not just applied by management to workers, but also by workers to management (Gouldner 1954: ch 11 and 12). Such 'punishment' was described by Punch in his study of corruption and reform efforts in Holland: 'informal resistance within the Amsterdam police was powerful enough to deflect investigations and to impede change' (1985: 199; see also Sherman 1974b: 270). More generally, tactics based on a 'policing model of corruption prevention' can backfire:

> Modes of supervision and control of narcotics [officers] tend to replicate the dissembling, duplicity, lying and threat used by officers *against* drug offenders... This mode of undercover and secretive enforcement of disciplinary rules ... creates an ambience of doubt and suspicion of colleagues. This condition furthers the already suspicious frame of mind of the officers, and sets him [sic] against the administrative strata in a very profound fashion. (Manning and Redlinger 1977: 150)

The need for specificity applies equally to consideration of complaint handling. It is widely accepted now that 'the complaint-handling process must be separated into different categories of problems and solutions' (Bayley 1991: ix). Treating all complaints as if they require the same type of investigation and assessment according to identical legal standards ignores the reality that there is a difference which needs to be acknowledged between, for example, an officer who is allegedly rude when speaking to a motorist and an officer who has allegedly beaten a suspect.[27] Bayley provides a convenient summary of the issue:

> many complaints can be handled satisfactorily to all concerned through conciliation. Such complaints are more misunderstandings than abuses of power. Even genuine mistakes of judgement are often not so serious that dismissal of police officers is required. In these cases expedited disciplinary hearings are sufficient to determine facts and recommend penalties, with the standard of proof being civil rather than criminal. . . Very serious abuses of power, however, where career-threatening penalties are appropriate, may require more court-like processes and a higher standard of proof. (1991: ix)

It may be argued that effective detection and prosecution of police corruption requires deviation from general standards of due process. However, Sherman points to this argument's 'fatal flaw':

> It may be a gross contradiction to expect police officers to uphold freedoms that they themselves are denied. If police officers feel that their rights are violated by their superiors, then they may be less willing to protect the rights of the public they police. The loss of freedom in society may be far greater from the police failure to serve democratic values than from the actual loss of freedom by police subjected to premonitory internal control policies. Yet a general police failure to serve democratic values could be exacerbated by the use of premonitory controls against police officers. (1978: 260)

Resolution of this dilemma is not just, as Sherman suggests, an empirical question of costs and benefits, but a matter of principle: at what point do the interests or rights of the individual police officer have to give way to the interests or rights of the public? As Sherman warns, 'the effort to avoid a possible cost of reforming corrupt police departments could ultimately result in the prevention of reform itself' (1978: 261).

9. Corruption and the regulation of illegal markets

> [I]n many cases the attempt to use the criminal law to prohibit the supply of goods and services which are constantly demanded . . . is one of the most criminogenic forces in our society. By enabling criminals to make vast profits from such sources as gambling and narcotics; by maximising opportunities for bribery and corruption; by attempting to enforce standards which do not command either the respect or compliance of citizens in general; by these and in a variety of other ways, we both encourage disrespect for the law and stimulate the expansion of both individual and organized crime. . . (Morris and Hawkins 1970: 27)

It should be beyond dispute that police corruption must be considered in the context of the substantive criminal laws which (notionally at least) the

---

27   See the *Police Service Amendment (Complaints and Management Reform) Act* 1998.

police are required to enforce. Police corruption must be taken into account as a likely social cost of the legislative creation and maintenance of 'victimless' crimes: this is a generally accepted conclusion of extensive academic and official investigations (eg Morin Commission 1976: 40-2; Morris and Hawkins 1970; see Sherman 1974b: 272-3; 1978: 299-301 on the need to deal with environmental influences conducive to corruption). The prohibition of substances and services for which markets exist place police officers 'upon an invitational edge of corruption' (Manning and Redlinger 1977: 150). The usual corollary of such comments would be discussion of policy options for decriminalisation or legalisation of relevant activities, notably decriminalising possession of small amounts of some drugs. There is increasingly significant support for such change. However, even if some such change is made, other prohibitions would continue. Indeed, the prohibition/ legalisation dichotomy is unhelpfully stark: the significant issue is not whether we choose prohibition or legalisation, but rather how we regulate markets in ways which minimise the harms caused both by the activities and by their prohibition (Maher et al 1998; Dixon and Maher 1999a). As Mugford (1992: 206) argues, no realistic proposal for reform of drug laws would leave the police without substantial continuing law enforcement duties: the opportunities and attractions of corruption can be reduced but not eliminated. Consequently, the emphasis here is on the need to appreciate how certain prohibitions and police corruption are linked, how the policing of such prohibitions affects policing more generally, and how developments in prohibited activities affect and are affected by police corruption.

i.   Corruption and the control of gambling: a comparative case study

While the most significant prohibitions are, of course, those relating to the use of various drugs, it is useful to begin with an example which shows the intimate links between policing and prohibited activities and, specifically, the way in which attempts to enforce prohibitions can push activities out of the effective reach of law enforcement. The example is the contrast between developments in the policing of illegal betting in England and New South Wales.[28] A common starting-point was an attempt to suppress working-class gambling by the prohibition of off-course cash bookmaking in 1906 in both jurisdictions. At this time, senior police officers were (in retrospect remarkably) sanguine about the prospects of being able to

---

28   For more detail, see Dixon 1996a. More generally, see Criminal Justice Commission 1991; Dixon 1991; ICAC 1994: Part 4; McCoy 1980; O'Hara 1988.

enforce such laws successfully. In England, this confidence soon disappeared as the unenforceability of the law and the police corruption associated with it became apparent. By the 1930s, senior officers were arguing for legalisation of off-course bookmaking: this eventually was brought about in the early 1960s. In the intervening period, police efforts were directed largely at containing and regulating off-course bookmaking (ie it was tolerated so long as public order was not disturbed and book-makers acted responsibly). No serious efforts were made to disrupt bookmaking by, eg, preventing the flow of information about race results on which the system depended. The result was that corruption existed, but it was largely small scale: police took what were effectively licensing fees from bookmakers who usually worked individually. Police efforts were designed to regulate, not to suppress: consequently, bookmaking did not develop the level of organisation or sophisticated communications systems which, as will be noted below, developed in New South Wales. When off-course bookmaking was legalised, bookmakers who had been working illegally were able to move into betting shops and operate legally.

By contrast, in New South Wales (and elsewhere in Australia) the working relationship which inevitably developed between police and bookmakers was undermined by a series of attempts to make prohibition effective. In response to scandals and pressure from influential groups, police attempted to crack down on bookmaking and, crucially, to eradi-cate it by limiting or banning the broadcasting of race results and the communications of odds from racecourses and by prohibiting newspapers from publishing betting odds or tips. The result was the reorganisation and development of illegal systems of communication. Information became a commodity around which illegal organisations were con-structed. Police crackdowns on bookmaking in hotels and other premises encouraged bookmakers to organise cooperative protective arrangements. In particular, bookmakers operated by telephone rather than in person. This necessitated a complex illicit telephone network and, later, use of cellular phones. A pattern emerged which has been familiar from attempts to police illegal gambling since at latest the 18th century: as Blackstone put it, 'the inventions of the sharpers' are 'swifter than the punishment of the law, which only hunts them from one device to another' (1769: 173). As police became more sophisticated in attempts to deal with such operations, so the illegal organisation became more complex, with small-scale independent bookmakers being replaced by coordinated groups. An additional consequence of pushing bookmaking into the telephone system was that a credit system was necessary (in contrast to England, where cash dominated). A large-scale illegal credit betting system required sanctions for punters who could not or would not pay losing bets: bookmaking therefore required the employment of debt enforcers, embedding it further in networks of illegal activity.

The outcome was an illegal bookmaking system in New South Wales which was very different from that in England in terms of organisation, functional links with other criminal activity, and relations with the authorities. Notably, police corruption was structural rather than small scale. In consequence, legalisation of off-course bookmaking was regarded as impracticable: it involved not, as in England, small-scale businesses which were almost respectable, but an organised activity with substantial, functional links to 'real crime'. While it was recognised that suppression by law enforcement was unlikely to be effective, legalisation was not possible: instead, the strategy adopted (which also had the attraction of revenue potential) was that of competing with the illegal market by attempting to provide an attractive legal form of betting via the Totalizator Agency Board.

This comparative example illustrates how specific types of illegal activity can be moulded in different ways by attempts to suppress or control it.[29] Indeed, the activity and the attempt to control it must be considered as being interactive and interdependent: each shapes the other.

ii. A positive view of corruption

The comparative example discussed above suggests the deficiencies of conventional accounts of corruption which present it as essentially negative, as being primarily concerned with the distribution of money, and as primarily a matter of individual (although possibly widespread) deviance. To insist on seeing corruption positively is not, it should be stressed, to imply approval: rather, it is to insist that to understand corruption in the context of the regulation of selling illegal services and substances, it must be seen as performing various roles and functions.

Most importantly, corruption must be seen as a way in which police manage the competing elements of their mandate. As noted above, law enforcement was promoted by police as their raison d'être. However:

> crime fighting has never been, is not, and could not be the prime activity of the police... The core mandate of the police, historically and in terms of concrete demands placed upon the police is the more diffuse one of order maintenance. (Reiner 1992: 212)

---

29 For discussion of how heroin markets in Sydney have been similarly shaped by police interventions, see Dixon and Maher 1998; 1999b; Maher et al 1998; Maher and Dixon 1999.

If suppression of prohibited services or substances is effectively impossible, the police priority must be to get some control over the activity: in such circumstances, 'the primary function of the police . . . is not the enforcement of the law but the regulation of illegal activities' (Whyte 1943: 138). Corruption becomes a tool of regulation: bribes serve as licensing fees, the tangible part of what can be an informal system of administration. Police may not be able to suppress the activity, but are able to influence or control who is involved, where it occurs, and how it is done. In this sense, corruption is to be understood not as venality, but as a mechanism of power and discipline:

> corruption is a product of the requirements of narcotics law enforcement and a theme found in the history of the enforcement enterprise. The structural nature of narcotics law enforcement has historically created the problem of [police] corruption. (Manning and Redlinger 1977: 150)

This presentation may overstate the rational organisation and police control of corruption and the activities on which it feeds. This is particularly so in the case of drug policing, where the vast amounts of money available and the size of the potential markets threaten to undermine relationships and arrangements. For example, the Mollen Commission argued that the 'explosion of the cocaine and crack trade in the mid-1980s fuelled the opportunities for corruption by flooding certain neighbourhoods with drugs and cash' (1994: 15). The result was a 'new character of police corruption', in which police did not merely allow drug-dealers to operate in return for bribes, but operated as dealers and as active violent criminals themselves. Corruption became less pervasive, but more threatening; rather than systemic minor corruption, the dominant pattern became localised serious corruption (1994: 16-17). Similarly, account must be taken of the effect of changes in drug markets. For example, the introduction or development of new drug commodities may have a telling effect on police corruption. A feature of the changes in New York police corruption which the Mollen Commission overlooks is the significance in respect of police drug-taking of the rise to prominence of cocaine. While few officers would use heroin, cocaine was a much more attractive and socially acceptable drug. The result is that corruption involving drug markets in the USA must take account of police officers' personal involvement in illegal drug use in a way which is not yet a serious concern in Australia, where heroin rather than cocaine continues to be the most significant illegal 'hard' drug.[30]

---

30   While the Royal Commission collected some evidence of illegal drug use by officers, its major concern was alcohol abuse (Wood 1997b: 504-9). The apparent expansion of street level cocaine markets may be grounds for concern here, as in other respects.

While regulation rather than suppression becomes the objective of policing illegal substances and services, this is rarely acknowledged, and the pretence of a commitment to enforcement is maintained. A result is that 'narcotics law enforcement is virtually always secretive, duplicitous and quasi-legal' (Manning and Redlinger 1977: 150). This contrast between what is done and what is said is a potent source of cynicism among police officers, contributing to broader disregard for the law in police culture and to cultural beliefs that police have to produce their own solutions to the dilemmas of their occupation. If enforcement is attempted, procedural rules are likely to carry little weight.

This provides another major example of the failure to provide officers with an appropriate and achievable image of good policing. The police have two audiences: those 'who have written their moral judgements into the law and demand . . . that the law be enforced' and those at whom the law is directed, whose values and standards do not necessarily correspond with public designations of deviance and criminality:

> Under these circumstances, the smoothest course for the officer to adopt is to conform to the social organisation with which he is in direct contact and at the same time try to give the impression to the outside world that he is enforcing the law. He must play an elaborate role and, in doing so, he serves as a buffer between different social organisations and their conflicting standards of conduct. (Whyte 1943: 138)

This section has argued that the connections between police corruption and prohibited substances and services are complex. In particular, it is vital to criticise accounts which suggest, somewhat simplistically, that police corruption is responsible for illegal activities – for example, that an illegal drug trade exists in Kings Cross 'because' of police corruption. Whatever their intentions, such accounts push explanation towards a search for factors in individual officers and in police cultures and institutions. It is more convincing to reverse the causal sequence, and to suggest that it is the illegality of the drug trade which provides the basis for police corruption. Such corruption can be understood properly only if its conditions of existence are seen as being rooted in much broader social and legal structures. Corruption and the distribution of illegal substances and services are inextricably entwined in relations of dependence, control, and regulation.

Finally, it should be made clear that the policing of illegal substances and services is not exceptional: it simply provides a clear example of the positive functions of corruption. There are other, equally significant instances. Notably, relationships between some police and major criminals have to be understood not just in terms of financial corruption, but rather as functionally related to modes of policing in which attempts are made to control and regulate criminal activities. Such control is, it is believed, unattainable through conventional law enforcement measures. Of central significance here is the use of informers (see above). As ICAC noted, '[I]nformation is used as currency. It is provide in exchange for something – money, or help with bail, or outstanding charges and sentences are probably the most common rewards sought' (1994: 1). It has also apparently led to the effective franchising of some serious criminal activity. Such arrangements have to be seen as more than merely individual deviance and criminality, an approach which invites the moralistic identification of folk-devils which is the usual mode in which serious police corruption is presented. It has to be understood positively as a regulatory strategy and as a means by which organisational objectives can be achieved.

10. Conclusion

The analysis provided here suggests that effective corruption reform efforts must confront numerous, intertwined issues in the legal regulation of policing. It has been argued that the place of law in New South Wales policing is unsatisfactory, with a considerable gap between the rhetoric of invoking the rule of law and the reality in which practices are often loosely regulated and crucial activities are performed by evading or ignoring the law. Particular problems in central areas of investigative law and practice have been indicated. Generally, there is a need to clarify the relationship between law and police work in the context of the developing paradigm of community policing. Specifically, investigative practices need to be legally regulated by putting aside the tired dichotomy of police powers versus suspects' rights and appreciating that clear and effective legal regulation can benefit all participants in the justice process. Current reviews of investigative strategies should also take account of the problems noted here.

As regards accountability in general, it has been suggested that lack of legal clarity and the (sometimes apparently functional) confusion of legal and political rhetoric make the current position unsatisfactory. In the area of complaints and corruption investigations, experience suggests the need for types of problems to be differentiated, for subjective and contextual factors to be considered, and for internal and external controls to be combined. Most significantly, but not surprisingly, effective procedures require a positive approach from the police themselves which can only be the product of wider organisational and cultural change.

Corruption, it has been argued, must be seen in a new way if it is to be tackled. While it is routine to reject the 'bad apple'/'black sheep' approach, its effects permeate many analyses which purport to focus on structural factors. Corruption has to be seen as being intimately connected to approved ways of working, and not just as deviance. In particular, corruption must be appreciated for its positive contribution to the policing of illegal substances and services (notably, of course, drugs and prostitution) and to the relationships between investigating police, informers and serious criminals. To change this means not just dealing with corruption, but more fundamentally providing officers with the skills with and contexts within which they can operate in a way which is desirable.

The good news from the research literature is that police organisations can be reformed; the bad news is that such reforms are often not durable (Mollen 1994; Sherman 1978). The implication of this observation should be that reform must go beyond dealing with the specific problems usually associated with corruption: the task must be a thorough reassessment of police organisations. In the context of the issues discussed in this paper, the priorities should be to develop a new understanding of the nature and benefits of legal regulation of policing and to nurture and communicate a clear vision of both what is good and what is bad in policing.

4

The Normative Structure
of Policing

David Dixon

1. Codes of ethics, codes of practice, and other police rules

This chapter[1] discusses various types of formal normative guidance which
are provided to police officers by their superiors and, particularly, by
external authorities. These range in *form* from Acts of Parliament to local
internal directives, and can include police instructions, standing orders,
circulars and policy documents, as well as court decisions and 'mission
statements, statements of values, standards of conduct . . . statements of
objectives . . . codes of ethics and codes of conduct' (Kleinig 1993: xi;
see also Kleinig 1996). They vary in *substance* from a specific instruction
or prohibition to general endorsement of a value or principle. Each form
can display variety in substance: while it would be expected that, for
example, statutes would be used for more serious prohibitions, they may
also include general statements of principle.[2] The form may change. For
example, the NSW Police Service's Statement of Values[3] began as an
internal document, subsequently was included in the *Police Service Act*

---

1   I am grateful to Naomi Sharp for her research assistance and to Christine Parker for
    commenting on a draft.

2   See eg the *Police Service Act* 1990 s 7. For a more general example of what Preston
    (1995: 17) terms 'aspirational' legislation regarding ethics, see the *Public Sector
    Ethics Act* 1994 (Qld).

3   Its ancestor – the 1870 'Maxims for General Guidance of Members of the Police
    Force' – is credited by Kleinig as being the earliest value statement in the form of a
    code discovered in his comprehensive international survey (1993: 25-6, 32-3). For a
    survey of contemporary Australian police codes of ethics, see Darvall-Stevens
    (1994). For Canada, see Offer 1994 and, for the USA, see Carter and Stephens 1991.

1990,[4] and currently forms part of a Code of Conduct and Ethics produced by the Service.[5]

Of particular interest are codes of ethics and codes of practice. This chapter will concentrate on these types of norms, suggesting how they should relate to each other and to other written norms. While recognising the problem of categorisation, in what follows, I use the terms 'code of ethics' to include what are variously called statements of values, mission statements and similar *exhortatory* norms, and 'codes of practice' to include police instructions, codes of conduct and similar *directive* norms. However, usage by authors quoted below is not consistent.

The focus here is on normative statements which are presented in a formal way as rule, code, or statement of value. However, the normative influence of other modes of expression needs also to be recognised. For example, the Scarman Report's statement of fundamental policing principles has been of significance comparable to the 1829 Metropolitan Police Instructions (which it substantially restated). It was a foundational text in the shift to 'community policing'.[6] A somewhat similar role in New South Wales was taken for a time by John Avery's *Police – Force or Service?* (Avery 1981). More generally, there is the informal normative guidance provided to police by the complex of values, standards, working practices which is conventionally labelled 'police culture'.[7] Indeed, the codes considered here are often designed to alter aspects of police culture.

2. Codes of ethics

i. Evaluating codes of ethics

The Queensland Electoral and Administrative Review Commission suggested that the main questions concerning the utility of formally codifying an organisation's desired ethical standards are these:

---

4   See Section 7. Contrast Kleinig 1993, in which it is assumed that codes are internal documents.

5   'Code of conduct and ethics' *Police Service Weekly* v9 (6), 10 February 1997.

6   See Scarman 1981: para 4.55-4.58. For the 1829 instructions on 'Primary Objects of Police', see Kleinig 1993: 27. Ironically, a police code overtly drawing on Scarman (the Metropolitan Police's 1985 *Principles of Policing*) 'caused barely a ripple', largely because of its length (61 pages) and the way in which it was disseminated – 'as though it were a Sinaitic deliverance whose acceptability needed no participation by those for whom it was intended' (Kleinig 1993: 18). It was replaced by a brief statement of common purpose and values (Metropolitan Police 1989). A comparison with the Avery-inspired Statement of Values in New South Wales is hard to avoid, with the added factor of extensive rank and file resistance to the reform regime.

7   Note criticisms that such usage artificially suggests homogeneity (Chan 1997; Dixon 1997: ch 1).

(a)   is a code an effective means of guiding and controlling standards of official behaviour?
(b)   is a code relevant to what are seen as 'the real concerns' of the organisation?
(c)   how can a code be implemented, and
(d)   whose interests should be served by a code? (EARC 1991: 27)

Codes of ethics often attract a cynical response. Indeed, it is difficult not to be cynical about elements of some such statements, for example the exhortation in the NSW Police Statement of Values to 'capitalise on the wealth of human resources'.[8] The Royal Commission reported that this Statement and a supplementary Code of Conduct were ineffective in reducing corruption. They:

> gave little by way of practical guidance ... were not tested for their relevance and impact ... [and] their generality meant that they were ... incapable of enforcement ... yet their existence was somewhat blithely seen by the Service as the solution to the problem. (Wood 1997b: 496)

Some provisions in such statements are justifiably described as 'platitudinous', while in others 'there is often an undercurrent of priggishness that magnifies the social place and importance of the service provider' (Kleinig 1993: 13, 17). If a code of ethics consists of 'bombastic sermonising' without connection to the perceived realities of police work, it may be counterproductive (Niederhoffer 1967: 27). Most observers of policing can recall frequent dismissive comments about the display of such statements in police stations. As the Royal Commission reported, the Police Service's Statement of Values 'had little meaning to the recalcitrant or corrupt officer, or to the subversive supervisor' (Wood 1997b: 496). A common attitude was displayed by an officer giving evidence to the Police Integrity Commission about his familiarity with the Police Service's newly issued Code of Conduct

> I didn't read the content of it. You know, you flick the pages over, read the headline and that's about it. I mean, we get issued with that sort of – you know, memos and things all the time. (PIC 1998: 66)

To many police officers, such codes are just more irrelevant paper generated by headquarters.

It is easy to disregard a code of ethics as a merely routine gesture in responses to corruption (eg Ward and McCormack 1987: 144). It is certainly the case that the intended audience of codes is often as much outside as inside the organisation. For example, the production and particularly the enactment of the New South Wales statement of values

---

8   *Police Service Act* 1990 s 7(f). See Avery (1989: 97) for explanation of what this is intended to convey.

had considerable symbolic intention: it was part of efforts to persuade government and the public that policing in New South Wales was changing. This is not unusual. As Kleinig suggests, 'most codes of ethics can be interpreted as public promises, vows or . . . commitments' (1993: 3). Clark argues more sceptically that 'codes of conduct . . . are really about trying to give us as . . . the payers of bureaucracies . . . some reason to believe that people act with rationality, with reason, and with due regard to their obligations to society' (1991: 83).[9]

However, cynicism about codes of ethics must be qualified by recognition that some police react positively to them, and indeed some apparently attach considerable significance to, and feel supported by, such official endorsement of particular standards. As well as providing a point of reference for individual officers seeking guidance on ethical practice, statements of values may also have a beneficial organisational effect: they may 'unite service providers through the creation or advancement of an associational or organisational ethos. . . Professional and occupational loyalties are embedded in the ideology of code commitment' (Kleinig 1993: 14). The role of police educators and trainers who are committed to ethical standards is clearly of crucial significance here.

A serious deficiency in the literature is the lack of empirical studies of the impact of codes of ethics. At least in the field of criminal justice, it appears that no substantial research has been done in this area.[10] The literature tends to focus on theoretical or conceptual discussion in 'applied ethics' or 'applied philosophy'. Too often, the result is the production of vague normative statements about policing which ironically reflect some of the perceived problems of codes of ethics themselves. Preconceived ideas dominate: either codes of ethics are vital for good policing, or are rejected as irrelevant and mere rhetoric. It is rare for these responses to be founded on research, whether specifically about the impact of codes of ethics or more generally about policing. For example, McCormack comments critically on the lack of research evaluation of the (very costly) Ethical Awareness Training Program which all NYPD officers attended following the Knapp Commission: 'How much of the post-Knapp improvement can be attributed to quality leadership, administrative reform, tighter discipline, or training no one knows' (1987: 164). Putting it the other way around, no one (including the Mollen Commission) was able to rely on a solid knowledge base in assessing to what extent failures in leadership, administration, discipline and training

9   This approach is similar to, and shares weaknesses of, the PSI's classification of 'presentational rules': see below.

10   A rare, albeit limited, empirical study of officers' understanding of and attitudes to value statements is reported in Felkenes (1984).

contributed to the re-emergence of major corruption in New York City in the 1990s. This should provide a powerful counter to the usual assumptions that research is a marginal luxury.[11]

ii. Targeting a code of ethics

Davis is pessimistic about the prospects for a police code of ethics. To be comparable with other professional codes, a 'code of ethics must set standards beyond ordinary morality. . . It must require something more than ordinary morality requires, lay down principles ordinary morality does not, or set an ideal ordinary morality does not' (1991: 20; see also Davis 1995). Similarly, Rohr argues that professions such as law and medicine deduce their ethical standards from 'understanding of what it is that makes them *different* from everyone else' (1989: 16, original emphasis). Their professional ethics are significant insofar as they relate to specific types of work, with personal ethics being irrelevant: it 'is quite possible for a surgeon with impeccable ethical standards in his professional life to be an absolutely irresponsible parent, a compulsive gambler, an incorrigible lecher, and so forth' (Rohr 1989: 16; see also EARC 1992: 7).

The nature of police work makes this distinction between ordinary and professional ethics harder to maintain: much such work requires officers to act according to basic standards of morality associated with ordinary values, rather than distinct professional ethics. As Davis argues, police have trouble enough to 'maintain ordinary standards of decency' (1991: 24) because of the peculiar stresses and temptations of police work.[12] While this accounts for the banality of some such statements, they should not necessarily be dismissed:

> A code can help to maintain ordinary moral decency in at least three ways. First, a code can simply serve to remind police of what is (and therefore of what is not) expected of them. Second, it can provide a common vocabulary for discussion of hard cases. Is this a use of unnecessary force?[13] Third, the emotional language so common in police codes might also help to inspire an officer to do more than she would otherwise do. (1991: 24)

---

11   See Chapter 6, Sections 2 and 3, below.

12   Davis usefully suggests some ways of tackling these problems, such as reducing dependence on undercover work and organising work patterns so that officers do not 'lose touch with the world beyond police work. Departments may even want to require "sabbatical leaves" every few years' (1991: 25). An obvious addition would be minimising the criminogenic effects of prohibiting various substances and services: see Chapter 3, Section 9, above.

13   This provides an example of value statements which 'reference so-called thick ethical standards – those kinds of standards that have a direct behavioural analogue' (Clark 1991: 86). Statements should either be in this form, or should be followed by explanatory notes. Rhetorical appeals to vague concepts such as the 'rule of law' (eg *Police Service Act* 1990 s 7(b)) are, by themselves, of little value.

These are modest, but not insignificant, objectives. However, Davis suggests that 'while reading a stirring code may do as much good as listening to a Sunday sermon or making a New Year's resolution, it is unlikely to do more' (1991: 25). As noted above, it may be a mistake to undervalue even such apparently modest effects of codes of ethics. While much of the corruption and misconduct disclosed by the Royal Commission did not raise complex ethical issues, the inherently discretionary nature of everyday policing does involve officers in making choices and taking decisions which, despite their less sensational and controversial nature, do require significant exercises of moral judgment. For example, an officer who finds several ounces of heroin and thousands of dollars while conducting a search faces no significant moral dilemma: the choice is to record what is found accurately, or not. However, the general duties officer who comes across a sick addict about to inject has to choose, inter alia, between arresting the addict, ignoring the incident, and destroying the drugs. Her or his choice involves moral and ethical considerations, as well as, inter alia, profane matters such as departmental and local policies, and (official and personal) willingness to commit time to arresting and processing the user. It is easy (for the Royal Commission and everyone else) to focus on the dramatic and the sensational. However, it may be that it is the everyday and the mundane which is of more long term significance for the Police Service.

An important argument made by Davis is that even codes which do not go beyond statements of ordinary morality could be made significant and effective by building into them a 'whistleblower clause' – that is one encouraging officers to report conduct violating the code.[14]

> Such a provision is . . . necessary to any police code that is to be more than a mere restatement of what law, market and ordinary morality exact. Part of the specifically professional responsibility of police, probably the most important, is helping other police to do the right thing. That may, on occasion, mean breaking the 'code of silence'. (1991: 25)

Providing support for officers who need to break the code of silence may be a significant contribution of a statement of values.[15] Indeed, Davis argues that 'secondary standards' such as 'making the conduct of each officer the professional responsibility of every other' are likely to be the most significant parts of police codes of ethics (1991: 26).

---

14   For example, Article 8 of the United Nation's 'Draft Code of Conduct for Law Enforcement Officials' and NSW Police 'Code of conduct and ethics' *Police Service Weekly* v9 (6), 10 February 1997.

15   See the section on reporting corrupt conduct in the NSW Police Service's Code of Conduct and Ethics, *Police Service Weekly* v9 (6), 10 February 1997 p 5; note also the *Protected Disclosures Act* 1994 (NSW).

The moral dilemma of the wrongdoer may be less than that of the member of the organisation who knows of wrongdoing but is not involved, or is marginally involved. It is important to provide resources for such people, helping them to step back from wrongdoing, by positive (encouragement, availability of other values) in addition to negative means (deterrents, threats).

iii. Distinguishing between codes of ethics and codes of practice

As suggested above, between a statement of values and a regulatory prohibition, there is a substantial grey area of various standards, codes and rules. As codes of ethics become more specific and closer to rules of practice, their potential value may grow 'as benchmarks, as moral minima. The more detailed and declarative a code is, the more likely it is that the standards it sets out will be regulatory (in intent, at least) rather than merely aspirational' (Kleinig 1993: 15). Nevertheless, the distinction has significance, not least in insisting on appropriate uses of codes of ethics. Treating codes of ethics as if they were rules which management imposes on workers 'gives ethics a bad name but also prevents members of organisations from using ethics appropriately' (Brown 1990: xi).[16] This requires both careful consideration of what it is that a code of ethics or statement of values is intended to achieve, and precision in drafting. Davis usefully distinguishes between rules, principles and ideals as possible constituents. In his analysis, rules require or forbid action of a specified kind.[17] Principles allow for more flexibility: they 'state considerations that should have a certain weight in choice of action' (1991: 15). If a consideration is one which must be taken into account for a good decision to be made, it is a principle. Ideals are less specific: they 'identify a state of affairs to be aimed at – and, if possible, achieved' (1991: 20) without requiring specific action. Because the standard set is higher, falling short of an ideal is not necessarily blameworthy (Davis 1991: 20, 16). Codes or statements which fail to distinguish rules, principles and ideals (by, for example, using the directive 'shall' rather than the exhortatory 'should', or vice versa) are likely to be confusing and ineffective.[18]

---

16   Brown cites the example of a corporation which requires its employees to sign an 'ethics code', in which they promise that they will notify management whenever they observe a worker violating any of the code's provisions' (1990: xi).

17   Note Hart's influential jurisprudential critique of this account of rules (Hart 1961).

18   For examples, see Davis 1991: 17-19.

This does not mean that a code or statement should consist only of norms of one type, but simply that if 'the code is to be a mixture, great care should be taken to make clear which statements are ideals, which principles, and which rules' (Davis 1991: 19). These distinctions may be useful in dealing with two types of ethical problems which a code of ethics needs to cover (Heffernan 1982): fairly specific issues of integrity (misconduct, such as taking bribes) and discretionary decision making (hard choices between various legitimate courses of action). It is suggested that, if a code of ethics is to be developed, it should have a pyramidal structure, starting with fundamental norms, and then progressively becoming more detailed and directive (Ethics Interest Group 1991; see for example the structure of the code in Victoria Police 1988). This can be explicitly connected to codes of conduct establishing more specific rules, which in turn should be tied to statutory provisions. The aim should be a thorough revision and reconstitution of the normative structure of policing.

While codes of ethics can legitimately be expected to have instrumental and symbolic effects, they must be 'intended to *reflect* and *express* but not to *create* the public obligations of professional or occupational life' (Kleinig 1993: 3). As Brown argues, '[e]thics belongs in the decision-making processes of an organisation' (1990: xi). Experience suggests that codes of ethics have little effect if simply imposed: they have to be products of a positive engagement with existing values and practices, so that they become permeated into police cultures. (See below on implementation).

This has implications for the contents of codes of ethics. While the need to avoid platitudes and inanities must be acknowledged, statements must not be too specific or rule-like: the 'best ethical guides do not tell people what they should do; rather, they show people how to discover the best course of action for themselves' (Brown 1990: xi). This is important practically – values which people espouse after a process of reflection and internalisation are more likely to be deeply held than those which are merely officially endorsed and imposed. But there is also a matter of principle involved here. Police should behave ethically because of a commitment to doing so, not just because they are following a code:

> Codes encourage an externalisation of conduct not just by divorcing conduct from its appropriate springs, but by detaching it from a certain kind of subjectivity that makes it an authentic expression of the person whose conduct it is. The reasons for engaging in ethical conduct must ultimately come from within, and not without... [Otherwise] it will lack authenticity and *moral* value, whatever other values it may possess. (Kleinig 1993: 20)

These arguments weigh against the conventional code of ethics which identifies, 'in more-or-less general terms, prohibited behaviours and activities' and provides '[l]ittle, if any, explanation of the rationale . . . other than by way of broad reference to traditions or assumed general principles' (EARC 1991: 28). Directive statements and prohibitions find their place in codes of conduct and other rules: codes of ethics should focus on 'being positive, educative, and principles based'. They should aim 'to encourage public employees to develop skills in identifying ethics-related issues and apply ethical principles . . . in deciding how to act in particular circumstances' (EARC 1991: 28). From this perspective, a code of ethics should be used not to provide solutions to ethical problems, but as a resource which provides 'deliberative skills,' terms and concepts and encourages police to use them in thinking and talking through the difficult choices which their work inevitably involves (Kleinig: 1990: 9; Heffernan 1982).

These comments and the procedure for producing a code of ethics suggested below indicate that the aim should be to produce something rather different from the rather hackneyed nostrums in most codes (see eg Kleinig (ed) 1993). A starting-point for a debate about what principles should be in a code of ethics could usefully be the statements of rights relevant to criminal procedure found in international human rights treaties.[19]

iv. Enforcing values?

Can a code of ethics of the kind proposed here be enforced? There is clearly a danger that a normative structure which is seen as toothless will be regarded as mere rhetoric. Kernaghan argues strongly for the enforcement of codes of ethics:

> There are employees of course who are influenced only slightly or not at all by the exhortations of codes of ethics. . . It is for these employees that a code of ethics may serve as an instrument of administrative control. Senior officials may utilise the code as a means of judging whether an employee has acted properly in a given situation and as a basis for disciplining an employee who has acted improperly. With a written code of ethics in their possession, supervisors will no longer be obliged to admonish employees by making reference to vague and uncertain conventions and under-standings. . . It is not necessary for all employees 'to get religion' in the sense of being converted to strong adherence to the tenets of the code. What is especially important is that those in formal positions of authority or in informal positions of influence accept the code as one standard by which an

---

19   This suggested by Newton (1995). See also Ashworth (1994) for an elaboration of the argument that rights should be foundational to policing and the justice process.

> employee's conduct is assessed in connection with promotion and other rewards. The employee will be expected to achieve certain ethical standards as well as technical standards. If the employee does not 'get religion', he [sic] may at least 'get the message' that occupational success and congenial relations with fellow employees depend in part on his demonstrating appropriate ethical standards. Thus a code may be used both as an instrument of control and a means of influence over administrative action. (1975: 8)

There are dangers in this vigorous approach to enforcing values, and some significant distinctions need to be maintained. Providing disciplinary sanctions for breach of the fundamental values which, it is suggested here, are appropriately included in codes of ethics would raise serious problems of definitional vagueness and excessive discretion (Kernaghan 1980: 211).

But treating codes of ethics in this way does not entail abandoning enforcement. If code of ethics are to be taken seriously by those resistant to getting religion, then they cannot be left as mere presentational wishlists: they must be connected (both in practice and in employees' minds) with organisational processes of reward and sanction. The latter cannot be neglected: it is probably in the area of penalties that there lies the greatest potential for the delivery of strong messages – both positive and negative – about the credibility of an ethics regime (EARC 1991: 35).

However, they are not in themselves suitable as prohibitory norms backed directly by sanctions (either via a disciplinary regime or as breach of contract). As suggested above, codes of ethics need to be articulated with more specific norms in rules of conduct and codes of practice. In this way, values can be enforced via focused provisions in other rules. Whenever possible, 'disciplinary actions should specifically refer to violations of ethical standards, as well as the specific actions being disciplined' (Hyams 1991: 129). Contraventions should be admissible in court proceedings where relevant (eg in considering admissibility of evidence).

It is particularly important in police departments that supervisors should have specific responsibilities for promoting and ensuring ethical conduct by officers (Dalglish 1991: 6). Compliance should be monitored internally and externally (Clark 1991: 87; Norton 1991). More generally, the policing of ethical behaviour itself raises significant ethical problems. This was notably the case in New York City, where (in the period of post-Knapp anti-corruption activity) 'field associate' and integrity testing programs raised problems of entrapment and deception (Henry 1990b). The field associate program (in which officers were recruited to report corrupt activity) was a radical attempt to undermine the dysfunctional aspects of police trust and the code of silence. Less dramatic methods may also be used to the same end. Limiting the length of assignments is often employed, although costs may include dilution or loss of expertise[20] and dissatisfaction with the social and family consequences of moving. Facilitating inter-state transfer of officers is already on the agenda for the national coordination of policing, and it may have some beneficial effects. Certainly, one of the unsung reasons for improvement in some English police forces in the 1960s and 1970s was the effect of amalgamating small forces: several officers whom I interviewed (cf Dixon 1997) spoke of the difference made by not knowing whether they could trust their colleagues in the larger, less intimate forces which resulted.

v. Writing and implementing codes of ethics

Cynical responses to codes of ethics may be reduced by care in the way in which they are produced and presented, and by moderating their content. Like other imposed norms, codes of ethics are likely to meet resistance from junior officers. As in other cases, such resistance may be reduced if norms are 'the result of co-operative dialogue' rather than 'top-down productions ... alien impositions, motivated not by a commitment to service but by the desire for control, or by political exigencies or just plain arrogance' (Kleinig 1996: 250). As Davis suggests, codes 'that seem to come from above generally do not touch the world below' (1991: 26).

A careful balance must be struck here. Police leaders will wish to put their stamp on the organisation's ethical code, particularly if the leadership is committed to reform. Also, the public has a legitimate interest in police ethics, and should be engaged by consultation in the process of writing a code which should 'be an opportunity for a wider community to ask itself what it may reasonably expect of the providers of particular goods and services' (Kleinig 1993: 22). This setting of principles and priorities at a relatively high level may ultimately prove to be a more constructive form of community involvement than consultative committees at local level which, if experience elsewhere is a guide, will all too often be frustrated by lack of specific information and inability to challenge a local area commander's (often resource-led) priorities.[21]

---

20   For example the resistance to the introduction of maximum periods of service in some English detective departments.

21   See Chapter 6, Section 4ii, below.

But the input of the public and of police leaders must not overshadow that of more junior officers. Overt efforts have to be made to draw on the opinions and experience of operational officers, indeed to draw on and adapt, rather than simply oppose and suppress, the occupational culture (Goldsmith 1991). They have to be given 'a central part in writing, interpreting, and enforcing the code' (Davis 1991: 26). Useful lessons may be taken from the NSW Road and Traffic Authority's 'Ethics Campaign' which emphasised that the values it promoted were those of the majority of the staff themselves. This could be credibly claimed because the campaign included fairly extensive staff consultation. Amongst a variety of other initiatives, a 'Code of Conduct and Ethics' was drafted, issued for comment, redrafted and again issued for comment before taking its final form. Davidow and Williams suggest that the 'fact that the campaign was to support the values of staff and not to impose rules from "up high" helped the acceptance of the campaign among staff' (1993: 382; see also Findlay and Stewart 1991; Sampford 1992). This is consistent with the approach suggested by the Independent Commission Against Corruption which starts 'from the assumption that those people who do the job are in the best position to know what ethical conflicts are going to arise' (Moore 1991: 91). This should lead to production of a code of ethics which is specific to an organisation rather than general.[22]

Such precedents are particularly worth noting in the context of contemporary New South Wales, where there is evidence of resentment amongst some police officers about assumptions that corruption and misconduct are ubiquitous and of harm to morale associated with the Royal Commission (Chan 1998). It is clearly vital not to alienate such officers by inappropriate action[23] but rather to involve them in the reform process. Inviting their contribution to the production of a code of ethics or statements of values (and other norms) would be one useful way of doing this. Experience elsewhere suggests that contributions may be more positive and constructive than cynics may expect (Norman 1988). The code of ethics which emerges will then be one which officers can feel is their own (ICAC 1994a: 268). As in other areas,[24] the police must take responsibility for dealing with problems: inviting officers to contribute actively to producing their own statement of values would be to treat them with respect and to encourage responsibility, providing police

---

22   This raises doubts about the worth of the National Police Professionalism Advisory Committee's reported plan to promote a common code of ethics for Australian police forces (Darvall-Stevens 1994: 28).

23   Such as the random breath-testing announced by the NSW Government on 20 September 1995.

24   For example, complaints and discipline: see Chapter 3, Section 8iii, above.

officers with a constructive (and not as at present merely defensive) way of talking through problems which have been publicly identified. A product of consultative rule-making should be the avoidance of inappropriate rules of the type which provoke cynicism. More positively, 'the very task of drawing up a code should be an opportunity for an organisation or association to look at itself – to ask itself what it is really about, what it is reasonable to expect of its members, what standards should determine its . . . affairs' (Kleinig 1993: 22).

This implies an approach to 'police culture' which is different from the usual disparaging references. An occupational culture is neither unusual nor uniformly undesirable. Indeed, ethics of various kinds are important constituents of police culture: it just happens that most of them do not accord with what philosophers prefer to categorise as ethics (Sherman 1982). The challenge is to see police culture as a resource (Goldsmith 1991) and to make best use of desirable elements. For example, the 'code of silence' is a product of the pressures for interdependence which police work entails. Rather than simply condemning this 'code', attempts should be made to adapt it, or to provide other ways of dealing with the pressures producing it.[25] Davis argues that a code of ethics could be valuable if it stressed 'an officer's responsibility for helping fellow police to do the right thing' (1991: 26). Rather than requiring silence and cover-up, police culture could encourage moral support, debate amongst officers about ethical conduct, interventions when misconduct occur and, ultimately, possibly even acceptance of whistle-blowing.[26] Henry notes that one effect of the post-Knapp anti-corruption strategy in the NYPD was that the:

> police subculture's unquestioning adherence to the code of silence has been seriously undermined, and many police who desire to remain honest throughout their careers have been freed of some of the constraints imposed by the code of silence. At the very least, these policies allow younger officers the opportunity to maintain their own integrity. (Henry (1990b: 54)

This approach depends upon an optimistic assessment of serving officers:

> If one assumes that most police officers are basically honest, hardworking people who wish to do a good job, a pervasive organisational effort to root out serious corruption provides these officers with an opportunity to resist peer group pressure in that direction. (McCormack 1987: 155)

---

25 Similar arguments are made by Ewin (1990) and Henry (1990b) about police 'loyalty'. See also Kleinig (ed) 1993; Kleinig 1997: ch 4.

26 For more discussion of whistle-blowing, see Barrett 1993; Grabosky (ed) 1977; EARC 1990; Wren 1985.

An effective anti-corruption strategy will, almost certainly, combine stick and carrot. McCormack suggests how one example of using the stick can provide room for good police and desirable elements of police culture to have influence:

> A strong proactive internal affairs initiative provides 'an excuse for being honest that may be acceptable to many of the rank and file. . . Under intense supervision, reluctance to engage in unethical conduct may be viewed not only as acceptable but also as prudent. As a result, many officers who are seeking ethical guidance may secretly welcome such efforts if policies are realistic and fair. (1987: 15)

This suggests the need for careful connection of stick and carrot (McCormack 1987: 154-63). Sticks can make carrots more appetising. However, especially in the wake of scandalous corruption disclosures, the stick is used most: it much easier for politicians and police leaders to show that they are acting against corruption by dramatic use of the stick. In addition, some support for use of the stick may be drawn from the literature on police corruption associated with the Knapp Commission (eg Sherman 1975). However, the case of New York illustrates the limitations of the stick, limitations which literature on the limits of deterrence should have made predictable (eg von Hirsch and Ashworth (eds) 1998: ch 2). As public attention and outrage fade, so the priority given to aggressive anti-corruption tactics fades away. The experience of Queensland shows how politicians can encourage this, as in (then) Police Minister Mackenroth's reported assertion that 'it's about time we put the Fitzgerald Inquiry and what has come out of it behind us and start looking to the future'.[27] If the fundamental organisational culture remains little changed, new corruption scandals must be expected to emerge (Mollen 1994; Wood 1997b).

Once a code of ethics has been introduced, how can ethical behaviour be internalised? It seems clear on both practical and philosophical grounds that production of a statement is not enough. Rather, as suggested above, a codes of ethics should be used to confirm and consolidate commitments which already have substantial roots. Again, it is clear that police education and training must play an important part in growing those roots. As Finnane points out, '[i]f literacy and education are the principal means available to our culture in the production of ethical conduct, then developments in police training in the twentieth century have only slowly advanced towards that end' (1990b: 221).

---

27 *Courier Mail*, 8 January 1990, p 10 as quoted by Henry (1990a: 21). Note also the calls for police to switch their focus from corruption reform to crime fighting, discussed in Chapter 6, below.

Nonetheless, some good work has emerged from the NSW Police Academy. Whatever problems there may have been in delivery and reception at the Academy, the vision of police as 'reflective practitioners' provides a good foundation for police reform (Bradley and Cioccarelli 1989, 1994; Bradley 1992; Cioccarelli 1994).

It is hardly contestable that ethics should be the concern of police education. A code of ethics may provide an initial focus for such teaching (Kleinig 1990; Massey 1993). But rather than being corralled in the conventional class devoted specifically to it, ethics should be integrated throughout the syllabus. Students should be encouraged to 'create and internalise their own moral codes' rather than having ethics presented as a 'topic'. In this form of ethical education, 'methods such 'as interactive discussions that focus on complex issues, decision making, monitored use of scenarios and case studies are particularly appropriate' (Braunstein and Tyre 1992: 32; cf Kleinig 1990). Ethical education must continue beyond initial training:

> In many organisations, the academy is the last time employees are exposed to ethical standards. It is not the last time they are exposed to officer safety training, nor is it the last time they receive training in technical skills. Technical skills training occurs throughout an officer's career, and so should training in ethical standards. (Hyams 1991: 129)

Ethical training should be thoroughly integrated into in-service and managerial training.

The Royal Commission's Report concluded similarly:

> It is essential that professionalism and integrity become the backbone of the Service, and that the theme 'integrity first' be regularly reinforced... This means that it should be included as a specific component in all training, not just as bare rhetoric, but worked into each course in a way relevant to it and delivered by recognised experts in ethics. (1997b: 281)

Education in ethics should be practical and pervasive: '[t]he teaching of ethics and integrity [should] be integrated, in a practical way . . . into every aspect of police education and training' (1997b: 282). The objective should be 'constant reinforcement of the importance of ethical policing' (1997a: 28).

While acknowledging its great importance, I do not wish to concentrate here on police education. There is a danger is marginalising the issue of ethics in policing by categorising it as the educators' business. If a code of ethics of values is to be more than rhetoric, then it must state values which are taken seriously throughout the organisation and which are affirmed and reinforced regularly: 'if police ethics is to be cordoned off to one area of the curriculum but otherwise ignored, then students could conclude that their superiors view it as a matter of public relations rather than an essential part of policing' (Heffernan 1982: 29). The significance of ethics should be reinforced throughout the organisation's operations (ICAC 1994b: 31-2). For example, '[r]outine communications should integrate ethical standards into policies and procedures and state the connection' (Braunstein and Tyre 1992: 30). Issues of values should be 'discussed at departmental meetings, reviewed at roll-calls and referred to in the decision-making process, both organisationally and individually' (Hyams 1991: 129). Police leaders should consciously present themselves as ethical role models.[28] Promotion criteria should include evidence of understanding of and adherence to ethical standards. Disciplinary proceedings should refer specifically to breaches of ethical standards. In general, as Braunstein and Tyre argue, '[e]thically sound police officers are most likely to be found in an atmosphere that clearly gives high priority to ethical behaviour and integrates ethics into every part of the department' (1992: 30).

Ethical behaviour should not simply be taken for granted, but should be rewarded: this is a feature of the more general need to change the character of police departments which have all too often been 'punishment centred bureaucracies' (Gouldner 1954) in which officers are subject to a mass of prohibitions, but fewer guides to good policing. As argued in Chapter 3 (above), police organisations must become as adept at identifying good practice and rewarding officers for carrying it out as they are at creating disciplinary rules and punishing officers for breaking them. In the process of defining 'good policing', the production of a statement of values may be a valuable step – but only so long as it is seen as part of a much broader process.[29] Finally, production of a code of ethics is not the end of the matter: it 'must be reviewed periodically to measure its effectiveness' and amendments made where necessary (Darvall-Stevens 1994: 26).

---

28   The importance of them making quite clear their commitment to the code of ethics is often stressed in the literature (Mangan 1992; Norton 1991; Dalglish 1991; Robinette 1991; Willingham and Tucker 1988).

29   The Royal Commission reported that there was need for 'a definition of "good policing" that is understood and accepted by the rank and file, [and] is based upon sound ethical standards and impartiality. . . A useful beginning has been made by the Service with the replacement of the vaguely defined and uninstructive Statement of Values by a broad and enforceable Code of Conduct and Ethics' (Wood 1997b: 38). As noted below, this overlooks the fact that the Statement of Values is part of the new Code. See also McConkey et al 1996.

vi. Values, codes and 'professionalism'

As Kleinig suggests, 'causal or historical factors' in the production of codes of ethics in policing and elsewhere 'include the desire for social enhancement, the protection of turf, a defence against external controls, a heightened sense of moral and social accountability, or the desire to consolidate group identity and provide a group ethos' (1993: 7). Stressing the link between codes of ethics and the attainment of 'professional' status, the Electoral and Administrative Review Commission usefully summarised the 'narrow professional purposes' of codes of ethics as including:

(a) the control of conduct of members in relation to their clients, and other members;

(b) the accreditation of educational standards within the profession;

(c) the control of the right to practise and the control of fee-setting; and

(d) the reassurance of governments and the public that the profession is properly regulated, thereby avoiding external regulation of standards of conduct and the scale of fees which may be charged. (EARC 1991: 25)

The burgeoning of statements of values, codes of ethics and the like is a product of two sometimes related, sometimes conflicting influences: 'a desire for professional status or accreditation' and 'a demand for accountability, both internal and external' (Kleinig 1993: x). The methods of seeking professional status and accreditation in policing are similar to those used elsewhere, are related, and are clearly influenced by similar managerialist literature (Bradley et al 1986). The central feature of professionalisation in policing has been the attempt to establish police as crime-fighting experts holding a monopoly of law enforcement. A major theme in policing literature is the irony of an organisation setting a standard for its own evaluation which was so unattainable: it is now trite to point out that conventional policing by means of random patrol and reactive investigation can have only a marginal impact on crime, that most police work does not involve law enforcement, and that much policing is carried out by private institutions (Jones and Newburn 1997; Johnston 1992).

It is important to consider what 'professionalism' is intended to provide to police. Davis argues forcefully that being a professional should not be identified with privilege, status and high income.

> Some professions have relatively low income, low status, and few privileges. Think, for example, of priests, teachers, or nurses. And many people with relatively high income, high status and great privilege are not professionals. Think, for example, of movie stars, 'professional athletes', or stock arbitrageurs. Police need to remember that. If they do not, any

> infatuation with ethics is likely to be short-lived and disappointing. Police do not have high income, high status or great privilege in any free society. They probably never will, code of ethics or no. (1991: 23)

Nor is it realistic to expect policing to be free of legal regulation in the way that some exponents of police professionalism suggest. At least so far as policing involves the state's interference with significant rights and liberties of citizens, it is vital that policing be closely legally regulated.[30]

What is left of 'professionalism' is its idealised core: the concept of a profession as 'a voluntary cooperative undertaking the [primary] purpose of which is public service' (Davis 1991: 23). If police are serious about wanting to be professionals, then their commitment to public service must be given credibility and substance. In this, production of a code or statement of ethics may be a useful step (although it must not be confused with actual achievement). If police set higher priorities – such as seeking to 'extend their political autonomy and influence and broaden their discretion (Holdaway 1983: 163; see also Ericson 1981: 222-7) or merely to make money and have a secure job (Davis 1991) – then claims to professionalism and codes of ethics will be of no more than presentational value.

The search for professional status often involves insistence on self-regulation and resistance to external control: indeed, codes and statements are often:

> put forward as evidence of a capacity for self-regulation... The code speaks of self-governance, of autonomy and dedication... [O]ne of the first projects of an occupation seeking to improve its place in the world – socially, as well as economically – is the formulation, adoption and promulgation of a code of ethics... A hall-mark of professionalism – at least in theory is self-regulation... Answerability within obviates the need for answerability without. (Kleinig 1993: 8, 11-12; see eg Barlow and Proctor 1980)

In the case of policing, this aspect of professionalisation has a particular significance which contains some apparent contradictions. Police have resisted or attempted to avoid political control and accountability by insisting that the mark of their professionalism is control by law. And yet police also reject legal regulation on the grounds that true professionals are endowed with wide discretion making tight rules inappropriate: theirs is a 'discretion-dependent expertise' (Kleinig 1993: 7). The apparent contradiction is resolved by recognition that the control by law which police espouse is a largely rhetorical invocation of the 'rule of law': they are happy to be accountable to 'the law', but not to laws, and to be controlled by the 'rule of law' in rhetoric, but not by the human and institutional

---

30   These points are elaborated below; see also Dixon 1997.

makers of laws (eg Lauer 1994). In Section 3 (below), police resistance to specific legal regulation and proposals for reconstructing the regulatory framework are considered.

vii. Prospects for codes of ethics

For codes of ethics to be of real worth, they must be expressions of a fundamental change in policing. If, as at present, they are simply a routine feature of the new managerialism which is familiar in almost every bureaucratic workplace, little can be expected of them. Equally, a code of ethics is likely to have little worth if it is recommended in a reflex response to the identification of ethical problems without considering what a code should include, how it should be implemented, and what it can be expected to achieve (eg Lee 1992).

It is possible that codes of ethics could be more than this. If 'community policing' is taken seriously as an alternative paradigm in policing (and not just as a way of packaging traditional policing), then fundamental values will change, and the process of defining and articulating them may be useful. Community policing involves a radical delegation of responsibility to operational officers:

> Crucial for understanding this new orientation – and indeed a critical premise for its success – is the principle that officers, in consultation with those they police, participate as equal partners with management in redefining their job roles, tailoring them to specific neighbourhood needs and problems. The assumption is that police and citizens are personally involved as coproducers of public safety and the improvement of the citizenry's quality of life. (Donahue and Felts 1993: 349)

It requires officers 'to define and redefine the vocation' of policing (Donahue and Felts 1993: 350). As suggested previously, community policing entails a new ethos, philosophy or ideology, the implications of which have not yet been worked out. The conclusion may be put starkly. If community policing develops as its proponents advocate, codes of ethics will be important. If it does not, and the old model of 'professional policing' reasserts itself either directly via new crime control strategies (Dixon 1999b), then they are unlikely to be worth the paper on which they are written.

It is important here to emphasise the need for ideological change (both within the police and in general population) in the way in which policing is conceived. The significance of policing must be appreciated in public, political culture.[31] Contrary to the prevailing 'thin, common-

---

31   For arguments about the general need for political understanding of the nature of public service, see Wakefield 1976.

sensical view of police work' (Bradley 1992: 138), it is inadequate to see policing as a profane, intellectually and morally undemanding activity to understand which the highest level of abstraction required is the metaphor of 'balance' between rights and powers. Without encouraging the rhetorical self-aggrandisement which mars too many police accounts (eg Lauer 1994), it has to be recognised that policing is a crucial social practice, in which relations between state and citizen have to be worked through in sharp and often difficult conflicts of interest. The cultural change to which a code of ethics and police training may contribute must include an understanding of the power which police officers have and of the responsibility which this entails. This is conventionally expressed in terms of social contract theory – the delegation of authority by society to police.[32] However, the limits of social contract theory in this as in other contexts must be acknowledged (Doyle 1992). 'Social contract' is, at best, an aspirational metaphor. It tends to draw attention away from the realities of the historical police mandate in societies which are structured by divisions of class, race, age and gender (Reiner 1992; Manning 1997). One does not have to be a Marxist to appreciate that bland commitments to 'serving the community' are problematic.

At present, too many police seem oblivious to the constitutional significance of the powers which they possess (to search, to arrest, to detain, etc). Too often, the appearance is given that they are administering 'a class of people who are not worth protecting or not capable of living decent lives. As irredeemable, they cannot be harmed by the officer's actions – so they are only fit to be exploited, ignored, or contained' (Cohen 1983: 242). The Royal Commission's Report recognises this to some extent, suggesting that police must be 'adequately instructed as to the use of their powers within a context that promotes impartiality, teaches legal values and principles, and reinforces the understanding that the law applies to police and that they hold an office which attracts special responsibilities rather than exemptions' (Wood 1997a: 38). The Report includes a valuable recommendation of a 'positive and sustained program' emphasising the importance both in principle and practice of operating according to due process and the rule of law (1997b: 427).

Putting the point more strongly, police should be aware of the significance, in a liberal democratic society, of the powers which have been given to them, of the need for specific justification of intrusion into individual liberty, and of the inclusive nature of citizenship (the promise

---

32   For example, Cohen and Feldberg (1991). For an example of a code explicitly based on 'social contract', see the French National Police Code of Ethics (Marin 1991: 293).

of equality) in a democratic society. It is not merely in police culture that change is necessary: our political culture more generally seems to lack understanding of foundational issues in relations between democratic states and their citizens. A major problem to be addressed is a widespread cynicism which pervades Australian criminal justice: this is discussed in more detail elsewhere (see Chapter 6, below; Dixon 1996b). To what extent is change possible, and what contribution could be made by a code of ethics of the type discussed above? Perhaps optimism of the will, but pessimism of the intelligence (Gramsci 1971) is the best guide.

In 1997, the New South Wales Police Service issued a new 'Code of conduct and ethics' which the Police Commissioner presented as 'a cornerstone for positive change and growth in the Police Service'.[33] The Royal Commission welcomed it (Wood 1997a: 38), but went on 'to recognise that in the past statements of weighty principle have not served to prevent corruption or misconduct. Publication of the Code should not be seen as a sufficient measure in itself to deal with the problems that it addresses. Rather it should be part of an overall strategy' (Wood 1997b: 497). Officers are informed that the Code's purpose 'is to make explicit certain behaviours which are unacceptable . . . and to provide an ethical framework for your decisions and actions'. What is described as an 'organisational code' includes a 'guide to ethical decision making'[34] and the Statement of Values which the Royal Commission had found to be so ineffective (Wood 1997a: 38; 1997b: 496; see above). It also deals with such matters as reporting corrupt conduct, the effect of criminal convictions, conflicts of interest, acceptance of gifts or benefits, discrimination and harassment, managers' responsibilities, customer rights, limitations of authority, professional competency and development, private conduct, public comment, protection of information, secondary employment, use of alcohol and other drugs, and provision for the Code's enforceability.

3. Rules, codes and instructions

i. Rules and policing

How significant are rules in policing? It is important to begin by making some distinctions between types of rules. An influential analysis of rules

---

33   See *Police Service Weekly* v9 (6) 10 February 1997.

34   This underemphasises the moral choices which officers must make, suggesting that decision-making should be guided by government and police service policy, evaluation of likely outcomes, consideration of potential conflict of interest, justifiability 'in terms of the public interest', and capacity to 'withstand public scrutiny' (op cit n 33 pp 4-5).

was provided by the Policy Studies Institute in its research (commissioned by the Metropolitan Police) on policing in London. The PSI suggested that there are three kinds of rules:

> *Working rules* are those that are internalised by police officers to become guiding principles of their conduct. *Inhibitory rules* are those which are not internalised, but which police officers take into account when deciding how to act and which tend to discourage them from behaving in certain ways in case they should be caught and the rule invoked against them. *Presentational rules* are ones that exist to give an acceptable appearance to the way that police work is carried out. It is important to realise that it is not only or even mainly the police who seek to put this gloss on the reality of policing behaviour. Most of the presentational rules derive from the law itself and are part of a successful attempt by the wider society to deceive itself about the realities of policing. (Smith 1986: 89)

In a research report on policing in Northern England, we suggested the addition of two categories: *reactive rules* are those created by police hierarchies in response to specific incidents and perceived problems, while *routinised rules* are those which may have initially been effective, but which have become ritualised and ineffective (Bottomley et al 1991: 193-4; Dixon 1997: 8). Such analyses have certain limitations. By concentrating on individual rules, they tend to underestimate the potential combined impact of groups of rules, which may include norms of various types. The PSI's work is functionalist in its assumption that a rule's effects are necessarily intended. By implication, it overlooks the possibility that a rule may become more (or less) effective as a result of its interpretation and implementation: rules are not self-executing: an apparently 'presentational' rule may be made to work in an inhibitory way as a result of 'organisational and institutional changes' (Baldwin and Kinsey 1985: 91). Nonetheless, these classifications provide a useful way of analysing rules. They suggest a lesson which is rather obvious, but is all too often ignored in discussions of legal regulation: the appropriate question is not 'Should we use rules?' but rather 'When should we use rules, and what kind of rules should we use?'

It might be might be thought that evidence of the rule-dominated nature of policing is provided by the voluminous books of rules and regulations which most police forces have produced. Bittner remarked that American police organisations were 'permanently flooded with petty military and bureaucratic regulations' (1970: 68, n 100). This was not simply bureaucratic excess: 'the requirement for administrative due process in police discipline', attempts to avoid civil liability by having 'guidelines prohibiting the act in question', and agency accreditation requirements have all encouraged the production of formal policies and rules (Cordner 1989: 18). In addition, rule-making was promoted as the best way of controlling police discretion by legal academics, notably KC Davis (1969: see below).

But this 'flood' itself belies legalistic/bureaucratic claims about the nature of policing (Dixon 1997: 1-8): 'the rules and regulations which typify police departments are so numerous and patently unenforceable that no one will (or could) obey' them all (Van Maanen 1974: 100). Until recently, amongst the rules and regulations for the New South Wales police, one could find this:

> Hair will be neatly cut and conform to the following requirements. . . Not to extend at the back below a line 1.5 centimetres above the shirt collar. . . Side-burns, if worn, not to extend below lines level with the points where ear lobes join the face, to be evenly tapered, not thick and bushy and must not increase in width throughout their length.

Such precision rubs shoulder with much broader rules: for example, 'Police who habitually quarrel with comrades will be liable to dismissal'.[35] At his appointment as Police Commissioner, Tony Lauer referred to 'the difficulty of relying on "two huge volumes" when no-one, including himself, knew exactly what was in them'.[36] As Bradley and his colleagues say, such rule-books 'should be seen as blueprints, guides to a possible reality, an abstract and partial account of how things could or should be, rather than an account of how things are' (1986: 121). While they see them as 'conceptions', a Metropolitan Police Sergeant described his force's General Orders as containing '140 years of fuckups. Every time something goes wrong, they make a rule about it' (quoted, Manning 1997: 149; this is a more colourful description of 'reactive rules': see above). Rule books have been a major characteristic and tool of police departments as 'punishment oriented bureaucracies'. Any observer of policing is soon aware of how limited is the effect of standing orders and force instructions on police. As part of more general changes in policing, several forces are responding by scrapping their voluminous rule books in favour of brief codes of ethics and objectives.[37] In January 1999, the NSW Police Service replaced its Commissioner's Instructions with a simplified and considerably reduced Police Service Handbook.

---

35   NSW Police Instructions (1989) 2.38 and 2.48.

36   *Sunday Telegraph*, 17 March 1991, p 3.

37   See Tendler 1988, and Hilliard (1988: 1489) on the replacement of 13000 pages of standing orders to West Midlands Police by 'a 300 page volume and a yellow card giving 10 criteria for the efficient performance of police duty'.

ii. Rules versus discretion?

The concept of professionalism which was associated with the mass production of police rules has been challenged by arguments from both within and outside the police that true professionalism requires wide discretion rather than rule-based direction (NSW Police 1988; Sparrow et al 1990). Drawing managerialist lessons from corporate practice, '[p]olice executives are . . . relying less on rules and constant supervision and more on selection, training and the articulation of values to create a culture that can properly guide officer conduct' (Moore and Stephen 1991: 5; see also Cordner 1989). At one level, this is simply the application to policing of what has become accepted wisdom in management literature: authority is to be devolved, responsibility is to be pushed down the line, and centralised direction is to be minimised (EARC 1991: 27). The new managerialism provides a rhetoric for and adds force to a much deeper change in theories and rationales of policing. The new policing associated with problem solving and community-oriented strategies (Moore 1992) distances itself from law and 'enthusiasm for these reforms grows precisely because of the perceived failures of the rule of law' (Mastrofski and Uchida 1993: 353). Just as law enforcement is no more than one part of the police function, so law loses its place as the prime legitimator of policing.

Such developments require a careful response. First, as argued in Section 1, the normative structure of policing needs to be reconstituted. On a basis of foundational values and principles, a structure of more specific rules, codes and instructions should be constructed. The process of consultative norm-making suggested for producing a code of ethics should be extended to other rules and instructions (Goldsmith 1991). Secondly, it is clearly desirable to rewrite the rules supposedly regulating most police services. This is likely to reduce drastically their current bulk. Along with scrapping redundant and ineffective rules, there should be a commitment for the future use of rules: reactive rule-making should not be the reflex response to perception of a problem. It must be stressed that this should not lead a general abandonment of regulation. In crucial areas of policing practice, good rules are vital, for example, to specify and define police powers and suspects' rights. More generally, the relative success of administrative rule-making in some areas (eg the control of police shootings in the USA: see Walker 1993: 25-33) attests to the potential value of such regulation. Similarly, the experiment with regulation by means of codes of practice in England and Wales deserves attention, and will be used as an example below. Thirdly, attention needs to be given to the process by which legal changes (both by legislative and judicial action) are absorbed by the Police Service and communicated to officers.

The general aim is to achieve an appropriate blend of norms (of various kinds) and discretion. How can this be achieved? The starting-point for modern analysis of this question is the work of KC Davis (1975, 1977). His extremely influential analysis argued that rules need not only be negative, restricting discretion. They can also be positive in chan-nelling the exercise of discretion by structuring and checking:

> Structuring includes plans, policy statements, and rules, as well as open findings, open rules, and open precedents... Checking includes both administrative and judicial supervision and review. (1977: 5)

Davis emphasised the value of administrative rule-making by police (and other agencies) themselves. However, as suggested above, the analysis applies equally well to rule-making by external authorities and to use of value-statements and codes of ethics as well as more clearly defined rules.

Davis has attracted criticism, notably for his failure to escape the Diceyan, legalistic attitude that discretion is inherently 'bad' and therefore necessarily to be minimised (Baldwin 1995). It is appropriate to point to the value as well as the inescapability of discretion: it provides ability to deal responsively to the endless variety of instances and requires police to take responsibility for their actions (rather than retreating behind claims that they are 'just enforcing the law').

> 'Hard cases' are not uncommon in police work. The very nature of the work often involves a careful assessment of individual and social interest that cannot be reconciled, and the wise exercise of discretion is required. (Kleinig 1993: 21)

The implications of this must be taken into account in writing rules: the aim should not primarily be to restrict discretion, but rather to provide for its best use. In this respect, guidance such as statements of principle or explanatory advice may be more useful than attempting to make a specific rule or prohibition. Kleinig warns that codes of ethics 'are rarely helpful to the making of (discretionary judgments in hard cases). They enumerate goals and standards without indicating priorities or procedures for handling conflicts between code requirements' (1993: 21). This should warn against relying too much on codes of ethics or rules, but perhaps underemphasises their role in articulation with more specific norms and their potential contribution in indirectly affecting discretionary choices by influencing police 'common sense' and culture. Here, value statements and codes have to operate in conjunction with other influences, such as training, external consultation, etc.

Fundamental to Davis's proposals for structuring discretion was an insistence on the need for openness in administration. This continues to be a problem in Australian police services: some officers still apparently believe that the sky will fall if, for example, the Police Rules and Instructions are made publicly available, or researchers have access to the institution. It finds expression, not so much in flat refusals to cooperate, but rather in seemingly endless swamps of bureaucracy and responsibility-shifting. Shernock (1990) convincingly identifies police alienation from and suspicion of the public as being a key factor in promoting unethical practices. The *public* discussion and production of a code of ethics and new police rules and instructions could be part of a continuing opening up of police services, and could consequently contribute to the reform process.

In brief, the dichotomy between rules and discretion is false. An elaborate structure of rules is inevitable, given the nature of policing. Such rules should not aim to suppress discretion, but to improve its exercise. Discretion is no more inherently undesirable than rules. Good policing inevitably involves officers taking responsibility for their decisions. The regulation of discretion should aim to assist officers in doing so.

iii. The *Police and Criminal Evidence Act* 1984 as an example of rule-making for police

It may be worth considering a specific example of normative restructuring in policing – the reconstitution of investigative practices associated with the introduction and subsequent adaptation of the *Police and Criminal Evidence Act* 1984 (PACE) in England and Wales. Some conflicting interpretations of the legislation's impact were noted in Chapter 3 (above; see also Dixon 1997). Here, the focus is on the strategic use of norms in and associated with PACE.

A notable feature of PACE has been the variety and adaptability of the modes of legal regulation employed. The basis is the statute itself. It is important that fundamental matters be given the authority of an Act of Parliament: for example, the inclusion of the right to legal advice in PACE s 58 was of both symbolic and practical importance. But the most interesting and (in a policing context) innovative use of rules has been the Codes of Practice dealing with stop/search, search of premises, detention and questioning, identification, and tape recording.

The codes contain a variety of material, ranging from straight-forward supplementary instructions to explanations of and advice on the interpretation of other rules. Much of the material is of the sort which in Australia might be included in Police Instructions. However, there are some telling differences. The codes have statutory authority and weight. A result has been extensive judicial consideration of their requirements and implications. They are produced, not as internal police documents, but as secondary legislation requiring the approval of both Houses of Parliament. There was extensive parliamentary discussion of the first codes. Drafts of codes are subject to a consultative process: this has proved to be more than a formality, with the Home Office paying attention to academic research findings and views of outsiders. The codes are adaptable (significantly more so than primary legislation), and have been revised twice since 1986.[38] These revisions allow account to be taken of experience and developments. As the consultative process suggests, the codes are public documents. A copy must be offered to detained suspects. As would be expected, PACE and the codes are supplemented by Home Office circulars (notably 22/1992 on 'Principles of Investigative Interviewing') and various force orders and instructions which attempt to explain, detail and relate to local contexts. In sum, PACE provides an important example of legal regulation, an exercise in rule-making which demonstrates many of the techniques and methods which are features of modern public law, but which are rarely thought of as being relevant to policing.

PACE's impact has varied according to the area of policing affected, the nature of the rules employed, their relationship with informal 'working rules', and the influence of contextual factors (Brown 1997; Dixon 1997). Despite its elaborate structure, PACE has not reduced policing to the mechanical application of rules. Some areas of policing have proved to be resistant to rules where activities are hard to supervise and are related to fundamental mandates and methods which the regulators paid insufficient attention. In particular, the attempt to regulate stop and search seems to have had little success despite the attempts in revisions of the codes of practice, circulars and local instructions to refine crucial issues such as the meaning of 'reasonable suspicion' and the relevance of 'consent' (Dixon 1997: ch 3). Indeed, stop and search continues to provide the best example for the PSI's category of 'presentational rules' (see above). If activities such as stop and search are to be regulated, rules have to be used as only one tactic in a much broader strategy of change (Dixon et al 1989).

The limits of rules have also been demonstrated in another important area – the questioning of suspects. In general, researchers conclude that

---

38   The current codes were implemented in April 1995.

PACE has had a substantial, beneficial effect on the crucial police practices of detaining and questioning suspects before charge (Dixon 1997: ch 4; Brown 1997; contrast McConville et al 1991). Police officers have clearly benefited from the clarification of their powers and duties.

However, it is a simplistic, positivist view of law which expects complete certainty. A crucial development in the impact of PACE has been the progressive interpretation by the courts of some sections: the result has been to leave some officers feeling that the 'sea change' has been into a 'sea of uncertainty' (Northumbria Police 1994). A notable example of this is the Heron case, in which a suspect's confession to the murder of a young girl was excluded from evidence (leading to his acquittal) despite the investigating officers' belief that they were acting within the rules, the lack of complaint from the suspect's legal advisers, and the approval of the Crown Prosecution Service. The trial judge's expansive treatment of the concept of oppression (in PACE s 76) caused consternation amongst many police officers. The point, of course, is that law has interpretative flexibility as a central characteristic. Such interpretations will change (despite the pleas for certainty), particularly as contexts change: in the case of interpreting 'oppression', a crucial factor was clearly judicial unease with continuing revelations about police malpractice.[39]

Of interest here is the police reaction to decisions. One, not surprising, response was for officers to demand specific and comprehensive instructions on what can and cannot constitute oppression. But other, more constructively, realised that this was impossible, and that regulation of investigative practice would require norms of a different kind. The result has been the growth of interest in 'ethical interviewing'. This provides, not a set of prohibitions and directives, but rather guidance on values and methods.[40] This example shows that the type of norms has to be chosen carefully to achieve desired purposes, and the potential for coordinating norms of various types.

4. Conclusion: the normative structure of policing

The limits of legal regulation can be readily acknowledged. Much police work does not involve law enforcement or duties with clear legal frames. Even when legal regulation is applicable, police have historically (for

---

39 See eg the Lord Chief Justice's comments in *R v Paris* (1993) 97 Cr App R 99 which provided the basis for the defence counsel's and trial judge's approach in Heron (Dixon 1997: 170-6; 1999a).

40 See eg National Crime Faculty (1998); Shepherd (1991). But note Newton's critique (1995) of the deficiencies of material provided to officers on interviewing.

both good and bad reasons) avoided it by relying on people 'consenting' (to be searched, to attend police stations for questioning, etc) so avoiding the requirements of legal regulation (Dixon 1997: ch 3). Discretion inevitably (for good and bad) pervades policing. Compliance with legal requirements will very often not be open to inspection by a court because a guilty plea is entered. If a legal power is overtly used, this is normally the result of a discretionary choice. Finally, legal rules are by nature open-textured and subject to interpretation. In brief, even at the heart of 'legalised' police work, ethical issues remain to be resolved by officers. This does not imply abandoning rules. Rather the aim should be a comprehensive reconstitution of the normative structure of policing by means of a review of the current laws, rules and instructions. In conjunction with this, the production of a new code of ethics would be a useful way of both providing a normative foundation for the regulatory structure and of encouraging police officers to consider their activities in a new way.

5

Police Culture

Janet Chan [1]

1. The concept of police culture

i. Definition

Social scientists who studied routine police work have for decades postulated the existence of a distinctive police occupational culture. Police officers are likened to members of an exotic tribe which has developed 'recognizable and distinct rules, customs, perceptions, and interpretations of what they see, along with consequent moral judgments' (Skolnick and Fyfe 1993: 90). Yet these rules are often unrelated to, and may even contradict, the formal written laws, regulations and guidelines regarding police practice. Skolnick (1966) suggests that this distinctive way of interpreting and responding to the world gives rise to a police 'working personality'. Manning and Van Maanen describe the following elements of the culture:

> The occupational culture constructed by the police consists of long-standing rules of thumb, a somewhat special language and ideology that help edit a member's everyday experiences, shared standards of relevance as to the critical aspects of the work, matter-of-fact prejudices, models for street-level etiquette and demeanour, certain customs and rituals suggestive of

1 The research assistance provided by Amy Meagher during the preparation of the issues paper for the Royal Commission is gratefully acknowledged. Except for minor editing and revisions, this chapter is in the same form as the issues paper originally submitted to the Royal Commission in September 1995. Sections of the text subsequently appeared in an abridged form in the discussions in chs 2, 4 and 10 of Chan (1997) in relation to police racism. Publishing this chapter in its original form provides a more focused and accessible summary of the development of the concept of police culture than that which is currently available.

how members are to relate not only to each other but to outsiders, and a sort of residual category consisting of the assorted miscellany of some rather plain police horse sense. (Manning and Van Maanen 1978: 267)

ii. Characteristics of police culture

The actual contents of the rules, standards and rituals of the occupational culture are, of course, not easily identified because of their 'unwritten' nature, and their being situated in the 'backstage' of police work. Ethnographic studies of policing have, however, uncovered some consistent features of this culture.

Manning (1978a: 11-12) has produced a list of basic assumptions contained in the occupational culture among American non-college-educated patrol officers. These assumptions include judgments about people in general ('People cannot be trusted; they are dangerous'; 'Everyone hates a cop'), beliefs about crime and justice ('People who are not controlled will break laws'; 'Stronger punishment will deter criminals from repeating their errors'), views regarding the role of police ('The legal system is untrustworthy; policemen[2] make the best decisions about guilt or innocence'; 'Policemen can most accurately identify crime and criminals'; 'The major jobs of the policeman are to prevent crime and to enforce laws'), and rules of thumb about police work ('Experience is better than abstract rules'; 'You must make people respect you'; 'Policemen must appear respectable and be efficient').

Reiner (1992: 111-29) summarises the cultural characteristics as including: a sense of mission about police work, an orientation towards action, a cynical or pessimistic perspective about their social environment, an attitude of constant suspiciousness, an isolated social life coupled with a strong code of solidarity with other police officers, a clear categorisation of the public between the rough and the respectable, a conservative stance in politics and morality, a machismo outlook that permits sexism, alcoholic and sexual indulgences, a prejudiced attitude towards ethnic minorities, and a pragmatic view of police work which discourages innovation and experimentation. Among these characteristics, the so-called 'siege mentality' and 'code of silence' have often been linked with the concealment and toleration of police misconduct.

---

2   Research studies carried out in the 1970s were conducted in relation to predominantly male police officers, although the masculine gender may have been used to represent all police officers, male and female. This comment applies to all such masculine references throughout this chapter.

iii. Assumptions about police culture

Several assumptions are implicit in most discussions about the police occupational culture: that there is a close relationship between the demands of police work and the existence of the culture, that the culture is relatively stable and uniform over time and space, and that the culture has a negative influence on police practice.

Relationship with demands of police work

The existence of a direct connection between the demands of police work and the development of the occupational culture has been suggested by a number of researchers. Skolnick (1966) sees the 'working personality' as a response to the danger of police work, the authority of the police constable, and the pressure to be productive and efficient. Reiner (1992) similarly suggests that the 'cop culture' develops as a way to help police cope with the pressure of police work. Van Maanen (1978a) points out that the nature of police work, the potential for danger, the shift work, the police uniform, the sense of isolation, and the proliferation of rules and regulations within police departments all contribute towards the formation of this culture. For example:

> The cynicism popularly attributed to police officers can, in part, be located in the unique and peculiar role police are required to play. Treated shabbily, hated, or feared by many of the contacts they have, police are asked frequently to arbitrate messy and uncertain citizen disputes. In such disputes, all concerned generally construct a particular account which exonerates them from blame. After a few years on the street, there are few accounts patrolmen have not heard. Hence, whether a claim is outrageous or plausible, police react by believing nothing and distrusting everything at the same time. Only one's colleagues can understand and appreciate such skepticism.
>
> The hardness commonly thought to be the mask of many policemen arises to fend off the perceived curse of doing society's dirty work. To be a sponge, absorbing the misery and degradation that pass daily through a patrolman's life, is an untenable position which would soon drive one from the police midst were it accepted. Therefore the proverbial 'shell' is constructed, which protects the patrolman from the effects of nasty encounters which would leave most persons visibly shaken. But in the patrol world such coldness becomes almost a legendary personal property. (Van Maanen 1978a: 120)

Stability over time and space

If aspects of the police culture are 'rooted in the recurrent problems and common experiences of police' and they 'arise as a way of coping with, and making sense of, a given environment' (Manning and Van Maanen 1978: 267), one would expect the occupational culture of policing to be fairly homogeneous among officers working under similar conditions. Indeed, referring to studies of police in the USA, in Europe and in Asia, Skolnick and Fyfe (1993: 92) observe that the 'fundamental culture of policing is everywhere similar ... since ... the same features of the police role – danger, authority, and the mandate to use coercive force – are everywhere present'. Manning and Van Maanen also comment on the culture's 'remarkable stability through time' and its persistence in spite of external efforts to change it:

> In the operational environment of the patrol division, the street level of policing, many old habits and traditions have survived largely intact despite the persistent efforts of officialdom to introduce new ideas, tighter organizational controls, and sophisticated technologies into the daily affairs of patrolmen. Even the introduction of better educated and more highly trained recruits has provided precious little encouragement for those seeking to alter the police culture from the inside. This latter point is particular crucial, for it suggests that there are powerful means available within the occupation that act to systematically discourage innovation while they encourage the status quo. (Manning and Van Maanen 1978: 267)

Negative influence on police practice

Although the police culture is seen as functional to the survival and sense of security among officers working under dangerous, unpredictable and alienating conditions, it is the negative, rather than the positive, influence that has become prominent in discussions about police culture. The Fitzgerald Report (1989: 202), for example, links the Queensland Police culture operating at the time to the 'deterioration of the Police Force': the so-called 'police code' has helped police 'verballing' and corruption to flourish within the force while protecting wrongdoers from detection and prosecution.

iv. Relationship with organisational culture

The term 'police culture' in most instances of usage refers to the *occupational* culture of policing. As Van Maanen (1978a: 116) points out, police are not unique in having developed a distinctive culture, since 'workers in all occupations develop ways and means by which they manage certain structural strains, contradictions and anomalies of their prescribed role and task'. Most police researchers, however, have concentrated their studies on the occupational culture of policing *at the street level*, although a well-recognised distinction has been made between the 'street cop culture', which yearned for the 'good old days' when 'the public valued and respected a cop, fellow officers could be counted on, and superior officers or "bosses" were an integral part of the police family', versus the 'management cop culture', which sought to clean up, professionalise and make the police more productive, efficient and responsive to the community (Reuss-Ianni and Ianni 1983).

Even though police forces are typically organised along the lines of a militaristic bureaucracy, police officers exercise extremely wide discretion at the street level. Decisions by street-level officers are usually made with little or no supervision:

> because police tasks at the lower levels are ill-defined, episodic, nonroutine, accomplished in regions of low visibility, and are dispatched in ways that most often bypass the formal chain of command in the organization, control over the work itself resides largely in the hands of those who perform the work (Banton 1964; Cain 1973; Manning 1977). In this sense, police agencies resemble symbolic or mock bureaucracies where only the appearance of control, not the reality, is of managerial concern. (Van Maanen 1983: 277)

Thus, these officers are demanded to act less like bureaucrats, who typically possess partial skills and are subject to external controls, but more like professionals, who typically possess complete skills and have internalised standards (see Scott 1966). Wilson has argued, however, that police are neither bureaucrats nor professionals:

> The patrolman is neither a bureaucrat nor a professional, but a member of a *craft*. As with more [sic] crafts, there is no generalized, written body of special knowledge; learning is by apprenticeship, but the apprenticeship takes place on the job rather than in the academy; the primary reference group from which the apprentice wins (or fails to win) respect are his colleagues on the job, not fellow members of his discipline wherever they may be; and the members, conscious of having a special skill or task, think of themselves a set apart from society and in need of restrictions on entry. But unlike other members of a craft – carpenters, for example, or journalists – the police work in an environment that is usually apprehensive and often hostile, and they produce no product . . . the value of which is evident and easily judged. (Wilson 1978: 68)

Regardless of whether street-level police officers are bureaucrats, professionals or members of a craft, police forces are *organisations* both in a practical and in a conceptual sense. Practically, police forces have a hierarchical structure, with functional and geographical divisions, and membership of the organisation is fairly well defined. Conceptually, police forces are 'open systems in constant interaction with their many environments, and they consist of many subgroups, occupational units, hierarchical layers, and geographically dispersed segments' (Schein 1985:

9). When conceived of as organisations, police forces develop their own *organisational cultures*, which obviously encompass the occupational culture, but are not equivalent to it.

Schein's definition of organisational culture contains elements which have been discussed earlier as important for understanding occupational culture and is useful as a general definition of any group's culture – culture is:

> a pattern of basic assumptions – invented, discovered, or developed by a given group as it learns to cope with its problems of external adaptation and internal integration – that has worked well enough to be considered valid and, therefore, to be taught to new members as the correct way to perceive, think, and feel in relation to those problems. (Schein 1985: 9; italics in the original)

For Schein, culture is the property of a stable social unit which has a shared history. Culture is a 'learned product of group experience' (Schein 1985: 7). Hence, it is possible to conceptualise the existence of different subcultures in different stable work units within a single police force. Although Schein distinguishes between three levels of culture, namely artefacts, values, and basic assumptions, he stresses that the term culture should be 'reserved for the deeper level of *basic assumptions* and *beliefs* that are shared by members of an organization' (Schein 1985: 6).

v. Relevance for understanding police conduct

Police culture would have remained within the pages of academic writings if it were no more than an interesting sociological concept. However, as pointed out earlier, elements of the police occupational culture have been linked with institutionalised police corruption, misconduct and police forces' resistance to change. The Fitzgerald Report (1989: 200), for example, found that within the Queensland Police Force at the time, there was a culture of 'contempt for the criminal justice system, disdain for the law and rejection of its application to police, disregard for the truth, and abuse of authority'. Fitzgerald has emphasised that the 'unwritten police code' was a 'critical factor in the deterioration of the Police Force':

> A practical effect of the code is to reduce, if not almost to eliminate, concern at possible apprehension and punishment as a deterrent to police misconduct. The code exaggerates the need for, and the benefits derived from, mutual loyalty and support... Under the code it is impermissible to criticize other police... The police code also requires that police not enforce the law against other police, nor co-operate in any attempt to do so, and perhaps even obstruct any such attempt. (Fitzgerald Report 1989: 202-3)

More recently, the Mollen Report (1994) made a similar link between police culture and police corruption in New York City:

> What we found is that the problem of police corruption extends far beyond the corrupt cop. It is a multi-faceted problem that has flourished in parts of our City not only because of opportunity and greed, but because of a police culture that exalts loyalty over integrity; because of the silence of honest officers who fear the consequences of 'ratting' on another cop no matter how grave the crime; because of wilfully blind supervisors who fear the consequences of a corruption scandal more than corruption itself; because of the demise of the principle of accountability that makes all commanders responsible for fighting corruption in their commands; because of a hostility and alienation between the police and community in certain precincts which breeds an 'Us versus Them' mentality; and because for years the New York City Police Department abandoned its responsibility to insure the integrity of its members. (Mollen 1994: 1-2)

This type of explanation for police deviance is an example of what is called 'subcultural' theories of criminality (see, generally, Downes and Rock 1982: ch 6). Originally used for explaining juvenile delinquency, subcultural theories postulate that delinquent groups conform to a subculture which condones deviant behaviour. When applied to police misconduct, subcultural theory views deviance as having been 'built in' to the nature and condition of police work; it also explains why it is so difficult to detect and prevent misconduct. Subcultural theories are attractive in that, by conceiving of deviance 'as a solution . . . to dilemmas' police officers face (Downes and Rock 1982: 115), they explain the apparent rationality of deviant behaviour to those inside the subculture. They also help those outside the subculture understand why it is usually difficult to 'correct' such behaviour. The main problem with subcultural theories is the way culture is conceptualised. Typically, it is conceived in 'functionalist' terms (see Schein's definition of culture in Section iv), which means that there is a kind of circularity in logic when the *cause* of deviant behaviour is equated with its beneficial *consequence*. For example, it may be true that a code of silence regarding corrupt activities among police officers can lead to internal solidarity *once such a code has been established*. However, it would not be quite as believable to explain a conspiracy to cover up corruption as something promoted by police officers in order to bring about internal solidarity (see Downes and Rock 1982: 90-3 for a critique of functionalism). The problem with police culture as an explanation for police deviance will be taken up in more detail later.

In any case it should be emphasised that subcultural theories are only one of many possible explanations of police misconduct. Other, perhaps equally powerful, theories include the lack of external control, the abundance of criminal opportunities, learning theory and thrill-seeking explanations. The Mollen Report (1994) explicitly pointed the finger at the 'abandonment of effective anti-corruption efforts' by the New York City Police Department as a direct cause of its serious corruption problems. The Report also highlighted the seduction of criminal opportunities available to police officers in some areas:

> constant, unrelieved exposure to the opportunities and temptations of corruption spawned in neighborhoods rife with drug dealing and violence may infect and destroy even the initially good cop, not just the 'rotten apples.' Even an officer with pride in the Department and in being an honest cop might eventually succumb to the constant nurture of a criminal environment. (Mollen 1994: 62)

Even the motives behind police corruption can be quite complex. Apart from the primary motivation of greed, there may be a whole range of other reasons for corruption: 'to exercise power over their environments; to vent frustration and hostility over their inability to stem the tide of crime around them; to experience excitement and thrills; to prove their mettle to other officers and gain their acceptance; and to administer their own brand of street justice because they believe the criminal justice system will administer none' (Mollen 1994: 21).

vi. Culture and practice

How, then, does culture affect practice? Although it is commonly assumed that there is a link between police culture and police practice, especially institutionalised deviant practice, the nature of this link has not been adequately examined in the literature. Part of the problem is that police culture itself is not a very useful concept unless there is a better understanding of what it is, how it is formed, how it is transmitted, how it affects practice and how it can be changed. A useful way of conceptualising culture is to view culture as shared organised knowledge which is held by members of a group (Sackmann 1991). This knowledge contains basic assumptions about descriptions, operations, prescriptions and explanations about the social and physical world. At the same time, members of the group operate in a particular social and political context which consists of certain structural arrangements of power, interests, and authority. Police practice is then the product of interaction between this shared knowledge and the structural conditions. In the following sections, I will elaborate on the dimensions of cultural knowledge relevant to police work, how culture is transmitted and the relationship between structural conditions and police practice.[3]

---

3   These sections discuss in greater detail the conceptual framework first presented in Chan (1996).

2. Police cultural knowledge

i. Dimensions of cultural knowledge

Using Schein's definition of organisational culture, Sackmann argues that the most useful way of conceptualising culture is to view it as shared organisational knowledge: 'the form of things that people have in their minds; their models for perceiving, integrating, and interpreting them; the ideas or theories that they use collectively to make sense of their social and physical reality' (Sackmann 1991: 21). Sackmann distinguishes between four dimensions of cultural knowledge. These are (a) *axiomatic knowledge* which represents the fundamental assumptions about why things are done the way they are in an organisation; (b) *dictionary knowledge* which consists of descriptive categories, definitions and labels of people, things or experiences; (c) *directory knowledge* which provides guidance on how things operate generally within the organisation; and (d) *recipe knowledge* which prescribes what should or should not be done in specific situations. This framework can be fruitfully applied to a discussion of police culture. There is a fair amount of evidence in the literature to support the existence of shared cultural knowledge among police officers, at least at the street level.

ii. Police mandate (axiomatic knowledge)

This refers to the fundamental assumptions about 'why things are done the way they are' in an organisation. Police traditionally see their work in terms of waging a 'war against crime', maintaining order and protecting people's lives and property. Reiner points out that officers often regard their work with a sense of mission: 'their sense of themselves as "the thin blue line", performing an essential role in safeguarding social order, which would lead to disastrous consequences if their authority was threatened' (Reiner 1992: 112). Manning (1978a: 8) observes that '[b]ased on their legal monopoly of violence, [police] have staked out a mandate that claims to include the efficient, apolitical, and professional enforcement of the law'. Manning calls this the 'impossible mandate' which is driven by public expectations rather than the reality of police work:

> To much of the public, the police are seen as alertly ready to respond to citizen demands, as crime-fighters, as an efficient, bureaucratic, highly organized force that keeps society from falling into chaos. The policeman himself considers the essence of his role to be the dangerous and heroic enterprise of crook-catching and the watchful prevention of crimes. The system of positive and negative sanctions from the public and within the

> department encourages this heroic conception. . . In an effort to gain the public's confidence in their ability, and to insure thereby the solidity of their mandate, the police have encouraged the public to continue thinking of them and their work in idealized terms. . . The public's response has been to demand even more dramatic crook-catching and crime prevention, and this demand for arrests has been converted into an index for measuring how well the police accomplish their mandate. The public's definitions have been converted by the police organization into distorted criteria for promotion, success, and security. (Manning 1978a: 12-13)

As a result of the acceptance of this 'impossible' mandate, police often make a distinction between 'real' police work and the work they routinely perform. Van Maanen describes this distinction he observed among American patrol officers:

> the young officer learns that there is a subtle but critical difference between 'real' police work and most of what he does on patrol. 'Real' police work is, in essence his *raison d'être*. It is that part of his job that comes closest to the romantic notions of police work . . . calls for a patrolman to exercise his perceived occupational expertise: to make an arrest, save a life, quell a dispute, prevent a robbery, catch a felon, stop a suspicious person, disarm a suspect, and so on. 'Real' police work involves the 'hot' call, the unusual 'on view' felony situation, or the potentially dangerous 'back-up' predicament in which an officer may have to assist a threatened colleague. . . Yet, because of this narrow definition of police work, little of his time on the street provides the opportunity to accomplish much of what he considers to be his primary function. Thus, 'real' police work to the patrolman is paradoxical; a source of satisfaction and frustration. (Van Maanen 1978a: 121-2)

iii. Police categories (dictionary knowledge)

Research studies have suggested that police officers develop ways of categorising their environment and the people they encounter in the community. American researchers have suggested that police officers develop notions of normal and abnormal appearances in relation to the public places they patrol. These notions of normality and abnormality are context dependent:

> Among the Americans, the police are occupational specialists on inferring the probability of criminality from the appearances persons present in public places. What is normal for a place is normal for the place at a time. The meaning of an event to the policeman at a place depends on the time it occurs. (Sacks 1978: 194)

In a study of a suburban Canadian police force, Ericson (1982: 86) notes a similar tendency for patrol officers to develop indicators of abnormality: these include '1) individuals out of place, 2) individuals in particular places, 3) individuals of particular types regardless of place, and 4) unusual circumstances regarding property'.

Reiner (1992: 117-18) has also commented on the distinction police make with regard to the general public, between 'the rough and respectable elements, those who challenge or those who accept the middle-class values of decency which most police revere'. Muir (1997: 155-6) describes a similar 'separation of people into the governables and the rebels . . . those who might revolt against police authority from those who would not'. Van Maanen observes a slightly different typology:

> the police tend to view their occupational world as comprised exhaustively of three types of citizens . . . (1) 'suspicious persons' – those whom the police have reason to believe may have committed a serious offence; (2) 'assholes' – those who do not accept the police definition of the situation; and (3) 'know nothings' – those who are not either of the first two categories but are not police and therefore, according to the police, cannot know what the police are about. (Van Maanen 1978b: 224)

In Australia police have been accused of forming stereotypical opinions about the criminality of certain ethnic groups (Australian Law Reform Commission 1992: 201) and regularly linking Aboriginal people with crime and social disorder (Cunneen and Robb 1987). Ericson's study in Canada found similar typifications of racial and ethnic minorities and young people with disorderly appearance and conduct who were considered 'the scum of the earth' (Ericson 1982: 66-7).

iv. Police methods (directory knowledge)

Directory knowledge informs police officers about how operational work is routinely carried out. To a certain extent these operational methods follow from the definitions and categories designated by dictionary knowledge. For example, in proactive policing, officers are 'chronically suspicious' and are forced 'to make snap decisions about the appropriateness of what people are doing' (Bayley and Mendelhson 1969: 93). Having developed indicators of normality and abnormality, roughness and respectability, police officers tend to target the unusual and the disreputable:

> Persons whose appearance indicates that they are not normal members of an ecological area, eg whites in negro areas, the apparently poor in wealthy areas etc, are subject to having a request made for 'their papers' and an interrogatory made as to the reason of their presence. (Sacks 1978: 195)

An important feature of police work is the capacity and authority to use coercive force if necessary. Bittner considers this capacity to use force as 'the core of the police role':

> every conceivable police intervention projects the message that force may be, and may have to be, used to achieve a desired objective. It is very likely ... that the actual use of physical coercion and restraint is rare... What matters is that police procedure is defined by the feature that it may not be opposed in its course, and that force can be used if it is opposed. (Bittner 1978: 35-6)

This capacity to use force by the police is 'essentially unrestricted', that is apart from the use of deadly force and the obvious restriction that force must not be used maliciously, there are very few guidelines regarding when 'forceful intervention was necessary, desirable or proper' (Bittner 1978: 33). This lack of regulation and guidance means that the concept 'lawful use of force' by the police is 'practically meaningless' (Bittner 1978: 330).

The use of force or the threat of force by police is often seen as a legitimate means of taking charge of situations, to maintain authority, to control suspects and to obtain information. Westley's (1970) study of an American police force found that the use of violence for the purpose of maintaining respect for the police was not seen to be illegitimate by almost 40 per cent of the 74 policemen surveyed. Baldwin and Kinsey's (1982) study of a British police force found that police would often use the threat of violence to obtain information or confession, but reserve actual violence to those who 'cut up rough'. Van Maanen (1978b: 224) suggests that people placed into the 'assholes' category by American police are vulnerable to so-called 'street justice – a physical attack designed to rectify what police take as personal insult'.

The use of force is, of course, only one of many ways of taking charge of situations efficiently. A Canadian researcher has commented on the tacit condoning of 'shortcuts' by officers, since legal procedures are seen as impediments to justice:

> Taking charge efficiently may seem to call for minor and sometimes major shortcuts in legal niceties. The officer may bluff or bully, mislead or lie, verbally abuse or physically 'rough up' the alleged offender. Senior officers are not concerned to eliminate such short-cuts, but merely to manage them, so as to keep citizens complaints ... at a minimum while getting the day's work done. The most important learning required of the rookie in his first six months is the ability to keep his/her mouth shut about the deviance from law and police regulations which veteran officers consider necessary if the police are not to be 'hamstrung' in their control of social order. (Lee 1981: 51)

In general, Manning's (1978c: 73-4) research suggests that police officers see their work as uncertain and unclear ('You never know what to expect next') and hence decisions are based on experience, commonsense and discretion, rather than 'an abstract theory of policing, the law, or police regulations'. Decisions can only be justified situationally ('You can't police by the book'). The centrality of experience as the foundation of police is taken for granted and seen as essential in the definition of occupational competence.

v. Police values (recipe knowledge)

This refers to the normative dimension of cultural knowledge. It suggests what should or should not be done in specific situations. It provides recommendations and strategies for coping with police work. Van Maanen's research of an American police force provides some significant observations. For example, officers learn to 'stay out of trouble':

> Essentially, this means that the officer will do what is assigned to him and little more. The novice patrolman soon learns that there are few incentives to work hard. He also discovers that the most satisfactory solution to the labyrinth of hierarchy, the red tape, the myriad of rules and regulations, the risks of street work, and unpleasantness which characterize the occupation is to adopt the group standard, stressing a 'lay-low-and-don't-make-waves' work ethic. And the best way in which he can stay out of trouble is to minimize the amount of work he pursues... Rookies were always accused of what was referred to as a 'gung-ho' attitude (rushing to calls and pushing eagerly for action). They were quickly taught, however, the appropriate perspective toward their work. For example, the aggressive patrolman who constantly was seeking out tasks to perform was the butt of community jokes. (Van Maanen 1978a: 125)

Officers also develop a sceptical attitude towards police supervisors and managers and learn not to expect much from the organisation:

> At times, patrolmen feel as if the department goes out of its way to make things uncomfortable for them... Critically, patrolmen discover that the department answers very few of their requests; for example, assignment shifts, new equipment, car repairs, expense reimbursements, and so on. And when the organization does act, it is usually after a long delay. In response to their situation, patrolmen assume a 'don't-expect-much' stance. They begin to realize that it is the rewards of camaraderie and small favors granted to them by their sergeant that makes their daily task either pleasant or intolerable. A few extra days off, a good partner, enjoyable squad parties, an agreeable assignment, or an extra long lunch become important rewards offered by a police career. (Van Maanen 1978a: 127)

One of the most pervasive attitudes in police organisations, and indeed in many bureaucracies, is that workers feel they must protect themselves against supervisors and dissatisfied customers:

> This 'cover your ass' perspective pervades all of patrol work. In a sense, it represents a sort of bureaucratic paranoia which is all but rampant in police circles. Again, the best way for patrolmen to 'cover their ass' is to watch

> carefully the kind of activities in which they engage. It is best therefore to not take the initiative on the street but rather react primarily to departmental direction. In this way, one seldom becomes involved in those potentially explosive situations which might result in disciplinary action for the patrolman. (Van Maanen 1978a: 127)

Consequently, written records of events are often manipulated by police officers to protect themselves against possible reviews by supervisors (Manning 1977: 191).

Another well-documented aspect of police recipe knowledge is the apparent 'code of silence' and solidarity among police officers when faced with allegations of misconduct. Westley's (1970) study in America found that, if faced with a partner's misconduct, 11 (out of 16) officers would not be willing to report this misconduct, and 10 would be prepared to perjure themselves in court to protect their partner. Skolnick and Fyfe noted that following the notorious beating of Rodney King by members of the Los Angeles Police, one of the indicted officers called for the resignation of the Police Chief Daryl Gates because he felt betrayed:

> The cops on the scene were responding to a code they believed in and considered to be moral. The code decrees that cops protect other cops, no matter what, and that cops of higher rank back up working street cops – no matter what. From the perspective of the indicted cops, Daryl Gates betrayed the code. (Skolnick and Fyfe 1993: 7)

The code, according to Skolnick and Fyfe, is typically enforced 'by the threat of shunning, by fear that *informing* will lead to exposure of one's own derelictions, and by fear that colleagues' assistance may be withheld in emergencies' rather than by violent means (Skolnick and Fyfe 1993: 110).

vi. The development and transmission of culture

As suggested earlier, police culture is assumed to have developed as an adaptive response to the nature and conditions of police work. Schein sees culture as the 'stable solutions' to a group's problems of external adaptation and internal integration:

> culture develops around the external and internal problems that groups face and gradually becomes abstracted into general and basic assumptions about the nature of reality; the world and the place of the group within it; and the nature of time, space, human nature, human activity, and human relationships. Culture can be thought of as the stable solutions to these problems, and the pattern of particular assumptions that represents these solutions can be thought of as the underlying 'essence' that gives any given group its particular character. (Schein 1985: 312)

For Schein, culture is transmitted by a learning process either through positive reinforcement of successful solutions to problems or successful avoidance of painful situations:

> culture is *learned*. . . But the learning process is complex because it is groups rather than individuals that are doing the learning, and it is cognitions and emotions, not only overt behavior patterns, that are learned. . . Structurally, two types of learning mechanisms must be clearly distinguished because they have different consequences for the stability of what is learned: (1) *positive problem-solving situations*, which lead to positive reinforcement if the attempted solution works; and (2) *anxiety-avoidance situations*, which produce positive reinforcement if the anxiety is successfully reduced and if the painful consequences that produced the anxiety are prevented. In practice these two types of situations are intertwined, but they have different motivational bases, different underlying learning mechanisms, and different consequences. . . (Schein 1985: 174)

Newcomers to the policing occupation typically learn the culture through anecdotes and 'war stories' told by more senior officers:

> During a newcomer's first few months on the street he is self-conscious and truly in need of guidelines as to his actions. A whole folklore of tales, myths, and legends surrounding the department is communicated to the novice by his fellow-officers, conspicuously by his FTO [Field Training Officer]. Through these anecdotes – dealing largely with 'mistakes' or 'flubs' made by policemen – the recruit begins to adopt the perspectives of his more experienced colleagues. He becomes aware that 'nobody's perfect,' and the only way in which one can be protected from his own mistakes is to protect others. Among members of a particular squad, this 'no rat' rule has deep and meaningful roots. Violations of the rule are met with swift (albeit informal) disapproval. (Van Maanen 1978a: 126)

This is what is commonly referred to as the 'socialisation process' that new members go through, so that they can see the world as more experienced officers do and they learn 'what is customary and desirable in the work setting as well as what is not' (Manning and Van Maanen 1978: 268).

It has been suggested, for example, that the recruits' experience at the Police Academy typically leads to a dramatic increase in cynicism (Niederhoffer 1967) because recruits are most susceptible to the influence of cynical veterans. Henry's (1992) study of police training in Queensland found that the new program, which involved recruits spending the first semester in a university-based program, followed by a second semester at the Police Academy, 'engenders much less cynicism among the recruits than did the traditional program, at least during the first six month semester' (Henry 1992: 14). The new training program was designed in a way that '[m]any of the factors contributing to the social isolation of police recruits, in particular the degree of contact with experienced police officers and the degree of physical and social isolation, have been extensively reduced or modified' (Henry 1992: 8). The long-term effect of this program remains to be seen, but if the American experience is any guide, one expectation might be that 'the current crop of police recruits will leave the Police Academy ill equipped to face the realities of police work' (Henry 1992: 15).

The recruit training program in New South Wales, which was substantially redesigned in 1988, received a positive assessment from a team of independent researchers from the UK (Centre for Applied Research in Education 1990). However, one of the most serious shortcomings of the program identified was the field training component (49 weeks of on-the-job training following six months of initial training at the Academy), during which probationary constables became 'assimilated in the traditional policing culture', rejecting the 'reflective professional' model of policing taught at the Academy (*PREP Course Documentation* 1993: 25). A recent study of ethnocentrism and conservatism among a cohort of 412 New South Wales recruits found that 'the Academy has done a good job in reducing or at least containing racist and authoritarian attitudes of recruits . . . [but] once recruits hit the streets, much of this good work is swept away' (Wortley 1993: 7; Wortley 1995). These results confirm the dominant influence of the street-level reality of police work on police attitudes and practice.

Schein's (1985) distinction between problem-solving learning and anxiety-avoidance learning is an important one for understanding police culture. Problem-solving learning is considered positive and rewarding:

> Once a workable solution to a given problem has been found, it is likely to be repeated the next time the same problem comes up. Solutions that no longer work are given up quickly because their failure is highly visible to the group; but, paradoxically, solutions that may work only part of the time may be clung to longest. (Schein 1985: 175-6)

On the other hand, anxiety-avoidance learning is negative and defensive:

> Instead of positive goal-oriented tension and mobilization of effort, anxiety involves feelings of dread (of being threatened from known or unknown sources) and varying degree of cognitive disorientation (of not knowing what is going on or what is ahead). Whereas problem-solving efforts mobilize attention on the problem, anxiety-based learning cannot be focused clearly if the source of the anxiety is not known. The individual or group is forced into a more random kind of trial-and-error learning, with less predictability of what will, in fact, reduce the anxiety. . . [A]voidance learning is often *one*-trial learning. Once something works, it will be repeated indefinitely, even if the source of pain is no longer active. . . Thus, all rituals, patterns of thinking or feeling, beliefs, and tacit assumptions about oneself and the environment that were learned originally as ways of

> avoiding painful situations are going to be very stable, even if the causes of the original pain are, in fact, no longer present. Just as we can label such learned behavior as 'defence mechanisms' in the individual personality, we can think of parts of a group's culture as being 'social defence mechanisms'... (Schein 1985: 177-8)

Many of the negative aspects of police culture seem to have been developed as anxiety-avoidance mechanisms rather than innovative problem-solving strategies. For example, dictionary knowledge and directory knowledge allow officers to place people and situations they encounter into ready-made categories and standard operational methods. Schein considers 'cognitive overload and/or an inability to decipher and categorize the multitude of stimuli impinging on the senses' as a major source of anxiety (*cognitive* anxiety) for people, so that a stable system of cognitions is 'absolutely necessary' for their own protection and survival (Schein 1985: 179). In addition, police officers' work involves considerable potential for risk and danger, which are sources of *role-related* anxiety. Hence these dimensions of knowledge reduce the level of uncertainty and anxiety in police work and make unfamiliar situations seem more predictable. As Muir points out:

> The potential of danger was always requiring a policeman to form a rapid first impression, to group people quickly according to whether they were likely to behave rebelliously or cooperatively. Because his job was to control the people's use of dangerous violence, he made judgments of mankind in terms of their potential for violence. Because he was a governor, he grouped the governed according to their governability. (Muir 1977: 157)

Similarly, recipe knowledge provides a way for officers to reduce *social* anxiety by offering recipes for avoiding trouble and preventing isolation within the police force. By observing the 'code of silence', for example, officers avoid the threat of being ostracised by colleagues and the danger of their withholding of assistance in emergencies.

The consequence of anxiety-avoidance learning, as pointed out earlier by Schein, is that the group has a tendency not to question their original assumptions, even if they were incorrect, because questioning the assumptions would be considered too anxiety-provoking or painful. Muir provides a good illustration of this attitude among police officers who preferred to be overly suspicious rather than overly trusting when approaching citizens. Officers used a 'minimax' strategy to minimise the maximum risk in their work:

> In the event that an assumption was erroneously suspicious, the policeman ended up unhappy but at least had the consolation that he was alive to appreciate his unhappiness. In the instance where the mistaken assumption was initially trusting, the policeman's mistake was not redeemed by the fact

> of personal survival. The mistaken oversuspicion meant wasting a citizen; the mistaken overtrust meant death. . . The minimax strategy . . . eliminated any incentive the policeman might have had to check whether his initial assumptions were correct or not . . . confirmation of the suspicious assumption was a waste of time. (Muir 1977: 166-7)

Anxiety-avoidance learning may also result in the group being defensive in the protection of their accepted rituals, beliefs and assumptions. The group may eventually lose its ability to change and innovate. As Sparrow et al (1990) point out, mistake avoidance and resistance to change seem to go hand in hand, especially when change is initiated from above:

> The legacy of militaristic management . . . poses problems as [police] chiefs work toward change. They have to grapple with the fact that patrol officers are deeply resentful of virtually anything new that comes out of headquarters. Patrol officers feel that nothing from headquarters ever made their job easier, and rarely failed to make it more difficult. . . This is the typical perception from the receiving [operational] end of the traditional process of centralized control: It all comes from headquarters; it is all imposed; it is all thought up by somebody else – probably somebody with a carpeted office who has time to sit and think these things up. We are too busy already; too busy doing 'real police work' to pay serious attention to any more of their fanciful schemes. We already have more rules and procedures than we can possibly remember. This is no time for trying new schemes out – it takes all day just to avoid making any mistakes. (Sparrow et al 1990: 147-8)

vii. The existence of multiple cultures

Many references to police culture have highlighted its similarities from one jurisdiction to another. However, it is wrong to assume that police culture is invariably uniform and stable throughout the police organisation and between jurisdictions. Reiner's (1992) review of the literature suggests that there are differences in organisational culture between police forces. Wilson's (1968) study, for example, distinguishes three 'styles' of police departments in the USA: the 'watchman' style which emphasises patrol work and the maintenance of public order; the 'legalistic' style which stresses bureaucratic and professional standards in law enforcement; and the 'service' style which gives priority to public relations and community service.

Schein (1985) suggests that whether an organisation has a single culture or multiple subcultures is an empirical question. Much depends on the existence of stable groups with shared experiences:

> Whether or not a given company has a single culture in addition to various subcultures then becomes an empirical question to be answered by locating stable groups within that company and determining what their shared experience has been, as well as determining the shared experiences of the

members of the total organization. One may well find that there are several cultures operating within the larger social unit called the company or the organization: a managerial culture, various occupationally based cultures in functional units, group cultures based on geographical proximity, worker cultures based on shared hierarchical experiences, and so on. The organization as a whole may be found to have an overall culture if that whole organization has a significant shared history, but we cannot assume the existence of such a culture ahead of time. (Schein 1985: 7-8)

Manning suggests that police organisations are structurally and culturally diversified:

> The police as an organization do not possess a 'common culture' when viewed from the *inside*. Instead, there is an elaborate hierarchical rank structure which replicates the social distribution of secret knowledge. Police organizations are segmented, specialized and covert to a striking degree. Social relationships among policemen are based to an unknown extent upon *differential information* and ignorance, a structural fact that maintains organizational stratification. (Manning 1978b: 244)

The division between the 'street cop culture' and the 'management cop culture' (Reuss-Ianni and Ianni 1983) has already been referred to. More recently, Manning (1993) has suggested that there are three subcultures of policing: command, middle management and lower participants. Chan's (1992) research in New South Wales found that officers in middle management positions held a distinctively negative view of the organisation. Differences were also detected between officers holding different functional responsibilities.

The idea of a unitary 'cop personality' or a monolithic police culture has been rejected by Manning and Van Maanen:

> The assignment of recruits, for instance, to different precincts, shifts, and beats will provide for different recruit experiences, as will the assignment of recruits to different supervisors, colleagues, and patrol partners ... the various task and structural arrangements within police organizations promote considerable segmentation in the perceptions of policemen toward such aspects of their work as task predictability, danger on the job, organizational production pressures, autonomy from supervision, and even encounters with citizens... Nor is the occupational socialization of policemen confined strictly to the early 'breaking-in' period of a police career ... the socialization of police is a continuous process that occurs at least to some degree, every time an individual crosses hierarchical, functional, or social boundaries within an organization... Potentially, any police career can take many twists and turns, periodically requiring an individual to adapt to novel circumstances and surroundings. (Manning and Van Maanen 1978: 271-2)

Reiner (1992) points out that several research studies in Britain, America and Canada independently noted similar variations in police perspectives. Muir (1977), for example, developed four categories of officers depending on their moral attitude towards the use of coercive force and their intellectual view of human pain and suffering. Similarly, Shearing (1981) created a typology of officers according to their responses to the subculture and to departmental policy. Reiner sees these categories as corresponding to functional and rank structures within the organisation:

> the same underlying types are postulated: an alienated cynic, a managerial professional, a peace-keeper and a law-enforcer. These correspond with the basic organisational division of labour between management/rank and file, and CID/uniform patrol. But the differing orientations are already discernible in samples of uniform patrol officers, prefiguring future career developments. (Reiner 1992: 132)

3. Structural conditions and police practice

i. The field of policing

As pointed out earlier, the close relationship between police culture and the structural conditions of police work has long been recognised in the literature. The link between police culture and institutionalised practice is also commonly assumed, although not clearly established. The danger of not exploring the linkages between structural conditions, cultural knowledge and institutionalised practice is that a simple-minded model of linear causality is often implied (see Figure 5.1). Such a model neglects the centrality of the police officers as active participants in the construction and reproduction of cultural knowledge and institutionalised practice. It also gives a misleading impression that it is possible to change cultural knowledge and institutionalised practice simply by changing structural conditions.

Figure 5.1: A Linear Model of the Production of Police Practice

STRUCTURAL CONDITIONS → CULTURAL KNOWLEDGE → POLICE PRACTICE

In this section, I would like to argue that the *active role* of 'police actors' (which include all members of the police organisation) forms a crucial link between these elements. Officers working under a given set of structural conditions (the 'field') develop and maintain certain cultural assumptions ('habitus' or cultural knowledge), and make choices about their actions (practice).[4] Hence changes to structural conditions are taken into account by officers in their practice. Whether a structural change results in any change in cultural knowledge or institutionalised practice depends on the nature of the change and the capacity of officers to adapt to the change. The relationships between the elements are neither uni-directional nor deterministic (see Figure 5.2).

Figure 5.2: An Interactive Model of the Production of Police Practice

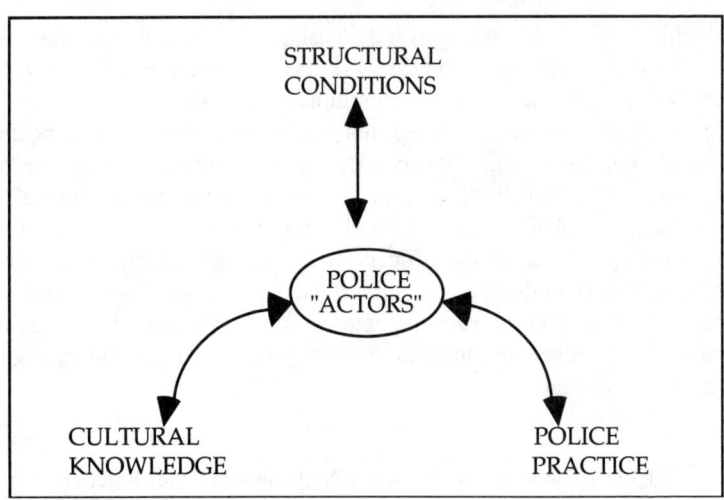

The following sections will explore the implications of this model by examining the external and internal structural conditions of police work, as well as the active role of police officers in the development and reproduction of cultural knowledge and institutionalised practice. Finally, the prospects for cultural change are discussed.

---

4   'Field' and 'habitus' are terms used by Bourdieu (see Bourdieu and Wacquant 1992) in his 'theory of practice'. In this chapter I have used 'structural conditions' to denote the field, and 'cultural knowledge' to stand for habitus.

ii.   External conditions

Police work is carried out under conditions shaped by social, economic, political and legal structures. These conditions give rise to the development of certain types of cultural knowledge and institutionalised practice. Only a brief overview of some of the conditions conducive to deviant practice will be attempted here.

Political context

In spite of the apparently apolitical nature of police organisations, policing is inherently political, since it is an institution 'created and sustained by political processes to enforce dominant conceptions of public order' (Skolnick 1972: 41; quoted in Reiner 1992: 2). As Manning (1978a: 18-19) points out, the law is itself a political entity, being the 'product of what is right and proper from the perspective of different politically powerful segments within the community'.

Finnane's (1994) historical account of policing in Australia is replete with examples of the political nature of police work, both in its more explicit form of controlling political dissent and in the routine tasks of maintaining social order. In Queensland, for example:

> the conservative political regime which governed Queensland after 1957 had gradually come to see policing as an integral part of the governing apparatus. This had intensified after the 1976 replacement of an autonomous Police Commissioner, Ray Whitrod (appointed from outside the Queensland force in 1970), with a sympathetic, conservative and dependable man from the ranks Terry Lewis... Over the following decade police were used as front-line troops in a tactical battle with street demonstrators protesting initially over uranium mining, then over free speech and assembly itself. Police were also used during this period as means of surveillance of troublesome politicians and other opponents of the ruling regime, as points of information and intelligence on electoral maters to do with the contentious 'gerrymander' or malapportionment operating in Queensland and generally, ideologically, as points of resistance to the government's social and political enemies. In short police were seen by the government as the 'thin blue line' between anarchy and order... (Finnane 1990: 164)

There is little doubt that the police culture condemned by the Fitzgerald Report (1989) was partly the product of the political condition at the time. The close relationship between the then Premier and the then Police Commissioner Terence Lewis from 1976 to 1987 was seen as the 'crucial political condition for the prevalence of recent corruption and misconduct' in the Queensland Police (Finnane 1990: 166).

Henry's (1994) analysis of police corruption in New York City also suggests the political environment can foster or impede corrupt practice:

> Police policy changes take place within a bureaucracy, and they are either impelled or constrained by a variety of subtle and overt external forces arising within a fluid and constantly shifting political landscape. These external forces include the type and extent of media coverage afforded to a particular issue, the relative strength or intensity of special interest groups and their ability to apply pressure directly on the police organisation or indirectly through the legitimate political structure, and the extent to which public pressures conflict with other existing or emerging political agendas. The fact that public opinion and public attention ultimately shape police policies and priorities cannot be ignored. (Henry 1994: 173)

Henry's analysis of published references to police corruption between 1972 and 1992 found that there was a general decline in media and academic attention to issues of police corruption. This period coincided with a gradual 'collapse' of the Police Department's corruption control system (Mollen 1994). Henry hypothesises that this easing of external pressure allowed police administrators to shift their attention and priority away from corruption controls.

Other commentators also suggest that police deviance can only thrive in a climate of public tolerance. Sparrow et al (1990) described the experience of a new police commissioner in Philadelphia, Kevin Tucker, who commissioned a survey of public opinion regarding the police. In spite of a major bungle and a serious corruption scandal in the police department, 70 per cent of the respondents rated the police as good or excellent overall, with only 5 per cent saying that they were doing a poor job. This high rating was given even though half of the respondents thought the police were rude, 49 per cent thought the police took bribes, and 66 per cent thought that the police used excessive force. These results suggest that there was an implicit 'deal' between the police and the public that 'if the police did a good job of fighting crime and responding to calls for service, they could be indulged a little in other ways' (Sparrow et al 1990: 133).

Morton's (1993) analysis of police corruption in Britain found that police often justified irregular practices by referring to this public tolerance:

> A typical police view is that the public does not much care about procedure provided results are achieved and provided that lapses in principle do not become scandals. Until then the police may effectively play by themselves. It is a similar attitude to that towards prison conditions – 'Well, they're only criminals, so why should we worry how they're treated?' (Morton 1993: 343)

Skolnick and Fyfe made a similar point about public support for aggressive policing in spite of the revelation of the beating of Rodney King:

> Today, permanently changing police organizational norms that tolerate and encourage brutality require change in the public expectations to which those norms are responsive. However repulsed viewers may have been by the graphic display of brutality shown in the King tape – and by the fury of the riotous response to it – there is considerable support among the public for an aggressive, kick-ass style of policing. (Skolnick and Fyfe 1993: 189)

The absence of public concern and political pressure to scrutinise the standards of police conduct means that there is little political risk for police organisations to ignore or pay only notional attention to police deviance. The experience of the *Cop It Sweet* scandal in New South Wales suggests that well-targeted media and public pressure could create political conditions which made it impossible for police misconduct to be tolerated or ignored (see Chan 1997: ch 8).

Legal regulation of illegal markets

The affinity between the regulation of certain classes of deviance and police corruption has been a subject of much debate. Finnane (1994: 176) asserts that '[b]ad laws help sustain corruption': the persistence of government regulation and intervention in Australia in areas such as prostitution, gambling, alcohol and drug consumption, has 'produced a context facilitating the corruption of police'. Manning is of the same view in relation to the American situation:

> [P]olice corruption is, in almost every instance, a consequence of trying to enforce admittedly unenforceable laws. The demand for services provided by homosexuals, by gamblers, prostitutes, and abortionists is high, and the supply is legally made unavailable to anyone who wants to remain in the so-called 'law-abiding' category. The laws, in effect, create the crime and the criminals. (Manning 1978a: 29)

The reason for police corruption to thrive in a legally suppressed market is that to gain control of the market, sellers must find ways to influence or neutralise police. On the other hand, police agents often have to resort to irregular or illegal means to obtain access to information or maintain contact with informants (Manning and Redlinger 1978: 152-3). It is not surprising that the Mollen Commission found that '[m]ost serious police corruption today arises from the drug trade' (Mollen 1994: 14).

The criminal justice system

The criminal justice system, especially the courts, exerts direct and indirect influences on how police officers carry out their work. The police, being the 'gatekeepers' of the criminal justice system, learn how to negotiate the practical requirements of criminal law to obtain successful convictions. Police often justify 'bending the rules' or administering 'street justice' by blaming the system for being 'too soft' on criminals. This apparent leniency is said to be a cause for cynicism to develop among officers:

> For most of these officers, the reasons for their cynicism arise from the jarring contrast between what the Department and society say they want from the police, and the experiences they have as police officers every day... While the Department's commanders, government officials, and community groups urge police officers to be aggressive crime fighters, officers often believe that the criminal justice system is too soft on criminal behavior... They see their authority being undermined and society's demand for law and order as a sham when the drug dealer they arrested on Monday is back on his street corner on Wednesday. They come to believe that true justice can only be served by their nightsticks or by insuring that the drug dealer will never enjoy his profit after they have taken it for themselves. Even officers who never resort to force or theft will close the gap between the requirements of the law and the demands of reality by falsifying the basis for arrests or searches to insure that the charges stick in what they see as the unrealistic rules of the courtroom. Simply put, they believe that integrity often makes them the only fools in a hypocritical system. (Mollen 1994: 63)

Not satisfied to leave the job of adjudication and punishment to other parts of the criminal justice system, some officers see procedural safeguards as unnecessary hurdles they must get through to obtain justice. Hence, some resort to dubious, aggressive or even illegal tactics to secure evidence or confessions, others go as far as fabricating evidence, committing perjury and other criminal offences.

Ironically, it is the same criminal justice system which seems to condone the use of illegally or improperly obtained evidence in criminal trials. As Dixon (1996: 296) suggests in relation to police detention of suspects for investigation in New South Wales prior to recent legislative changes, 'police have been able, indeed were encouraged, to detain suspects unlawfully or by means of legal trickery and loopholes because legislators paid no attention to the issue, judges routinely allow unlawfully obtained evidence to be used in their courts, prosecutors advised police to exploit legal loopholes and defence lawyers did not challenge such evidence and encourage guilty pleas'. The NSW Law Reform Commission's inquiry into criminal procedure found that there was little judicial support for the exclusion of improperly obtained evidence:

> Many of the submissions received by the Commission made the point that it was uncommon for confessional evidence which the trial judge had determined to be 'voluntary' to be excluded in the exercise of discretion on the basis of unfairness or prejudice to the accused, and that it was even more rare for voluntary evidence to be excluded on the basis of the public interest test... The Commission received many submissions from members of the judiciary which emphasised that there is a compelling community interest in ensuring that the accused persons who are factually guilty are found guilty by a court. Thus, there is a real reticence about excluding probative evidence at trial in order to 'punish' the police for some wrongdoing. (NSW Law Reform Commission 1990: 17)

Another ironic fact about the criminal justice system is that attempts to use criminal law against police malpractice are fraught with difficulties. An outspoken former Director of Public Prosecutions in Victoria has observed that police officers were less likely to plead guilty and much more likely to be acquitted in a criminal trial than normal (Bongiorno 1994: 38). In general, police officers enjoy significant advantages over ordinary citizens in the criminal justice process: they are far more competent in handling themselves during investigative interviews and courtroom cross-examinations; they are more likely to be supplied with competent, experienced defence counsel by their unions; and their membership in the police force means that they are investigated by officers who are in some sense 'friendly' to them and backed up by witnesses who are generally sympathetic. Occasionally, intimidatory tactics are used by friends of accused officers against witnesses, and it is not unusual for the defence to be in possession of confidential documents from police sources (Bongiorno 1994: 39).

iii. Internal organisation

Most police forces are still organised along the military model, with uniforms, chain of command, progression through the ranks, strong disciplinary rules, and formalised training. This model of organisation seems fitting for an institution which sees its mission as the legitimate use of coercive force in the 'war against crime'. The military metaphor usually translates into a disciplinary regime that insists on the proliferation of rules and regulations: '[w]hat sorts of rules and regulations exist in such a setting are in some ways less important than that there be plenty of them and the personnel be continually aware that they can be harshly called to account for disobeying them' (Bittner 1978: 42).

In contrast to this seemingly hierarchical model of organisation, much of police work at the operational level calls for individual judgment, localised responses and discretionary decisions. Far from being rule-driven, policing is characterised by 'situationally justified actions' (Manning 1977), that is, actions are taken as the situations demand, and then rationalised afterwards in terms of the available rules. Hence, police organisations are considered a form of 'symbolic bureaucracy . . . which maintain an image of complete adherence to bureaucratic rules when internally they conform to such rules little or not at all' (Manning and Van Maanen 1978: 3-4).

Schein (1985: 225) has suggested that the most powerful primary mechanisms in which leaders of organisations typically embed and reinforce organisational culture are: '(1) what leaders pay attention to, measure, and control; (2) leader reactions to critical incidents and organisational crises; (3) deliberate role modelling, teaching, and coaching by leaders; (4) criteria for allocation of rewards and status; (5) criteria for recruitment, selection, promotion, retirement and excommunication'. Other mechanisms, such as organisational structure, systems and procedures, design of physical space, stories and legends, and formal statements of organisational philosophy, are seen as secondary. They work to reinforce culture only if they are consistent with the primary mechanisms.

The research literature provides some indication of what leaders of police organisation typically pay attention to. Accountability in police organisations traditionally takes the form of explicitly and continually paying attention to internal discipline, such as dress code, departmental procedures, and so on, rather than auditing how officers make decisions and deal with citizens. Rewards are typically given for staying out of troubles and for 'good pinches':

> there is little doubt that emphasis on military-bureaucratic control rewards the appearance of staying out of troubles as far as internal regulations are concerned, combined with strenuous efforts to make 'good pinches', ie, arrests that contain, or can be managed to appear to contain, elements of physical danger. Every officer knows that he will never receive a citation for avoiding a fight but only for prevailing in a fight at the risk of his own safety. (Bittner 1978: 46)

The military metaphor breaks down even further where the police supervisors, far from leading their officers into battle, are perceived to be no more than disciplinarians. Bittner describes the typical relationship which emerges between police officers and their superiors:

> supervisory personnel are often viewed by the line personnel with distrust and even contempt. . . But like all superiors, police superiors, do depend on

the good will of the subordinates, if only to protect their own employee interests within the institution. Thus, they are forced to resort to the only means available to insure a modicum of loyalty, namely, covering mistakes. The more blatantly an officer's transgression violates an explicit departmental regulation the less likely it is that his superior will be able to conceal it. Therefore, to be helpful, as they must try to be, superiors must confine themselves to whitewashing bad practices involving relatively unregulated conduct that is, those dealings with citizens that lead up to arrests. In other words, to gain compliance with explicit regulations, where failings could be acutely embarrassing, command must yield in unregulated or little regulated areas of practice. (Bittner 1978: 47-8)

Van Maanen (1983: 280) similarly noted a 'high degree of mutual dependence and reciprocity' between officers and their sergeants: 'He is dependent on them to do their work smoothly, without causing untoward concern among the public or others in the department and they are dependent on him for shielding them from the consequences of the mistake they will, in good faith and bad, make'. Because officers mostly work out of their supervisor's sight, the emphasis is on *results* (arrests, for example) rather than means. This lack of supervision of police work, coupled with power and discretion, creates ample opportunities for irregular practice and corruption (Morton 1993: 342). At the same time, to stay out of trouble, officers develop anxiety-avoidance mechanisms rather than problem-solving strategies.

The Mollen Commission Report provides useful case-study data on how leaders of a police department contributed to the culture of corruption through their reactions to organisational crises. The Commission found that the New York City Police Department had become 'paranoid over bad press'; they were more concerned with the damage brought about by negative publicity than with the problem of corruption. As a result, anti-corruption efforts were all but abandoned:

> The principle of command accountability, which holds commanders responsible for fighting corruption, completely collapsed. Supervisors and commanding officers were largely complacent about maintaining integrity. Few were concerned with corruption on their watch – unless it exploded into an embarrassing corruption scandal. One officer in a high-crime precinct related how his commanding officer went so far as to announce at roll call that he knew his officers were committing acts of corruption, and gave them this bit of advice: if you get caught, keep your mouth shut. Obviously, any officer who hears that message will conclude that his bosses are content to let corruption continue – despite the Department's rhetoric to the contrary. (Mollen 1994: 3)

Lower level officers were justifiably sceptical about their leaders' public display of commitment to fighting corruption. The Mollen Inquiry found widespread disenchantment with and cynicism about the Department.

This fostered an even stronger bond of loyalty and solidarity with fellow officers:

> Many officers we interviewed believe that the Department suffers from a large measure of hypocrisy. They believe that the Department's commitment to integrity is more rhetoric and reality. They also believe that the Department is more responsive to political influence and media pressure than the needs and attitudes of its own officers. When officers view themselves and their superiors as political pawns rather than impartial officers of the law, they resent it and question the integrity and motivations of the very Department whose uniform they wear. Regardless of the truth of the perception, the point is such impressions are widespread and have a corrosive impact on morale, character, and integrity... Favoritism is another source of officers' cynicism about the Department's integrity... Even worse, many police officers believe that for the favored 'boss,' the same rules of integrity do not apply. In their view, while the Department will quickly penalize street cops for minor infractions, it protects favored commanders from their own incompetence and indiscretions... Officers' cynicism toward the Department fuels the worse aspects of police culture. It further makes officers' bonds of loyalty to fellow officers, honest and corrupt alike, greater than their loyalty to the Department, and often the law. (Mollen 1994: 63-4)

It would appear that leaders of police organisations, through the types of activities they pay attention to and reward officers for, are primarily responsible for contributing to the development and reinforcement of negative aspects of police culture.

iv. Active role of police

Police 'actors', meaning individuals or groups within a police organisation, form the crucial link between structural conditions of police work and the production of cultural knowledge and institutionalised practice on the other. This link is often missing in discussions of police culture and institutionalised practice. The main point being made here is that structural conditions do not completely determine cultural knowledge and cultural knowledge does not totally dictate practice. Working within the structural conditions of policing, members have an active role to play in developing, reinforcing, resisting or transforming cultural knowledge. They are not passive carriers of police culture. In a similar way, to borrow the game analogy used by Bourdieu (1990), officers who have learned 'a feel for the game' (cultural knowledge), are not restricted to a limited number of 'moves' (modes of practice) they can make.

This perspective of organisational culture and institutionalised practice is increasingly being recognised by organisational theorists (see Powell and DiMaggio 1991). Instead of viewing institutionalised behaviour as the product of the internalisation of values and attitudes, theorists are finding other types of models more useful and more powerful. For example, instead of explaining corrupt police practice in terms of the inculcation of corrupt values among officers through a vaguely understood process of socialisation, we can view officers as active decision makers who are nevertheless guided by the assumptions they learn and the possibilities they are aware of. Their acquiring of cultural knowledge creates schema and categories which both help them organise information and lead them to resist evidence contrary to these schema. Their awareness of structural possibilities provides 'menus of legitimate accounts' (Powell and DiMaggio 1991: 15) or a 'vocabulary of precedents' (Ericson et al 1987) which they can use to justify their actions. Hence, institutionalised practice is partly the product of a 'practical consciousness' (Giddens 1984) or a 'logic of practice' (Bourdieu 1990) which is not based on rational calculations but learned 'commonsense' and skills. However, practice is also partly guided by the actor's awareness of how action can be retrospectively justified rationally, that is what types of justification are organisationally permitted.

Examples of this way of conceptualising police institutionalised practice can be found in the literature, although they are not common. Shearing and Ericson, for example, describe how police officers play an active role in constructing and reinforcing the police culture. The transmission of culture is achieved by passing on a collection of stories and aphorisms which instruct officers how to see the world and act in it. Stories are 'cognitive devices used to gain practical insight into how to do the job of policing' (Shearing and Ericson 1991). They present officers with ready-made schema and scripts which 'work' and which assist officers in particular situations to limit their search for information, organise information in terms of established categories, constitute a sensibility out of which a range of action can flow, and provide officers with a repertoire of reasonable accounts to legitimate their actions. Yet stories do not totally dictate behaviour; they merely capture the collective wisdom of generations of police experience and provide a 'tool kit' for officers to get on with their work. Shearing and Ericson recognise that officers do not all possess the same competence in using this toolkit and that individual initiatives are still required. Hence, there is an indeterminate and creative dimension in actual practice. Moreover, officers help create the seemingly factual and objective existence of police culture by their regular reference to these rules and recipes when retrospectively justifying their own actions.[5]

Another example of this perspective is found in Fielding's research on police recruits in Britain. Fielding suggests that the individual officer is the 'final arbiter or mediator' of the structural and cultural influences of the occupation (Fielding 1988: 10). While the culture may be powerful, it is nevertheless up to individuals to accommodate or resist its influence:

> One cannot read the recruit as a cipher for the occupational culture. The occupational culture has to make its pitch for support, just as the agencies of the formal organization exert their influence through control of resources. The stock stories of the occupational culture may be effective as a means of ordering perception which maximizes desirable outcomes. If they contradict the recruit's gathering experience they are likely to be dismissed. (Fielding 1988: 135)

This type of analysis can be extended to the group or organisational level. It is a well-recognised perspective in organisational theory that organisations do not simply react to their environments; they *enact* them (Weick 1979). This means that organisations – or, more precisely, *people* within organisations – are not passive entities; they take an active part in the construction of their environments. When applied to policing, this has significant implications for understanding how structural conditions impact on organisational practice. Smith's (1994) analysis of the Queensland police bureaucracy prior to the Fitzgerald Inquiry, for example, illustrates how a police organisation could enact its political environments to ensure its own survival. For many years, the Queensland Police Force succeeded in exerting major influence on law enforcement policies, obstructing the implementation of reforms, and using propaganda to promote a favourable public image, in spite of the presence of entrenched corrupt practices.

Recognising the active role played by police actors (and groups of actors) is an important antidote to the simplistic view that deviant institutionalised practice is *caused* by a deviant police culture, which is in turn a necessary product of the conditions of police work. Constructing better theories is not a pointless academic exercise. Better theories provide a way out of the 'blind alleys' of traditional ways of thinking about culture; they uncover possibilities and useful alternatives for reform.

---

5   A useful way to think of this is again to borrow Bourdieu's game analogy. Sports players make their moves almost instinctively during a game, guided by a feel for the game they have acquired through training and experience. During the game there is little time for rational calculation – players do what has to be done under the circumstances. Yet it is possible for a sports coach, or the players themselves, to construct retrospectively strategies or rational explanations for what happened during the game.

4. Cultural change

i. Prospects for cultural change

The danger in the current fad in management circles about 'cultural change' is the belief that organisational culture can be readily changed to improve corporate performance (Czarniawska-Joerges 1992; see also Ouchi and Wilkins 1985). Schein (1985: 5), however, has reminded us that 'culture is a *deep* phenomenon' and it is incorrect to assume that 'culture can be changed to suit our purposes'. Change can also be traumatic: sociologists who observe the taken-for-granted aspects of everyday life find that prolonged attempts to disrupt accepted norms of behaviour can lead to a breakdown of the apparent orderliness of reality (Garfinkel 1967; Morgan 1986: 129). Schein also warns managers not to assume that they can manipulate culture; more likely, managers are being controlled by culture without even being aware of it. Managers are also told not to assume that 'all aspects of the culture are relevant to the effectiveness of the organisation' (Schein 1985: 315).

To the extent that institutionalised police deviance can be linked to aspects of the police culture, it makes sense to try to change the culture. However, there are no foolproof blueprints for reform.

Schein (1985: 271) argues that the prerequisite for cultural change is that the organisation must be 'unfrozen and ready to change, either because of an externally induced crisis or because of internal forces towards change'. Depending on the stage of development of an organisation, the forces that can unfreeze and change culture are supposed to be quite different. For police organisations which are at 'midlife', Schein suggests mechanisms such as planned change and organisation development, technological seduction, change through scandal, explosion of myths, and incrementalism. For organisations which are at 'maturity' (characterised by 'increasing internal stability and/or stagnation' and 'lack of motivation to change'), mechanisms such as coercive persuasion, turnaround, reorganisation, destruction and rebirth are suggested (Schein 1985: 272). Once the organisation is unfrozen, Schein argues that the following elements must all be present for the change process to succeed: '(1) a turnaround manager or team with (2) a clear sense of where the organisation needs to go, (3) a model of how to change culture to get there, and (4) the power to implement the model' (Schein 1985: 294-5).

Like other writers whose work are directed at managers, Schein's approach is essentially top-down with a great deal of emphasis on leadership. The experience of the NSW Police Service, however, has been that a decade of top-down reforms have not made sufficient difference to institutionalised corrupt practice. Apart from the top-level executives who regularly engage in the discourse of 'change', there is little evidence that the majority of officers at the operational level are willing or ready for change. Hence, the impetus to change has mainly come from externally induced crises. The *Cop It Sweet* scandal, for example, exposed the gap between the Police Service's espoused policy (eg, community based policing based on non-racist principles) and operational officers' practice (eg, routine use of racist slurs against Aborigines), forcing the organisation to initiate change (see Chan 1997). The need for continuing external pressure to change is partly the rationale behind the Mollen Commission's recommendation for an independent external agency to oversight the fight against corruption in the New York City Police Department:

> If history proves anything, it is that when the glare of scrutiny shines on the Department, it can and will successfully police itself. But history also proves that left to its own devices the Department will backslide, and its commitment to integrity will erode... Only a truly independent body, working with the Department but beyond its control, can sustain this commitment – and make the fear of failed corruption controls more powerful than the fear of corruption's disclosure... But independent oversight alone will not do the trick. The primary responsibility for combating police corruption should and must remain with the Department. (Mollen 1994: 6-7)

In New South Wales, two independent external bodies of oversight already exist: the Ombudsman and the Independent Commission Against Corruption (ICAC) both have powers to monitor aspects of police operations and push for change. However, research has suggested that externally imposed changes are often resisted by the organisation, so that change either remains at the 'damage control' level or simply a paper exercise. Studies of police organisations have also observed a high level of disenchantment and cynicism towards management among operational officers My analysis of the Police Service's implementation of the Ethnic Affairs Policy Statement (EAPS) has shown how difficult it was for an external agency to impose change on the police organisation and for police headquarters to impose change on operational units (Chan 1997: ch 7). This should come as no surprise given the embeddedness of cultural knowledge and the ineffectiveness of cosmetic efforts such as policy statements and operational guidelines in challenging assumptions and changing attitudes. Schein suggests that a strategy of 'coercive persuasion' should be used in situations 'where elements of the old culture are dysfunctional but strongly adhered to':

> The key to producing change in that situation is first to prevent exit and then to escalate the disconfirming forces while providing psychological safety. This is difficult to execute, but precisely what effective turnaround managers do. By using the right incentives, they make sure that the people whom they wish to retain in the organization find it difficult to leave. By consistently challenging the old assumptions ... they make it difficult for people to sustain the old assumptions. By consistently being supportive and rewarding any evidence of movement in the direction of new assumptions, they provide some psychological safety. If psychological safety is sufficient, members of the group can begin to examine and possibly give up some of their cognitive defenses. (Schein 1985: 294)

The lessons from research are clear: change is traumatic, it has to be directed and continuous, people must be willing to change, and, finally, planned change is difficult to achieve, especially when it is imposed by one group upon another:

> All change, then, is motivated. However, many changes do not go in the direction that the motivated persons wanted them to go. In other words, much of what actually happens as a consequence of initial change efforts may be unplanned and unintended because the change agents may have miscalculated the effects of their action or may have been unaware of other forces that were simultaneously acting. Such miscalculation is especially likely when members of one cultural unit make efforts to change behavior, values, or assumptions in another cultural unit, without fully understanding how their own behavior will be interpreted in the other cultural unit. The result may be new behaviors that neither group intended and that require either cultural redefinition or new cultural assumptions altogether. (Schein 1985: 301)

It is perhaps no surprise that the Mollen Commission's recommendations include a wide range of internal reforms in addition to external structural changes (Mollen 1994). I have argued elsewhere (Chan 1997) that changing police culture requires changes both in the 'field', the external and internal structural conditions of policing, and in the 'habitus', the content of cultural knowledge. Changes in the level of public awareness and pressure for reform, legislative reform, improvement of accountability structures, reward systems and auditing procedures are all important structural reforms which are essential. However, my concern in this paper is to highlight how changes in cultural knowledge can be approached. The next section, therefore, outlines the prospects of 'professionalism' as a way of transforming police practice.

ii.   Professional policing practice

If we take Brogden and Shearing's (1993: 108) observation that professionalism is seen as offering an 'alternative set of goals, means, and values to those of the occupational culture', it is possible to use my previous framework for analysing institutionalised practice to postulate how professionalism can result in professional practice. To summarise my previous argument: institutionalised police practice can be conceptualised as a product of the interaction between the 'field' (ie structural conditions of police practice such as legal, political, economic, organisational, etc) and the 'habitus' (ie cognitive structures acquired by police officers which are commonly referred to as the 'cop code' or informal occupational culture), mediated by the active role played by police 'actors' (ie police officers and managers). It is therefore possible to hypothesise, by analogy, that professional practice is the product of the interaction between the field and the habitus, mediated by police actors. Only the habitus no longer contains the cultural knowledge identified with the 'cop culture', but that derived from the 'professional ideal' (see Figure 5.3).

Figure 5.3: An Interactive Model of the Production of Professional Practice

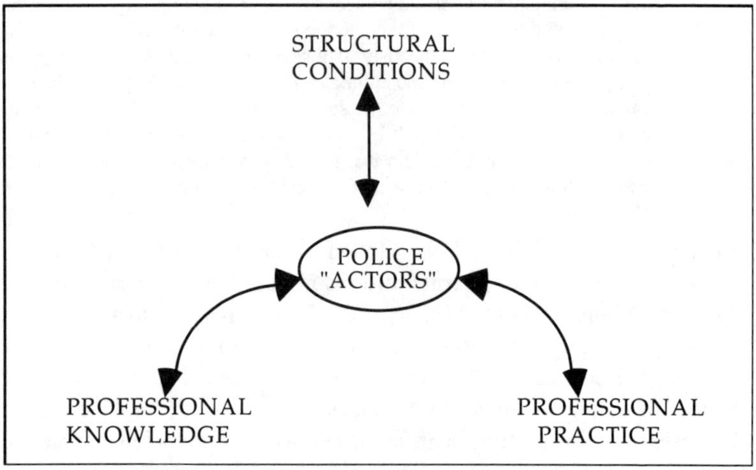

It is hazardous to typify professionalism, as there are different conceptions of this ideal, just as it is dangerous to stereotype police culture, since multiple cultures exist. As Manning has warned, the rhetoric of professionalism is by no means uniformly understood:

> rhetoric can take on different meanings even within the organizational hierarchy. To patrolmen, the term 'professionalism' means control over hours and salary and protection from arbitrary punishment from 'upstairs'; to the chief and the higher administrators, it relates to the public-administrations of efficiency, technological expertise, and standards of excellence in recruitment and training. (Manning 1978a: 10)

However, as Bittner points out, the absence of models or even meaningful discussions of what constitutes 'good police practice' ensures that professionalism remains an abstract ideal:

> presently good and bad work practices are not distinguishable, or, more precisely, are not distinguished. Worst of all, we have good reasons to suspect that if some men are possessed by and act with professional acumen, they might possibly find it wiser to keep it to themselves lest they will be found to be in conflict with some departmental regulation. The pending task . . . [has to do with] discovering those good qualities of police work that already exist in the skills of *individual practitioners*. It is not enough to discover them, however, they must be liberated and allowed to take their proper place in the scheme of police organization. By making the possession and use of such skills the controlling consideration in the distribution of rewards, we will have a beginning of a professional system for controlling police practices. (Bittner 1978: 50)

Thus, at the risk of oversimplification and being misinterpreted as providing a blueprint for reform, I offer the following interpretations of professionalism, primarily as a way of stimulating debate and further research (see Braithwaite 1992 for a discussion of similar issues). It should be clear from earlier sections that I am doubtful that professional practice can be produced by any other means than *activating processes* within and outside of police organisations to change the field and the habitus of policing.

Figure 5.4 provides a simplified model of how the field and habitus of traditional policing differ from those of professional policing. The left-hand side of the table is no more than a summary of previous sections. The 'field' component of the right-hand side of the table is simply the opposite of the left-hand side; while the 'habitus' component is taken directly from what the NSW Police Service's principal operational strategy community based policing and its 'statement of values'. It may seem ironic that these values and strategies are cited as model of professionalism, given the evidence presented to the Royal Commission that for a disturbing number of police officers, such values were largely ignored in practice. But that is precisely what the problem is: the gap between the organisation's 'espoused theories' and members' 'theories-in-use' (Argyris and Schon 1978, cited in Schein 1985). Moreover, by specifying that aspects of the field must also be changed to support these professional ideals, I try to emphasise that structural conditions and professional knowledge are equally important for the production of professional practice. This view has been stated by Bittner years ago:

> It must be said, however, that the true professionalization of police work, in and of itself, is no weapon against sloth and corruption, no more than in the case of medicine, the ministry, law, teaching, and social work. That is, the professionalization of police work still leaves open the matter of its control.

Figure 5.4: Traditional and Professional Policing

Traditional Policing	Professional Policing
THE FIELD:	
Wide discretionary powers	Clearly defined legal powers
Ineffective external accountability mechanisms (courts, ombudsman, media, parliament, videotaping, etc)	Strong and effective external accountability mechanisms
Ineffective supervisory and management structure	Effective supervisory and management structure
'Core business' of police directed at underclass and street offences	'Core business' of police directed at problem solving and crime control
Implicit public support of 'noble cause' misconduct	Strong public intolerance for lack of integrity in police conduct
THE HABITUS:	
Axiomatic Knowledge (mandate)	
War on crime	Problem solving
Order maintenance	Crime prevention
Organisational interests	Service provision
Dictionary Knowledge (categories)	
Rough vs respectable	Non-judgmental approach to people
Indicators of suspiciousness (people out of place, etc)	Appreciation of diversity in cultures and lifestyles
Stereotyping of minorities	Understanding of social and historical positions of minorities
Directory Knowledge (methods)	
Look for the unusual	Get to know the community and make service responsive to needs and feelings of community
Use force to take control of situations	Involve community in policing and problem solving
Take short cuts	Follow prescribed procedures
Recipe Knowledge (values)	
Cover your 'arse'	Place integrity above all
Stand by your mate	Uphold the rule of law
Keep the lid on	Preserve rights and freedom of individuals
Stay out of trouble	Strive for citizen and police personal satisfaction
	Ensure that authority is exercised responsibly

> But if we are not willing to settle for having physicians who are merely honest, and who would frankly admit that in curing diseases and dealing with patients they have to rely on 'playing by ear,' it is difficult to see why we would devote all our energies to try to make the police honest without any concern whatever for whether or not they know, in a technical sense, how to do what they are supposed to do. (Bittner 1978: 49-50)

Finally, the crucial role of police officers and police managers in organisational change should be re-emphasised, since there is 'no such thing as spontaneous change' (Schein 1985: 299). Schein has emphasised the role of leadership: 'Leaders create cultures, but cultures, in turn, create their next generation of leaders' (Schein 1985: 313). However, *it would be a mistake to equate leadership with organisational rank or position:* leadership is necessary from every level and every division of the organisation, not simply from the top. What is required of leadership, according to Schein, includes: perception and insight, motivation and skill, emotional strength, ability to change cultural assumptions, creation of involvement and participation, and depth of vision (Schein 1985: 322-5).

Obviously, the organisation must create a suitably supportive climate to encourage and reward such leadership. This may be what the Mollen Commission is talking about when it suggests that the support of 'honest cops' should be enlisted:

> The Department can do much to strengthen the resolve of each officer to resist the opportunity and tolerance for corruption by attacking the deep-seated cynicism too many officers feel about the Department and replacing it with an abiding respect for their Department. To do that, the Department must convince its officers that it is ready to enter a new and inviolable pact with them: unremitting support, guidance, rewards, and incentives in exchange for their professionalism and pride in a Department that is renown for its skills and integrity. (Mollen 1994: 65).

5. Summary and conclusions

In summary, police culture can be understood as a set of basic assumptions or organisational knowledge shared by members of the policing occupation or subgroups within police organisations. Cultural knowledge is developed when members of a group discover that certain assumptions or methods of operating are useful for overcoming problems encountered by the group. In time these assumptions and rules of thumb become abstracted into general schema for interpreting the social and physical reality of police work. Cultural knowledge is then transmitted by a learning process either through positive reinforcement of successful solutions to problems or successful avoidance of painful situations. Many of the negative aspects of police culture are the result of anxiety-avoidance learning rather than problem-solving learning. Consequently, these negative aspects become a type of group 'defence mechanism' which is virtually unchallenged and which impedes change and innovation. However, police culture is not monolithic and unchanging. Although many studies have highlighted the similarities of cultures in different jurisdictions, variations are also found between police forces and within police forces. Within police organisations, differences in cultural knowledge are associated with differences in rank, functional responsibility, as well as individual officers' orientations.

Police cultural knowledge is clearly a product of the structural conditions of police work. Externally, the absence of political pressure to deal with police deviance, the opportunities created by the regulation of illegal markets and the failure of the accountability system to guard against unlawful police practices all create conditions conducive to deviant cultures and corrupt practices. Internally, police work is organised as a military-bureaucratic structure with numerous layers of rules and regulations. Accountability tends to concentrate on disciplinary matters and arrest statistics rather than excellence in service delivery. These working conditions contribute to the development of a culture of solidarity among lower level officers, concealment of mistakes, and cynicism towards upper level supervisors and managers. Nevertheless, police officers and police organisations are not passive carriers of the police culture. They take an active part in the construction of their environments and aspects of cultural knowledge. In fact, officers help create and reinforce the notion that a stable and inviolable 'cop code' exists by regularly referring to such a code to justify their own actions. Individual officers have the capacity to resist and transform the negative aspects of police culture, although a radical cultural change cannot be sustained without a great deal of commitment and reinforcement from inside and outside the organisation.

Since culture is a 'deep phenomenon' (Schein 1985: 5), it is both difficult and traumatic to effect change. A police organisation must be ready to change for change to be successful. Although the impetus for change may come from external bodies or an organisational crisis, changes imposed from outside are often resisted by the organisation, while changes initiated from the top are sometimes ignored by officers at the operational level. Moreover, changes do not always produce results in the intended direction. There is a need for continual monitoring and reinforcement of the change strategies.

Professionalism in policing has been seen as a normative alternative to the negative aspects of the police culture. Even though professionalism could be used as a weapon to increase police powers rather than improve police service, it is still important, as a start, to distinguish between good and bad police practices. Obviously the professional model will not replace existing cultural knowledge unless such a change is reinforced by internal and external structural conditions. Police organisations should therefore provide a supportive climate to encourage and reward leadership from every level and every division to promote and sustain a culture of professionalism.

6

Reform, Regression and the Royal Commission into the NSW Police Service

David Dixon

1. Reform and regression

Assessment of developments since the publication of the Royal Commission's Final Report must be ambivalent.[1] On one hand, major changes have been (and continue to be) made in the Police Service. Notably, the managerial and command structure has been thoroughly rearranged, complaints procedures have been reformed, new education and training programs have been developed, new crime policing strategies have been introduced, and, last but by no means least, there has been a major turnover in personnel, particularly in senior positions. Given the difficulty of effecting change in such an organisation, these achievements must be acknowledged. On the other hand, there are grounds for the concern that the 'desire and momentum for reform' (Wood 1997a: 4) which the Royal Commission engendered is slipping away.[2]

In 1998, the murder of a police officer, a series of attacks on elderly people,[3] and the firing of shots at a police station[4] provided the catalyst for a regressive reversion in public discourse. Once again, it came to be

---

1   I am grateful to Jill Bolen, David Brown, Janet Chan, Mark Finnane, and Lisa Maher for comments and advice on drafts of this chapter.

2   One indication of this was the Ombudsman's expression of concern about delays and managerial inefficiencies in the Police Service's response to evidence of police misconduct (NSW Ombudsman 1998a).

3   See 'Granny bashing: man held' *Daily Telegraph*, 24 May 1998.

4   See 'Law and disorder: our police under fire' *Sydney Morning Herald*, 2 November 1998; 'Anarchy pulls the trigger' and '18 bullets that changed a city' *Daily Telegraph*, 2 November 1998.

dominated by demands for action to deal with a breakdown in law and order, 'the rising tide of violence that floods the streets of almost every community in NSW' which will soon make Sydney 'an international byword for random savagery'.[5] According to one popular newspaper,

> We are afraid. It is not safe any more to walk down the main streets of Sydney at night... Crime is rife. No matter what time it is, the threat of having a knife placed at your chest for just a few dollars is imminent... [T]here is only one solution. We need to be tougher on crime. We need stronger laws and harsher punishments.[6]

The standard accompaniment was to demand more police provided with additional powers, responding more quickly to calls for service. With an election looming, the Government was keen to oblige: the Premier set the tone, declaring that he had 'had enough of hearing about the rights of criminals and thugs'[7] and that the 'time has come ... to make a fundamental decision about how we want our streets, our neighbourhoods and our lives to be'.[8] The Police Association (despite the Royal Commission's criticism of its earlier role and despite its expressions of support for the reform process: Wood 1997b: 211-12, 531-2) reverted to its accustomed role of treating police powers as an industrial relations issue (Griffith and Simpson 1998: 5-7; Dixon 1997: 222).

In some influential quarters, concern for police reform became not just irrelevant, but unacceptable: according to one prominent talk-back radio commentator, you are either with the police or in their way. In this topsy-turvy world, public respect for the police is said to be improperly undermined by accusations of corruption and the accusers are allocated some responsibility for assaults on police.[9] According to such accounts, the Royal Commission was concerned with the corrupt activities of a number of individuals who have been identified and expelled. This is despite Wood's cogent critique of 'bad apple' accounts of corruption (1997a: 26-7), his insistence that '[s]o far as the NSW Police Service is concerned, the findings of this Royal Commission must dispel, for all time, any explanation based upon individual deviance or opportunistic corruption' (1997a: 28), and his demonstration that the source of the Police Service's problems lay not in individual venality but in organisational structures and cultures.[10]

---

5   'Streets of shame' *Sunday Telegraph*, 15 March 1998; cf Hogg and Brown 1998.

6   'Victims demand action on crime' *Sunday Telegraph*, 15 March 1998.

7   'Premier sticks to his knives' *Sunday Telegraph*, 28 June 1998.

8   Legislative Assembly, *Hansard* 31 March 1998, p 3440.

9   'Hard questions for a horrified city' *Sydney Morning Herald*, 2 November 1998.

10   As in other respects (see below), the Wood Commission's critique of 'bad apple' accounts echoed the Lusher Report (1981).

It may be objected that this is to pay more attention to media accounts than they deserve, and that the significant story concerns the hard grind of change within the police service. What do you expect from the tabloid press and talk-back radio? Understandable as this reaction (particularly from police officers committed to the reform process) may be, this approach is fundamentally misconceived. First, it underestimates the extraordinary influence which the popular media have on criminal justice policy in New South Wales. Second, and more generally, policing and reform efforts do not operate in a social and political vacuum. The significance of the interactive relationship between policing and its socio-political context is exemplified by the history of the Queensland Police Service (Bolen 1997) and by that of the New York City Police Department between 1972 and 1992, when 'a general decline in media and academic attention to issues of police corruption ... coincided with a gradual "collapse" of the Police Department's corruption control system' (Chan 1997: 81, citing Henry 1994). The maintenance of reform campaigns depends significantly upon pressure from the public discourse about policing. If, as has happened in New South Wales, this discourse is dominated by 'law and order' rhetoric, then one should not be surprised if the impetus for reform and change is lost.

A particular difficulty is getting some police officers to recognise concern about policing practices. Two examples may be provided suggesting that some officers feel immune from the reform process. Even when the Royal Commission had revealed the vigour of its investigative capacity (see below), some continued to engage in misconduct and corrupt activity, and their superiors failed to take basic steps to detect and prevent it. In 1997, the Police Integrity Commission's Operation Jade investigated Task Force Bax, a special unit established to tackle crime in Kings Cross, which 'had been repeatedly flagged as a high risk area for police corruption' (PIC 1998: 43). It found that Detective Sergeant Robert Irwin had an apparently corrupt relationship with a convicted heroin dealer ('J2'), leaking sensitive police information (including the existence of a covert informant) and accepting money.[11] His Commander had 'failed to recognise and respond to a clear telltale sign or indicator of corruption', had managed Bax in ways which 'had been highlighted in the Royal Commission's Final Report ... as key reasons why corruption had gone unexposed in the Police Service as a whole' (PIC 1998: v), and had failed to implement basic anti-corruption measures. This was 'astounding since Task Force Bax commenced at the time the Royal Commission was

---

11 The PIC concluded that there was 'no evidence revealed during the public hearings of network-based corruption within Task Force Bax' (1998: 32).

running and evidence of serious police corruption and the failure of management to prevent it was being adduced on a daily basis' (PIC 1998: v). The PIC also found that Detective Sergeant Craig 'Snidely' McDonald, a close associate of Irwin, felt able to ask another officer (J1) to join his 'family' and start 'playing first grade' by having J2's finger-prints removed from police evidence (PIC 1998: 27). In this case, the trust proved to be misplaced, much to the credit of the officer who reported the incident and collected evidence against yet another 'elite squad'.[12] The PIC anticipated that its 'public hearings, and the arrests that followed will serve to deter officers contemplating acts of corruption' (1998: vi). Expecting that the type of officer whose view was that 'the only thing that caused a problem at the Royal Commission was blokes under pressure shitting themselves'[13] would be deterred by the PIC is perhaps too optimistic. More realistic is the PIC's indication 'that informal networks of corrupt officers persist in the Police Service' (PIC 1998: iv). It should be of concern that the episode indicates the disdain of such officers for the reform process.

At another level, some officers seem to have ignored or forgotten the Commission's work remarkably quickly. When research was published in late 1997 which reported that apparently unlawful and improper practices in the treatment of Indo-Chinese heroin users had carried on during the Commission's tenure (Maher et al 1997), some officers reacted indignantly. It was as if criticism of police officers' integrity was incredible and unacceptable, despite the fact that the research merely provided empirical evidence of what the Royal Commission had reported: in 'a disturbingly large number of cases, the Royal Commission received complaints of money and property having been stolen by police in the course of routine police work'. The Commission concluded that 'theft and extortion from criminals had become regular features of policing in some sections of the Service' (Wood 1997a: 114).

Clearly, the Royal Commission cannot be held responsible for the degeneration of public discourse. Justice Wood stressed that 'the public exposure of corruption ... and the formulation of policy recommendations, will ... achieve little unless very great attention is given to the process of implementation' (1997a: 81). Wood went on to repeat Mollen's warning that 'when the glare of scrutiny shines on the Department, it can and will successfully police itself. But ... left to its

---

12 See PIC 1998; 'The breaking of Task Force Bax' *Sun Herald*, 14 December 1997. Note also the treatment of a new officer who complained about a colleague's process corruption: 'The grim blue line' *Sun Herald*, 10 May 1998.

13 Detective Sergeant 'Snidely' McDonald, quoted, 'Nowhere to hide' *Sydney Morning Herald*, 13 December 1997.

own devices the Department will backslide, and its commitment to integrity will erode' (Mollen 1994: 6, quoted Wood 1997a: 82). However, there are significant respects in which aspects of the Commission's Report made this possible. Consequently, this chapter will focus on what are perceived to be weaknesses in the Royal Commission's approach. However, it is necessary to begin by giving appropriate acknowledgment to the Commission's considerable achievements.

2. A 'state of systemic and entrenched corruption'

i. The Commission's investigations

Assessment of the Royal Commission cannot be limited to its reports. Its investigative activity[14] was itself a major achievement in exposing a 'state of systemic and entrenched corruption' (Wood 1997a: 84). The establishment of the Commission in May 1994 was met with considerable scepticism: it was widely expected[15] that Justice Wood would conduct a judicial inquiry which would focus on well-publicised allegations about corruption, notably involving some notorious officers and their relations with criminals. This ground was already thoroughly, if unproductively, turned (ICAC 1994a, 1994b). For almost a year, it seemed that the Commission was performing the function so often taken by such inquiries: symbolising commitment to tackling a problem, but deflecting pressures for real change. As resources were poured into the Commission's establishment and premises, scepticism grew.

Doubters were made to reassess the Commission when, in June 1995, its investigative strategy was unveiled. The Commission had used the time since its establishment to look at the present rather than the past, and had done so by means of proactive investigations. As a demonstrative example, the Commission revealed that Trevor Haken, an officer who was heavily involved in major corruption, had 'rolled over' and had, for several months, been cooperating with the Commission. Notably, a videorecorder installed in the car which he used had recorded his corrupt dealings with police and criminals. The exposure of this material began with a tape showing Haken giving money from bribes to a senior detective.

---

14 There is a very useful overview of the Commission's 'methodology and inquiry' in Wood 1997c: App 2, and a detailed 'Royal Commission Chronology' in App 19.

15 Exercising considerable restraint, Justice Wood relegated to a footnote the dismissal by the then and the former Premiers, the Police Commissioner, and Police Association officials of the Commission as a waste of time and money: see Wood 1997a: 84, n 381.

A strategy then was laid out. Officers would be called to give evidence. They would be confronted with video or informant evidence of their involvement in corrupt activity, and would then be asked to reconsider their position.[16] This material was skilfully exploited by the Commission. Brown suggests that '[s]uch readily understandable and widely conveyed images grabbed public attention, helped build up a strong momentum for further revelations, swept aside the remnants of the "rotten apple" thesis and created a strong public and political demand for reform' (1998: 229).[17]

The confidence of some officers that they were untouchable was shaken: others rolled over and gave evidence about their and others' misconduct. The Commission was able to collect and present evidence about a wide range of alleged corruption and other misconduct involving, inter alia, senior officers (an assistant commissioner and the Police Commissioner's chief of staff), whole squads, detective groups, and an inter-jurisdictional task force. The Commission's list of topics indicates the scale and range of corruption discovered: 'process corruption; gratuities and improper associations; substance abuse; fraudulent practices; assaults and abuse of police powers; prosecution – compromise or favourable treatment; theft and extortion; protection of the drug trade; protection of club and vice operators; protection of gaming and betting interests; drug trafficking; interference with internal investigations, and the code of silence; and other circumstances suggestive of corruption' (Wood 1997a: 83-4). An early casualty was Police Commissioner Lauer, who resigned in February 1996: while there were no allegations that he had been involved in financial corruption (cf ICAC 1989), his claim that there was no structural corruption within the Service made his position untenable in the light of the Commission's findings. The Royal Commission has to be assessed, therefore, not just as a judicial inquiry, but also as an investigative, policing agency. In eliding this distinction, the Commission is part of a diversification of policing as new agencies (private as well as public)

---

16   The ultimate humiliation was suffered by Wayne Eade, a senior detective whose denials were countered by a videotape apparently showing him using illegal drugs, discussing the purchase of further drugs and pornographic videos involving children, and having sex with a prostitute: see 'Breaking the brotherhood' *Sydney Morning Herald*, 1 May 1997.

17   With the benefit of hindsight, this is over optimistic. In the longer term, these images ironically contributed to the re-emergence of 'rotten apple' accounts by officers and others who found it easy and necessary to distinguish their (process and other) corruption from the gross misconduct by the Commission's targets. In turn, this allowed the reform process to be understood as a matter of managerial administration, rather than as a cultural and structural reformation to which all officers had to be committed contributors.

are introduced to the field (Findlay, Odgers and Yeo 1994: ch 3). The Commission obtained significant cooperation from one such, the NSW Crime Commission. Such agencies are distinctive in the special powers with which they are provided and the limited effectiveness of the accountability to which they are subjected. The Royal Commission has left a permanent addition: the Police Integrity Commission (PIC) was established to carry on the work of investigating corruption (1997b: 524-6).

The PIC is the most tangible product of two concerns. First, the Royal Commission made no pretence that it had uncovered all corruption in the Service. In the context of the discussion of structural and cultural factors which promote misconduct, it would be hard to read the Commission's treatment of specific incidents, individuals and groups as other than examples. Indeed, soon after publication of his Final Report, Justice Wood was expressing concern about continuing corruption.[18] Secondly, the shadow of earlier inquiries and reform efforts hung over the Wood Commission. In New South Wales, the Royal Commission's investigation followed more than a decade of internal reform and external scrutiny. According to (then Commissioner) Tony Lauer, the NSW Police Service between the mid-1980s and mid-1990s underwent 'a total reformation in terms of its organisational structures, philosophy and practice' (1995: 75). In 1994, an application for an Australian Quality Award (itself some indication of self-confidence) reported on a 10-year program of developing 'professional, accountable, responsible and innovative police officers' (NSW Police 1994: 3). The 'Avery reform era' has been held out as 'a successful model in police change management' (Etter 1995: 288; cf Sparrow et al 1990).

However, the Commission delivered a damning judgement on these attempted reforms: they were uncoordinated, ill-informed, superficial and ineffective (1997b: 207-12). External pressure for change had been to little effect: the Commission expressed 'concern that both the ICAC and the Ombudsman in New South Wales have investigated, exposed and made recommendations about corruption in the NSW Police Service with little resultant change or acknowledgment by the Service' (Wood 1997a: 144; cf id, 144-50; ICAC 1994). Elsewhere, the reform process in Queensland initiated by the Fitzgerald Report (but also building on earlier reform activities) had run into the sand of Queensland's politics (Bolen 1997; Prenzler 1997; cf CJC 1997). Wood's senior counsel, Gary Crooke, brought his crucial experience of Fitzgerald to the Royal Commission.[19]

---

18 'Big names escaped commission net: Wood' *Australian Financial Review*, 28 May 1998.

19 For Justice Wood's acknowledgment of Crooke's contribution, see 1997c: A1.

Similarly, the Mollen Commission in New York, which provided a continuing point of reference for Justice Wood, was followed by discoveries of further corruption in the New York City Police Department.[20] Most recently, serious corruption has again emerged in London's Metropolitan Police and elsewhere in England.[21]

ii. The Commission's reports

The reports of the Commission represent a significant achievement. While, as will be argued below, general and specific criticism can be made, these must be put in the context of references which were very wide. The inclusion of the paedophile reference[22] made the Commission's task enormous. It deserves credit for not taking what must have been an inviting option of narrowing the inquiry down. On the contrary, it adopted a wideranging definition of corruption, giving 'process corruption' the serious attention that it deserved (1997a: 26, 36-8, 84-95). The Commission's most important message was that the focus of reform should not be on individual wrongdoers and their corruption, but on the institutional and cultural contexts which produced, maintained, and tolerated them:

> The long term solution to the problems uncovered lies only partially in the investigation and prosecution of corrupt individuals. The more significant reform lies in addressing the structure, attitudes and professionalism of the Service, with a view to preventing the occurrence of such conduct. Failure to achieve this reform can only result in the cyclical reappearance of the very same culture and conduct that led to the setting up of the current inquiry. (Wood 1996b: 2)

From this perspective, corruption is a symptom of a deeper malaise: tackling the latter is the priority. Consequently, the Commission did not merely recommend further layers of anti-corruption bureaucracy and regulation, the approach which Anechiarico and Jacobs (1996) argue is so

---

20 For a useful summary of NYPD anti-corruption efforts, see Anechiarico and Jacobs (1996: 157-70).

21 See 'Yard's clean-up now spans three decades' *The Times*, 28 January 1998; 'Corruption crusade running out of time' *The Times*, 16 May 1998; 'Condon's Untouchables ready to finger collars' *The Times*, 25 July 1998; 'Corruption drive to end police perks' *The Times*, 15 August 1998. See also HMIC 1999; Newburn 1999.

22 In December 1994, the Royal Commission's terms of reference were extended to include not just police involvement in the investigation of paedophilia (about which evidence of corruption had emerged), but also the law concerning paedophilia, trial processes, and the arrangements for preventing sexual abuse of children in state care or supervision. The Royal Commission's Report on these matters was issued in June 1997 (Wood 1997d). This part of the Royal Commission's work is not considered here: for discussion, see Cossins 1999; Simpson 1998.

damaging to effective government.[23] This meant that, despite its formal terms of reference, the Royal Commission's focus was widened to include the whole spectrum of police and policing. A comprehensive inquiry was impossible, given the deadline, the need for a reform process to get underway, and the pressure to complete specific corruption-related investigations. Consequently, there are (as will be indicated below) areas of thinness in the Commission's discussions and recommendations. In addition, much of the responsibility for constructing a reform process was delegated to the Police Service, and specifically to Commissioner Ryan.

One problem which the Commission faced in its attempt to go beyond a narrow study of corruption was the paucity of academic research on Australian policing: the Commission was in a very different position than, for example, the Royal Commission on Criminal Justice (in England and Wales) which was able to draw on a wide range of excellent recently completed or current projects (for a useful summary, see Home Office Research and Statistics Branch 1994). Policing research in Australia is in its infancy: most of the growing literature consists either of naïve, quantitative empiricism or legal and political commentary: theoretically informed, empirical studies of any quality can be counted on one hand. The usual pleas about lack of research access are hardly convincing in New South Wales, where the Service has generally had a good record of facilitating research.[24] Unfortunately, the view that researchers merely restate what is already known and create damaging publicity appears to be gaining ground. It would be regrettable if, as seems may be the case, the Service becomes less open to research: good research has intrinsic benefits (cf Brereton 1998 and below) and police defensiveness can contribute to the 'culture of corruption' (Chan 1997: 91). Both the Royal Commission and the Mollen Commission in New York demonstrated the costs of being 'more concerned with the damage brought about by negative publicity than with the problem of corruption' (Chan 1997: 91).

In some of the areas where significant research was available, the Commission made good use of it. Mark Finnane's work (both in his chapter above and in a series of publications including his *Police and Government* (1994)) clearly assisted the Commission's historical sensitivity which has been noted above (see Wood 1997a: ch 3). Similarly, Janet Chan's work (in her chapter above, and in her *Changing Police Culture* (1997) and other publications) contributed to the

---

23   Indeed, removing police corruption from the Independent Commission Against Corruption's responsibilities recognised the inefficiency of overlapping jurisdictions. But note the critique of Anechiarico and Jacobs by Doig (1997).

24   But note Finnane's complaint (ch 2 above) about the inaccessibility of NSW Police archives.

Commission displaying a much more sophisticated understanding of the key concept of police culture than is common either in general usage or, for example, in the Fitzgerald Report. The diversity within police cultures was acknowledged (Wood 1997b: 216). By seeking to explain the sources of police culture, the Commission avoided the circularity of using 'culture' as a grab-bag descriptor for what is wrong in policing and then invoking it 'as the cause of corruption and misconduct' (Delahunty 1998: 14; cf Chan 1997). Culture was seen not just negatively, but both in terms of its functions and its potential: 'what must be harnessed now is the energy, commitment and loyalty which have in the past underpinned the brotherhood, but within a framework of sensible, achievable and careful planned reform' (Wood 1997a: 204; see also 1997b: 216). Crucially, Chan demonstrates that changing police culture requires that attention should be paid not just to informal rules, practices and values, but also to 'the social, economic, legal and political sites' which constitute 'the conditions of policing' (Chan 1997: 92). This serves to emphasise the scale of the task with which the Commission was faced.

Reform of the Police Service did not wait until the Commission reported. In some areas, this meant that the Commission's Final Report was commenting on initiatives which were already under way.[25] Some of these were recommended in the Commission's Interim Reports (Wood 1996a, 1996b), to which in turn the Service had contributed, directly or indirectly. Reform was generally developed in a process of interaction between Police Service and Commission. However, in some areas, the agenda for reform was clearly led by the Police Service and simply sanctioned by the Royal Commission. A notable example came in the treatment of criminal investigation, a crucial area in which the Commission's role was largely as an approving commentator on developments in train, rather than as an active party. Given its criticism of the 'failure of the Service ... to bring detectives into a truly integrated Service' in earlier reform projects (1997b: 211) and of 'the historical approach to criminal investigation which has kept it separate from other activities ... has led to the formation of an investigative power base and engendered a sense of elitism amongst detectives' (1997b: 424), the Commission had little (less than half a page) to say about central and regional detective units: 'It is appropriate that the ultimate decision for [sic] the retention and structure of the agencies should be left to the Service, so long as it takes into account the problems and inefficiencies detected and identified' (1997b: 254). This reticence is certainly surprising, given the

---

25   See Wood 1997a: 6-11. By contrast, reform of the Queensland Police Service awaited the completion of the Fitzgerald Inquiry (Bolen 1997).

Commission's analysis of the role played by high status, central and regional detective agencies in corruption. The success of the Police Service in ensuring that the new Crime Agencies do not reproduce the faults of the old CIB will be vital to the reform process.

iii. Life after death: Appendix 31

The Wood Commission made an innovative attempt to ensure that its program of reform would not be set aside or forgotten. Its final recommendations were that there should be an 'external strategic audit' which should 'report on success and failure, and to advise on measures to improve the reform process' (1997b: 535). A 'blueprint' for the audit process is provided in Appendix 31 (1997c: A246-54). This has a familiar appearance as the product of the retreat facilitator's white board. However, it has real substance, requiring continuing investigation of crucial matters. For example, the key reform area, 'Changing culture and values', will require police managers to identify and articulate their goals, and to make external comparisons. A rigorous program of audit is outlined. This is to be carried out by private sector auditors engaged by the Police Integrity Commission, beginning in 1999. Appendix 31 has achieved the status of a continuing examination paper which the Police Service must pass. The extent to which the Wood Commission leads to real change in the Police Service will depend to a considerable degree on the rigour with which the audit process is carried out.

3. Managing policing

If the Commission's volume on reform has a dominant discourse, it is that of managerialism. It began by insisting that '[a]t the core of many of the problems that have emerged lies the traditional approach of the Service to its staff. . . [A] limited authoritarian and conservative outlook . . . has permeated the upper levels of the Service in the past' (1997b: 207-8). The lengthy chapter on 'Transforming the NSW Police Service' dealt with a series of specific issues of police organisation, employment, education, promotion, termination, performance management and the like (1997b: 237-325). As noted above, a vital text in the reform process has been the Report's Appendix 31 (Wood 1997c: A246-54) which provides a program for auditing the progress of reform: with its identification of 'key reform areas', 'core changes', 'threshold and ongoing activities to audit', and 'assurance strategies', it relies upon a conventional managerialist template. A major influence on the Commission was its 'Transformational change and reform process consultant', Dr Peter Crawford (Honorary professorial fellow at the Graduate School of Management at Macquarie University) (see 1997c: A12, 35). Managerial change is seen as being 'at the heart of the reform process', in which change is engineered not by the discredited methods of command and control,[26] but by having police officers change the Service from within 'by setting proper professional standards and then doing whatever it can, in a managerial way, to lift their performance' (1997b: 330).

Rejecting 'the view that (the Service) is possessed of special features which require it to be managed in a unique way' (1997b: 208), the Commission called for the Police Service to be subjected to processes of managerial reform which have become familiar to the public sector in the last decade: flatter management, devolution of responsibility to base units, identification of core business, and replacement of restrictive and directive rules with revised statements of values and codes of ethics. The Report recommended measures which 'have long been adopted by progressive and well-managed organisations in the community' (1997b: 523). Anyone who has noted developments in British policing in the 1990s would find all this very familiar and, indeed, somewhat bland (cf Leishman et al (eds) 1996). There is certainly room for some more substantial and critical discussion of issues such as the identification of core functions: recent British experience has shown how controversial the application of managerialist wisdom to policing can be. As Chan suggests, the new managerialism has had limited success in controlling policing and has never become hegemonic because of public demands for more punitive measures in response to exposures of corruption:

> The new accountability's project of managing the risk of official misconduct is continually frustrated by evidence of its failure and the attendant swing back to punitive control strategies. Police accountability is demanded more aggressively now in New South Wales than ever: while people have lost trust in the integrity of their public institutions, they are increasingly placing their trust on the promises of more and better accountability which has repeatedly failed them. (Chan 1999: 266; cf Davids and Hancock 1998)

The rhetoric and failings of managerialism present a relatively easy target for criticism. More difficult is the presentation of positive alternatives, both generally and in specific relation to policing. It is widely recognised that the English debates about accountability in the 1980s were unproductive: the obsession with local political accountability generally failed

---

26   See Chapter 4, Section 3ii, above.

to go beyond slogans, leaving largely unexplored crucial concepts such as control, democracy, and community (cf Jones, Newburn and Smith 1994). It has been left high and dry by a new politics of centralised control linked to a corporatised public sector in which accountability is more rhetoric than substance. But as yet we lack strategies or even a language which would allow us to go beyond this to offer a developed alternative to managerialism. This must be a significant goal for those interested in the regulation not just of policing, but of contemporary institutions more generally.

A key question is whether managerialist reforms can contribute to the cultural change which the Commission saw as so vital: 'No matter what structural changes or safeguards are introduced, corruption is ultimately a matter of individual choice, which can only be influenced by peer pressure, example and close supervision' (Wood 1997a: 162). This does not represent a naïve individualism: the Commission made clear that 'selection or rejection of the corrupt road depends not just on individual choice, but on the existence of an acquired and taught mind-set that neither encourages nor tolerates unethical behaviour' (Wood 1997a: 204). While the Commission's analysis of the problem of corruption fully recognised the role of culture, it was not dealt with directly in the proposals for reform.[27] The Commissions seems to have assumed that managerial changes would affect culture, but the specific manner in which this was expected to happen was unexplored. As Chan suggests, '[t]he danger in the current fad in management circles about cultural change is the belief that organisational cultures can be readily changed to improve corporate performance' (1997: 232). The well-worn nostrums of the new managerialism may underestimate the task.

The fate of earlier reform efforts suggests that this may be the case. The Royal Commission's recommendations are less original than they may appear. While fashions in terminology have changed, the Royal Commission echoed the 1981 Lusher Report in significant respects (Lusher 1981; cf Chan 1997: 124-5; Finnane: ch 2, above). Under John Avery, the Police Service was equally committed to 'emerging ideas that flat is beautiful . . . that layers of management should be few; that the best headquarters are small; that commanders should have a clear idea of what they are expected to accomplish; be held accountable for performance; and their accountability should be fairly matched with resources and authority' (Jackson 1991: 18). Indeed, what is striking is the similarity

---

27   However, 'changing culture and values' was included in Appendix 31 as a 'key reform area' to be audited (Wood 1997c: A247).

between the Avery and the Ryan programs rather than their differences.[28] This should not be surprising in the light of experience elsewhere: police reformers are notably prone to paying more attention to the fact that previous administrations failed than to what they attempted. This was the case with Justice Wood, ironically despite his recognition of the need to break out of the corruption-reform cycle. All too often, managers fail to review and evaluate previous programs of reform from a genuine research base.[29] As noted above, the lack of research on Australian policing hampers reform efforts.

The Wood Commission was consistent with its predecessors in another, ironical sense. Such bodies frequently note the limitations of management by 'law and order', deterrence and 'command and control'. Yet they are themselves expressions of such approaches: as Janet Chan suggests, 'a powerful inquisitorial body to deal with police corruption' is established 'because the "normal" criminal justice processes had failed'.[30] Reforms efforts within police departments have similar problems. One example is Ryan's approach: embarking on a program of fundamental change to a 'militaristic', 'stagnant' and 'rule-bound' Service, he felt that he had to begin by adopting a management style that was 'firm, hard and autocratic . . . because that is what the organisation understood' (quoted Baker 1997: 6). The problem is that (understandable as Ryan's choice may be) it has set the tone for his Commissionership.

A second example of bureaucratic style crushing possibilities of change is provided by the fate of the Service's Professional Standards Councils. These began as a grassroots initiative in Kings Cross, providing a forum for officers to discuss the ethical dilemmas which occur in policing an area which includes Sydney's red-light district. The Wood Commission encouraged the development of such councils (1997b: 494-5). The response of police management was to direct that they should be established throughout the Service. This imposition from above and the failure to allow for existing local arrangements resulted in a promising initiative coming to grief. All areas now have Professional Standards Councils, but they are widely regarded as ineffective and marginal. The Commission recommended that there should be 'ongoing evaluation by an external body such as the ICAC (Independent Commission Against

---

28   Cf Chan 1997: ch 6; Etter 1995: 286-8. Tony Lauer's commitment to reform (1995: 101-2) is also similar to current rhetoric. Contrast Peter Ryan's claim that he is responsible for 'introducing . . . concepts' of 'modern management thinking which emphasises flat structures and wider spans of responsibility' (1996: 14).

29   I am grateful to Mark Finnane for this point. See also Chapter 4, Section 2i, above for comments on the costs of failing to evaluate 'ethical awareness training programs'.

30   Personal communication, 28 April 1998, see also Chan 1999.

Corruption). Measures such as these require careful research and testing to establish their correct role, and to ensure that they receive adequate organisational and managerial support' (1997b: 495). The failure to implement this recommendation contributed to the fate of the PSCs. A third example is the Code of Conduct and Ethics which was introduced in the conventional way as a top-down imposition, despite the research suggesting that such codes are likely to be ineffective (see Chapter 4, Section 2i, above).

4. Accountability

The breadth of the Commission's task, both in its inquiry and investigative functions, was vast. Perhaps inevitably, but unfortunately, the result was that some crucial areas were not adequately discussed. This and the next section will discuss two prominent examples: accountability and drugs.

i. Parliamentary accountability

The issue of accountability is controversial at the levels both of Commissioner-Minister relations and of police-community consultation. First, the Commission argued that the constitutional relationship between Commissioner and Police Minister, which had been the subject of several disputes (Joint Select Committee upon Police Administration 1993; NSW Ombudsman 1993), should be resolved by statutory allocation of operational matters to the former and policy to the latter. The Commission distinguished policy and operations by providing examples of matters which it considered to be operational: 'the particular location of a number of police officers; the opening or closing or relocation of a police station; the creation of a Task Force; the targeting of a particular category of conduct and the means by which it should be achieve' (1997b: 244). By implication, this confined 'policy' to matters of generality. Reliance on this dichotomy is disappointing. First steps in consideration of police accountability should be Lustgarten's discrediting of the policy-operations distinction (1986) and Hogg and Hawker's demonstration that the uncertainty of relations between police and government was not so much a problem as a facilitative device (1983). Yet the Commission and subsequent debate proceeded as if policy/operations was a viable basis for political and strategic development.

It appears that the primary concern was to protect the Police Commissioner from politically motivated and ill informed interventions, while retaining ministerial accountability (1997b: 244-5). The Commission's priority was expressed best in referring to 'the pressing need to provide the new Police Commissioner with the power to properly manage the Service' (1997b: 379). Given the degenerate state of criminal justice politics in New South Wales, there may be good reasons for this, and the enthusiasm for political accountability which permeated academic debate in the 1980s seems inappropriate. Nevertheless, the end result was an arrangement in which the division between policy and operations was seen as fundamental but remained (inevitably) undefined and in which much relies upon the ability, trustworthiness, and professionalism of the Police Commissioner.

Similarly, the Commission's recommendation that the Police Board should be abolished (Wood 1996: 10-13) and its immediate implementation by the Government were driven by the perceived need to free the hands of the Police Commissioner, who had made clear his demand for 'the opportunity to actually proceed with the reform (of the Service) without having to respond to intrusive demands from stakeholders for an account of progress' (Ryan 1996: 4).[31] The various weaknesses and failures of the Police Board and the enthusiasm for managerialism provided an inadequate foundation for rejecting wholesale any civilian involvement in police management.[32] Indeed, the Commission's support for Peter Ryan's appointment seemed to determine the recommendations regarding high level accountability. Whether this provided the basis for long-term constitutional arrangements may be questioned. As Brown suggests, '[e]xtensions and concentrations of power should be justified in structural terms as appropriate to the office, not with an eye to the characteristics or personality of the office holder or an assessment of the political conjuncture' (DB Brown 1997: 223).

Even in the short term, some difficulties with the Commission's approach emerged. Only a few pages after the entrenchment of the policy/ operations divide, the Report noted the dispute over the Commissioner's decision to replace the Special Branch (discredited after revelations of its activities) with a 'Protective Security Response Group' with similar duties (1997b: 251-4). This would seem to come clearly within the Royal Commission's definition of 'operational' decisions. However, the Police

---

31 See also 'Police complaints hinder arrests, says Ryan' *Daily Telegraph*, 21 July 1998. Ryan's view of his role is indicated by the suggestion that he is 'like the cowboy in the John Ford westerns who had to leap from his galloping horse onto the runaway stage coach and stop it plunging into the ravine' (Ryan 1997a: 3).

32 There is civilian oversight by the Police Integrity Commission and the Ombudsman, but such accountability is by nature largely retrospective, rather than the prospective control that managerial involvement potentially allows.

Minister intervened, proposing a number of specific 'safeguards' and then suspending the Group's introduction until the Commission reported on the matter.[33] He 'stated that the replacement of Special Branch was a policy issue for which he would take responsibility' (Wood 1997b: 253). The proposed safeguards included integrity testing, intra-Service accountability, work allocation procedures, and the introduction of an 'operating manual' (Wood 1997b: 253). These were, in the Royal Commission's definition, unquestionably 'operational' matters.[34] Here was a stark example of the limits of the policy/operations divide. However, the Commission made no reference to its own discussion of accountability, simply supporting the introduction of a PSRG under specified conditions. The matter was resolved, in a traditional manner (cf Hogg and Hawker 1983) by compromise and negotiation.

Another example comes in the discussion of police education. The Commission stated: 'There is universal concern as to police dominance over training and education, and growing interest in this field. As a consequence, it is clear to the Commission that education and training should be treated as a policy matter for the Minister' (1997b: 281). The point is asserted, not argued: no reason was given for distinguishing between education and other sources of concern, such as deployment of staff or investigative techniques. 'Universal concern' and 'growing interest' are hardly appropriate criteria for distinguishing policy and operational matters.

Finally, it seems unlikely that a government so sensitive to 'law and order' politics will allow the Commissioner the political freedom which Justice Wood's formulation suggested.[35] Before Peter Ryan's appointment, Premier Carr showed his willingness to intervene: in September 1995, Carr ordered 'the random breath testing of all police officers . . . the deployment of all-night patrols by foot police and sniffer dogs' and regular rotation between districts of probationary constables.[36] Attempts by Ryan to rationalise police deployment have produced a series of local political controversies about the closure of police stations from which acknowledgment of the Commissioner's operational independence has

---

33   See 'Whelan kills off Ryan's new branch' *Sydney Morning Herald*, 17 April 1997.

34   Provision for audit and review of (what became) the Protective Security Group was inserted in the *Police Service Act* 1990 Pt 3.

35   A revised statutory relationship between Minister and Commissioner was one of the very few recommendations which the Government explicitly rejected: according to Police Minister Paul Whelan, 'There's no real cause for it to happen at this stage because the government does not tinker in operational decisions' quoted 'Reform rejected as too esoteric' *Sydney Morning Herald*, 15 May 1998.

36   See 'Carr: how I'll beat corruption' *Sydney Morning Herald*, 20 September 1995.

been notably absent.[37] Further tensions concerning comments on drug law reform and the announcement of a new policy on community policing strained relations between Commissioner and Government.[38]

While political accountability is undoubtedly a complex issue, it is disappointing that the Commission made so little progress in tackling a matter which had been the cause of notable disputes in the period immediately before its establishment (Joint Select Committee Upon Police Administration 1993). It is indicative of trends in public administration that the major innovation in accountability which the Commission proposed was the 'external strategic audit' of the reform process which has been noted above (Power 1997; Wood 1997c: App 31).

ii. Community consultation

The Commission recommended a two-tier structure of community consultation at local and managerial levels. It provided an admirable summary of the deficiencies of attempts at local community consultation in England and Wales (which have been the subject of considerable research), Canada, and New South Wales (1997b: 384-90). Unfortunately, the Commission misdiagnosed what it described, and consequently went on to propose a system built upon the flaws which have been responsible for failure elsewhere. Consultation in England and Wales has been a source of frustration because it involves no redistribution of power: police may hear what community representatives have to say, but have no obligation to change policy or practice in consequence. (Given what some 'community representatives' have to say, this is often a good thing.) The distribution of knowledge also imbalances the relation of power: typically, consultative committee members report concerns about low-level social problems. The local commander (or his/her) representative reports on crime rates and inadequate resources, so explaining the subordination of local concerns to other priorities. The police as the source of relevant information set the agenda for meetings. Committees also reflect local power imbalances, with their membership reflecting local political, organisational, and commercial interests rather than being representative of the police service's 'customers',[39] particularly those such as young and black people who are most likely to deal with the police as 'conflict customers' (sic, Harris Research Centre 1993).

---

37   See 'Ryan's Bid: Shut "Vote Catcher" Stations' *Sydney Morning Herald*, 30 June 1999; 'Whelan vows: no police closures' *Sydney Morning Herald*, 6 September 1999.
38   'Stay out of politics Ryan told' *Daily Telegraph*, 26 September 1997.
39   This managerialist term is unfortunately gaining favour in New South Wales: see eg 'Code of conduct and ethics' *Police Service Weekly* v 9(6), 10 February 1997, p 8.

This brief sketch is inevitably a caricature, but not an unfair one (Morgan and Newburn 1997: 52). It points to a key problem: community consultation which proceeds without any distribution of power is likely to be frustrating and, ultimately, unproductive.

Unfortunately, the Commission overlooked this clear finding of the English research literature. It treated the development of local consultation as 'very much a matter for the Service' (1997b: 391). Local commands should take responsibility for organising and initiating consultation. The priority in choosing those to be consulted was 'local government and local groups such as the Chamber of Commerce' (1997b: 391). If one deliberately set out to recreate consultative committees which are dominated by police, serve as mechanisms for transmitting information and opinion from police to public (rather than vice versa), and exclude the sections of the community most likely to have contact with police, one could hardly do better than implement these suggestions.[40]

At the higher level, the Commission discussed the possibility of establishing 'an on-ongoing council ... to provide strategic advice' (1997b: 392-3) but shied away, citing several objections. However, the real problem would seem to lie in what was cited as an advantage of this approach: such a Council might develop strength as a means of accountability, acting as 'an independent check on the power of the Police Commissioner' (1997b: 393). Having just dismissed the Police Board's pretensions to such a role and insisting on giving a free hand to Peter Ryan, the Commission not surprisingly moved on to a safer proposal. It recommended establishing 'a pool of people with expertise in relevant fields ... from which separate committees could be formed on a needs basis, chaired by the Commissioner or his representative, to address particular issues' (1997b: 393). This proposal had the possible advantage of providing some transparency in a process by which the Police Service seeks external advice, some of which, it would appear, has been of doubtful value in the past: willingness to offer an opinion needs to be distinguished from research and professional experience.[41] But as a mode of consultation, the flaws are evident: consultation was to be on terms set by the Commissioner and with those whom he chose to appoint to these committees. It was claimed that this would allow the Commissioner to

---

40 The exclusion of young people is a particular concern. As Delahunty points out, the Commission's praise for the 'Service's efforts to promote consultation with young people through the ... Youth Working Party ... neglected to mention' that the working party's membership is entirely from the Police Service and the Police Ministry (1998: 15).

41 For example, the inadequacies of the Police Service's sources of expertise on 'Asian Crime' are discussed in Dixon and Maher 1998: 65-6; 1999b.

'access people who are successes in their own right, have relevant expertise, are not politically aligned, and who would accept the appointment as altruistic citizens' (1997b: 394). The reference to political alignment is concerning: while recognising the need to avoid the political cronyism so often evident in New South Wales, it is simply naïve to treat criminal justice as an apolitical area. Finally, it is hard to see how such ad hoc committees could connect, as was expected, with local level committees.

The Police Commissioner has expressed his frustration about the constraints of accountability:

> I would like to see us being given the chance to get on with the job, quite frankly. It's taking up a huge amount of my time and the time of my senior managers. It also affects operational police because they are constantly looking over their shoulders.[42]

Police officers are encouraged to put the Commission behind them and to get back to fighting crime. Indeed, the Commission is sometimes presented as a diversion which criminals exploited as police took their 'eye off the ball'. The reform process is to go on, but it is essentially the business of management: Commissioner Ryan told his officers 'to start concentrating on getting crime down' and to 'leave the reform process to me'.[43] In arguing for an expansion of the powers in the Bill which became the *Police and Public Safety Act* 1998 (see below), Peter Ryan said 'the important thing is that people have to trust the service to use these powers judiciously'.[44] The Police Minister commented that such 'tough powers would never have been given to the old police service. . . They couldn't be trusted with them'.[45]

Such sentiments are hardly surprising. However, the response should be that the Police Service has not yet earned sufficient trust for accountability to be slackened, that some humility about the breach of trust which the Royal Commission uncovered might be appropriate, that external scrutiny is a necessary continuing anti-corruption measure, and that, far from forgetting the Commission, police officers should be reminded of it every day. If policing in New South Wales is to be fundamentally refashioned (as Wood showed it needs to be), then the active involvement of every officer in the process will be needed.

---

42   Quoted, 'Heroin: the main enemy' *Sydney Morning Herald*, 15 May 1998. See also 'Police complaints hinder arrests, says Ryan' *Daily Telegraph*, 21 July 1998. For a critical response, see NSW Ombudsman 1998c: 11.

43   'Self-indulgent junkies' *Daily Telegraph*, 22 September 1997. See also Ryan 1997b.

44   'Crackdown on knives unites Ryan and the force' *Sydney Morning Herald*, 17 March 1998.

45   'Police seize 1100 weapons in four-month blitz' *Sunday Telegraph*, 15 November 1998.

5. Illegal drug markets and police corruption

Recognising that '[m]uch of the corruption identified in this inquiry was connected to drug law enforcement' (1997b: 223), the Royal Commission recommended a variety of measures relating to drugs. Prominent amongst these was the establishment of legal 'injecting rooms' (1997b: 226-7) and support for a trial, to be conducted initially in the Australian Capital Territory, of an experiment in providing legal heroin to registered users (1997b: 228-9). These recommendations dominated responses to the Commission's Report, with the Premier effectively rejecting both before its ink was dry.[46] A key influence was the hostility of the tabloid press and talk back radio commentators to 'giving up the war on drugs'.[47] This insistence that any significant drug law reform would open the way to complete decriminalisation paralysed the political process. The tone was set for early discussion of the Report: those who were sceptical about the likelihood of change could point to the Government's dismissal of the Commission's recommendations on this matter. There was some political misjudgment in the Commission's failure to pre-empt this entirely predictable response.

However, Justice Wood's contribution to the drug reform debate did not end with his Report. In his brief speech to the Drug Summit staged by the NSW Government in May 1999, he made a powerful case for trying alternatives to an unsustainable status quo. This was impossible to dismiss as mere tactics of a zealot committed to complete legalisation.[48] Wood's intervention had a significant influence upon the Summit's deliberations and, subsequently, upon Government policy. Cautious as the policies announced in July 1999 were, the inclusion of a trial of a legal safe injecting room symbolised a significant shift in what was politically possible.[49]

In other respects the Commission's discussion of drug policing reflected the practical constraints upon it. There was much good sense in the dismissal of 'rhetoric based upon a "war on drugs"' as 'empty, and incapable of fulfilment' (1997b: 224) and in its endorsement of harm minimisation and its emphasis on the need to develop a strategy of harm minimising law enforcement. Decriminalisation was seen as a matter which could only be properly considered by a 'comprehensive national inquiry' (1997b: 228) but which, in any case, could not provide the

---

46   The headline reporting the release of the Commission's Report was 'Carr's go-slow on drugs' *Sydney Morning Herald*, 16 May 1997.
47   'Legalisation a sign of defeat' *Sunday Telegraph*, 18 May 1998.
48   See NSW Drug Summit, Report of Proceedings of 20 May 1999.
49   'Government Response to the Drug Summit – July 1999'.

panacea which some of its proponents assume. Decriminalisation trips all too easily off the tongue: the difficulties of market regulation which any such move would entail are usually underestimated. In any case, political reality dictates that, for the foreseeable future, the relevant significant question will be how to police prohibition in the most effective, least socially harmful way (Dixon and Maher 1999a; Maher and Dixon 1999). The Commission pays less attention than it might have done to this harsh reality: the prospect here is not of 'breaking the cycle of corruption' but the much less dramatic one of minimising the corruption which continuing prohibitions will foster.

The Commission's understanding of drug policing was limited: it rehearsed the usual distinction between users and suppliers (1997b: 224, 229), arguing that law enforcement should focus on the latter. This was based on several misconceptions about drug markets, most of which stem from the pyramidal model of the drug economy. Contemporary research on drug law enforcement suggests that there is no clear distinction between users and suppliers at street level (see below) and that commitments to targeting suppliers have been ineffective and have usually led to prosecution of minor players (Maher et al 1998). The Commission commended the Police Service's support for harm minimisation (1997b: 226-7). However, it failed to recognise this commitment as a particularly strong example of a problem which elsewhere it saw as characteristic of the Service: a yawning gap between policy and practice. Research suggests that harm minimisation is not understood at operational level and that, in significant respects, drug policing practices currently increase harm, not just to public health, but also to police-public relations (Dixon and Maher 1998, 1999a; Maher and Dixon 1999; Maher et al 1997, 1998). However, the issue is not just familiar problems in policy implementation: at policy level, harm reduction is challenged by other commitments to crime control and order maintenance. The Police Commissioner has stated that 'his strategy is to arrest as many drug dealers and users as possible so the police could gain intelligence to clear up other crimes'.[50] For example, intensive policing in Cabramatta has as its objective the dispersal of the drug market as a way of improving 'quality of life' in the city centre. Such strategies run contrary to harm reduction, and research has indicated their criminogenic and pathogenic consequences (Dixon and Maher 1998, 1999a; Maher and Dixon 1999; Maher et al 1998).

---

50   'Heroin: the main enemy' *Sydney Morning Herald*, 15 May 1998.

6. Police powers

Since the publication of the Royal Commission's Final Report, there has been extensive legislative activity in this area, much of it responding directly to the Royal Commission's recommendations. There is room to choose just three examples: these deal with small-scale drug selling, the detention and questioning of suspects, and street policing powers. Collectively, they illustrate the Commission's excessive reliance on police definitions of problems, inadequate consideration of how police powers affect policing practice, and inappropriate willingness to legalise unlawful police practices.

i. The *Drug Misuse and Trafficking Amendment (Ongoing Dealing) Act* 1998

The *Ongoing Dealing Act* creates a new offence (punishable by 20 years imprisonment) of supplying a prohibited drug in whatever quantity on three or more separate occasions. Its origins were in the work of the Model Criminal Code Officers' Committee (1997: 180-3) and the Royal Commission (Wood 1997b: 229-30). It is a direct product of the inadequate understanding of drug markets and drug policing which has been indicated above. Its particular significance is as an example of incoherence in drug policy and as an illustration of the grip of entrenched, but inaccurate, stereotypes.

The Act's target is the street dealer who takes care not to be found in possession of more than very small amounts of drugs (either by hiding larger amounts in accessible public places or by swallowing drugs when approached by officers). The dealer here is a popular folk devil: someone who profits by pulling innocents into addiction, and who is too crafty for the blunt instruments of the law to catch. The drug dealer is, according to the Premier, 'close to subhuman'.[51] For such a marginal person, the creative response of accumulated penalties seems fully appropriate.

Unfortunately, reality is inconveniently less tidy. People who sell illegal drugs on the streets (of Cabramatta, Australia's principal street-level drug market, at least, and it appears to be the principal target) are not just dealers. They are also, overwhelmingly, users (Maher et al 1997, 1998). As users, they are officially perceived as victims.[52] They are to be the immediate beneficiaries of glossy official commitments to harm

---

51 Bob Carr, quoted 'Crime in the Cross isn't the best but it could be worse' *Sydney Morning Herald*, 23 September 1998.

52 However, the Premier's version is less charitable: see 'Self-indulgent junkies behind rising crime rate, says Carr' *Sydney Morning Herald*, 22 September 1997.

minimisation: they are to be counselled, helped, treated and provided with methadone maintenance and needle exchanges. They straddle the divide between folk devil and victim, yet the *Ongoing Dealing Act* gives complete priority to their identity as dealers. This basic failure to understand the empirical reality at which legislation is thrown shows both the inadequacies of our legislative processes and the insubstantial nature of commitments to harm minimisation.

ii. The *Crimes Amendment (Detention after Arrest) Act* 1997

This long-awaited legislative response to the decision of the High Court in *Williams* (Dixon 1997: ch 5, and ch 3 above) provides police with the authority to detain a suspect for investigative purposes between arrest and charge. Police had, of course, detained suspects for questioning before 1997, but to do so they had had to exploit loopholes in the law, claim that suspects 'voluntarily attended' at stations, or simply rely on magistrates and judges to accept unlawfully obtained evidence. The *Detention after Arrest Act* is, without doubt, much better than proposals in the Bills which preceded it (Dixon 1997c: 223-6). Notably, maximum investigative detention times are specified (although actual detention may be extended by 'time-outs'), some suspects' rights are specified, and a regulatory scheme of some detail has been developed.

The problem is not so much with the legislation per se as with the measures to make this reform effective. First, detailed regulation in codes of practice has been left to the police, rather than being carried out under Parliamentary supervision, as in the English system on which the process is supposedly modelled.[53] Second, the failure to provide public funding for duty solicitor schemes and other legal aid at police stations means that a suspect's right to legal advice will, in most cases, be merely rhetorical. Most suspects cannot afford legal advice and encounter great difficulties in getting legal advisers to come to stations. The usual response to this argument is to say that such legal advice schemes would be desirable, but are impossible within the constraints on the legal aid budget. This is to misunderstand the integral role of legal advice in an effective and efficient justice process. It is like saying we can't afford a whole car, so we'll make do with three wheels and put with the scraping and banging from one corner. Lawyers are not an optional extra. This argument is not

---

53   See the 'Code of Practice for Custody, Rights, Investigation, Management and Evidence' NSW Police Service, February 1998, an unfortunate example of the police obsession with acronyms.

based on any naïve idealism about defence lawyers: having done empirical research on them in England, I am all too aware of their deficiencies (Dixon 1997: ch 6). Nonetheless, the English experience demonstrates the positive contribution that lawyers can make and the potential for action to improve the services which they provide. The Royal Commission claimed that the Bill which subsequently became the *Detention After Arrest Act* 'adopted' the NSW Law Reform Commission's recommendations (1997b: 465). This was superficial to the point of being misleading: the Law Reform Commission had insisted that suspects' rights should be made substantial by the provision of resources, notably legal aid for duty solicitor schemes at police stations (NSW LRC 1990; Dixon 1997: ch 5).

More generally, the problem with the Act is not intrinsic, but rather in how it was presented to and received by the police. Much has been made of the similarities between the *Detention After Arrest Act* and the *Police and Criminal Evidence Act* 1984 (PACE). Implicit in most comparisons is a reference to the beneficial impact which PACE is widely reported to have had on policing in England and Wales (D Brown 1997; Dixon 1997: ch 4). What tends to be inadequately understood is that the impact of PACE was due to a number of contextual factors, rather just than to the intrinsic merit of the provisions. Only the most significant will be noted here (cf Dixon 1997: ch 7).

First, PACE was the product of a long political controversy. It was presented to and received by the police as a major reform, one requiring a significant change in organisational and cultural practices. Second, it exploited tensions within the police between detectives and uniformed officers: giving power and responsibility to dedicated uniform custody officers was a crucial tactic in changing the dynamic of police stations. Third, the courts took seriously the role of policing the police by excluding unlawfully obtained evidence. They did so much more readily than cynics (such as myself) had expected. This was because the effects of police malpractice in investigations was being made clear enough even for the Court of Appeal to see, as in case after case after case it became indisputable that people had been wrongly convicted. (The Birmingham Six and the Guildford Four were merely the most celebrated: see Dixon 1999a.)

None of these factors appears to be present in New South Wales as the *Detention After Arrest Act* is implemented. There has been a long legal controversy, but it has never attracted much public attention. There have been few signals to police that the power which they have been given – to detain suspects before charge for investigative purposes – is of political significance in terms of the relationship between state and citizen. The passage and implementation of the Act raised barely a murmur in the media, while the Police Association used it as a target in its campaign for more resources, presenting it as yet another administrative burden on police officers and a further drain on operational capacity.[54] Second, there is no indication that the custody manager will or is being encouraged to play the active supervisory role of her or his English counterpart. Third, and most significant, magistrates and judges were responsible for tolerating the farce in which police who had no power to detain for questioning did so as normal practice for many years (Dixon 1997: ch 5). There is no reason for optimism that their attitudes have changed significantly. This is because there has not yet been the fundamental challenge to legal complacency which swept through the English justice process in the past decade (Dixon 1999a). New South Wales has had its miscarriages of justice, of course, some of them celebrated and some of them recognised (Carrington et al eds 1991). Yet they have not carried sufficient weight to change entrenched attitudes. This is due in part to some factors deeply entrenched in the cultural politics of crime and justice in New South Wales. The victims of miscarriages have been from the other side of that fissure between us and them, respectable and unrespectable, good people and crims, which defines crime in Australian culture. When victims of miscarriages are political/religious oddities,[55] Aboriginal, socially marginal, or (most often) identified as 'crims', the wrongs done to them simply do not count enough.

iii. The *Crimes Legislation Amendment (Police and Public Safety) Act* 1998

Inter alia, this legislation makes carrying a knife in a public place an offence, extends police powers to stop and search, and provides police with authority to demand the name and address of witnesses and to move people on (so complementing the powers in the *Children (Protection and Parental Responsibility) Act* 1997 to remove young people from public places under certain conditions).

Perhaps the most depressing aspect of the *Police and Public Safety Act* was the air of unreality in which it was produced. While politicians

---

54 'New custody law "takes police off beat"' *Sydney Morning Herald*, 17 February 1998. See also the cartoon on the cover of the Police Association's *Police News* for May 1998, which depicts a custody manager trying to waken a detainee who has gone to sleep while the officer reads out screeds of rights.

55 On the convictions of Tim Anderson, see Chapter 3, Section 6, above.

(goaded by the popular media) played their increasingly ridiculous game of 'My policy is harsher than theirs', there was no public acknowledgment of some basic facts about the way in which street policing has long been conducted in New South Wales. Police regularly stop and 'check' people, recording their details. For example, in the Cabramatta CBD, 16,000 people were stopped and checked between mid 1997 and mid 1998 (Cassidy 1998). Some of these people will be searched. The decision to do so is not determined by the availability of legal powers: it is inconceivable that, before the Act was implemented in July 1998, an officer who had reasonable suspicion that someone was carrying an offensive weapon would not have searched for it. Such searches would be facilitated by the potent combination of the suspect's ignorance of the law, their belief in the power of the police, and their prediction of the likely consequences if they refused. The myth of 'consent' provided an explanation, if such accounting was necessary (Dixon 1997: ch 3). People – particularly young people – were told to move on, to split up, to get off the street, to go home, if they were seen as being in the wrong place at the wrong time. This is common knowledge to anyone who has researched or even casually observed street policing.

Pointing this out does not necessarily imply criticism. Law is one resource in, not the determinant of, street policing (Dixon 1997). Good street policing may be done without extensive legal authority, just as bad street policing may rely on a raft of formal powers. Nor does it mean that the *Police and Public Safety Act* is insignificant: it legitimises police actions and encourages officers to be more active in street policing. But to talk as if it was authorising police to do something that they did not do before was quite misleading.

Equally misleading was the idea that the *Police and Public Safety Act's* prohibition on carrying knives had any direct, general effect. Those outraged respectable correspondents to the Press who complained about having to leave their Swiss Army knives at home missed a rather important, basic point: the likelihood of them being stopped and searched is almost non-existent. The Act creates (despite its form) not general prohibitions and powers, but rather resources for the police to draw upon. With no serious attempt to structure and define reasonable suspicion, it is indeed a generous resource. Perhaps the best comment on this legislation was provided by the Police Minister: 'This is instant law, this is as quick as instant coffee.'[56] Unfortunately, he meant this as a recommendation of the legislation.

---

56   'Whelan and Ryan clash over anti-knife laws' *Daily Telegraph*, 30 April 1998.

iv. Police powers in criminal justice

What unites these three examples is the paucity of the understanding of criminal justice upon which they are based. Making legislation on the back of myths and fictions is a good indication that, despite all the rhetoric to the contrary, politicians do not take issues of law and order seriously. Unless practice in criminal justice is understood, legislation extending police powers is inevitably problematic.

Perhaps the most difficult issue of both principle and practice in this area is the legalisation of conduct by police which was previously illegal or of doubtful legality. As indicated above, several of the new powers do not provide legal conditions for new practices. Rather, they provide legal conditions for longstanding practices.[57] It is vital to recognise this for two reasons. First, the implications of legalising illegalities should be openly considered in terms of the message which doing so sends to a Police Service which is supposed to work within the rule of law. If law merely authorises what police practice determines to be necessary, then the rule of law is devalued. Of course, it has to be acknowledged that the responsibility for police choosing to operate unlawfully cannot be allocated unproblematically to them: in some important instances such as post-arrest detention, legal and political vacillation and negligence left the police with little option. Second, the implementation of new legislation raises particular problems if its function is to regulate an existing practice rather than to introduce a new one. Considerable, specific effort needs to be exerted to ensure that practice is changed. A starting point must be to connect concern about process corruption to proposals for extending police powers, rather than seeing them as confined to separate fields. As the Royal Commission recommended (1997b: 427-8), police powers, currently scattered through various criminal law statutes, are to be consolidated. Unfortunately, it seems likely that this important opportunity for a fundamental review of police powers will be wasted.

Providing police with new powers may be necessary: but doing so without adequately controlling their use or protecting the rights of suspects subject to them is inviting the problems of the past to reproduce

---

57   Note also the *Law Enforcement (Controlled Operations) Act* 1997 which not only responds to the High Court's decision in *Ridgeway* (1995) 129 ALR 41, but goes much further, authorising the Police Commissioner or his Deputy to exclude from criminal liability any action by a police officer 'in the course of and for the purposes of' a controlled operation (s 16). Note also the *Law Enforcement and National Security (Assumed Identities) Act* 1998 which authorises the creation and use of 'assumed identities', notably in undercover operations, by means that would otherwise be unlawful : see Legislative Assembly *Hansard*, 10 November 1998, 18-20.

themselves.[58] As in the case of accountability, the Commission did not deal adequately with an issue has been at the heart of the Service's difficulties. The readiness of Parliament to extend the powers of a police service which so recently was the subject of the Wood Commission's damning critique is consistent with the dominant concern to move on which has been criticised above.

The Government's response to an incident in which a police station was sprayed with semi-automatic gunfire exemplifies the problem. The Police Commissioner, taking advantage of public concern, pressed for new powers. The Premier responded by commenting 'If police can identify another power they need to protect order and public safety, they will get it.'[59] Within days, a Bill providing new powers to establish road-blocks, search cars and demand the identification of drivers and passengers was introduced and was passed soon thereafter.[60] The inspiration was clearly English legislation introduced to counter terrorist activity.[61] The episode provides a notable example of the 'normalisation' of police powers, of reliance on legislating powers as a solution to emergent problems, and of a willingness to allow police to set the agenda for change.

The failure of reform campaigns to endure is common: as noted above, New York and, currently, London provide excellent examples of the cyclical nature of corruption and reform. One reason why reform efforts deteriorate so quickly is the tendency to give priority to other objectives. In New South Wales, the current concern to equip the police with new powers in the war on crime may, paradoxically, be a step down the road towards the next Royal Commission.

---

58   Pressure to restrict the right to silence of arrested suspects (Ryan 1997a) without providing funding for legal advice is a worrying example. On the English precedent for this restriction, see Dixon 1997: ch 6.

59   'Carr gives go-ahead to roadblocks' *Sydney Morning Herald*, 3 November 1998. This commitment was repeated after reports of drug dealing in the Sydney suburb of Marrickville: 'If the police commissioner ever comes to me and says "I need additional powers to arrest drug dealers", it goes without saying he gets those from the Carr Government': see 'No mercy for drug dealers, says Carr' *Sydney Morning Herald*, 12 December 1998.

60   *Police Powers (Vehicles) Act* 1998: see Legislative Assembly *Hansard*, 10 November pp 3-4, 12 November 1998, 45-6; 'Peter's power' *Daily Telegraph*, 11 November 1998. Meanwhile, the Opposition promised to extend the *Police and Public Safety Act*: 'Libs would give police unprecedented power' *Daily Telegraph*, 4 November 1998.

61   *Criminal Justice and Public Order Act* 1994 Pt VI.

7. Corruption as deviance or normality

There was a significant (perhaps contextually inevitable) tension in the Commission's discourse on corruption. On one side, the Commission dismissed 'bad apple' accounts of police corruption (1997a: 26-7) and recognised the structural nature of corruption as produced by the nature of police tasks (Wood 1997a: 28-31), police culture (1997a: 31-3), and the prohibition of goods and services for which substantial demand continues (1997a: 34-6). The Commission recognised that 'corruption within policing tends to be a cyclical phenomenon. Following a period of scandal and disclosure, there comes commitment and reform which lasts for a time, and then the cycle begins again' (1997b: 523).

On the other, the Commission (like so many who before it) was 'animated by a vision of corruption-free government' (Anechiarico and Jacobs 1996: x). Belief in achieving this ideal is a political necessity. Having recognised the structural and cyclical nature of corruption, the Commission insisted that this time it will be different: '[t]he occasion of this Royal Commission, and the strength of the present climate for change, provide an opportunity to challenge the inevitability of that cycle' (1997b: 523). Peter Ryan uses a different metaphor: he seeks 'to draw a line in the sand. I want to leave history where it rightly belongs. While acknowledging that those who do not learn the lessons of the past are condemned to repeat them, I am determined to look forward and go forward. Those who want to dwell in the past are of no value to me or the Service' (1996: 9).

Associated with this was exaggeration of the effects of corruption: the Royal Commission suggested that if process corruption 'is not checked, it will eventually destroy or so destabilise the Police Service and other institutions of criminal justice, such as the Courts, to the point where all confidence in and respect for them is lost' (1996a: 46). Such hyperbole is unhelpful, serving to disguise the really worrying nature and effects of process corruption. Rather than some alien cancer, process corruption has been the normality of criminal justice in New South Wales. It did not threaten to destroy or destabilise the system: it became a functional part of it. It is not helpful to erect an ideal image of the system and to marginalise as deviance what have become regular elements of it, not least because doing so encourages underestimation of the scale of the reform which is necessary. Far from threatening public support and respect for the system, process corruption has given (at least some sections of) the public what it wants. A problem in tackling process corruption has been public support for police who cut corners, as expressed by some juries refusing to convict police officers on charges associated with process corruption (see Dixon 1996b). As Janet Chan's and Mark Finnane's essays in this volume make clear, corruption has to be understood as integral to the cultural and historical construction of policing. It is part of it, not some alien excrescence upon it.

A more realistic approach would be to challenge the bi-polar account of corruption as deviance and abnormality, and the absence of corruption as propriety and normality. The political predilection for the utopia of a society free of corruption appears to be a feature of periods when Royal Commissions and other inquiries are running.[62] As the political moment passes, more modest aims may become more attractive. If corruption cannot be suppressed, then government's realistic aim is to minimise the harm which it causes.[63] The choice of words here is deliberate: there is a valuable comparison to be made between the control of corruption and the control of illegal drugs. Just as suppression has been replaced by harm minimisation as the objective of drug control policy, so we need to be more realistic about what corruption control can achieve. As Peter Ryan says, 'a corruption-free service' is impossible: what he aims for is 'a corruption-resistant one'.[64] This does not express any acceptance of corruption any more than harm minimisation involves acceptance of illegal drug use. It suggests no more than that realism is needed about what can be achieved, that fantasies of suppression are unhelpful, and that considerable work in developing a new understanding of corruption and its control is necessary. If this is not done, it seems very likely that in 10 or 20 years another Royal Commission will be sent out to slay the dragon.

8.   The policing of minorities

In his second interim report, Justice Wood indicated that the policing of minorities was 'an important existing term of reference' (Wood 1996b: 129), referring to the direction to inquire into the 'impartiality of the Police Service . . . in investigating and/or pursuing prosecutions' (Wood 1997c: A38). It was pointed out that such issues are especially important in relation to the disciplinary system and anti-corruption measures because of the particular vulnerability to 'extortion and corrupt conduct'

---

62   I am grateful to Mark Finnane for this observation.
63   See the Royal Commission's comments on the need for 'risk minimisation strategies' (1997a: 41). The Ombudsman described the Police Service's slowness in adopting risk minimisation as 'disturbing' (1998c: 5). Lessons could be learnt from the Chicago Police Department's development of a sophisticated computerised risk assessment: see Kappeler et al 1998: 238-9.
64   Quoted, 'I'll never give up' *Sun-Herald*, 6 June 1999.

of 'some minority or disadvantaged groups ... [who] lack an effective capacity to complain'. It was also noted that 'verbal and physical harassment, insult and intimidation of these groups tends to be more pronounced either because of bias or ignorance of racial, cultural and gender issues' (1996b: 129).

This commitment raised hopes that the Commission would treat racism as a structuring factor which facilitates and entrenches misconduct and corruption.[65] However, the lack of attention to such issues in the Final Report was disappointing.[66] The Final Report did little more than rehearse the connection between lack of partiality and 'the existence of personal attitudes based on race' and other characteristics (1997a: 38), an approach which trivialises racism as an individual (rather than as a structural and cultural) matter. Race was introduced to the section on community consultation in brief and predictable terms: developing a community policing model required 'recognition of social diversity: this is critical in a multi-cultural society' (1997b: 389). In only one case study, the Commission dug a little beneath the surface: this concerns the mistreatment of Ken Jurotte, 'one of a small number of senior Aboriginal police' (1997b: 419) whose problems as a 'whistleblower' were over-determined by racism and prejudice amongst his subordinates, colleagues, and superiors (1997b: 412-19). Even so, the implications of this study were not explicitly woven back into the Report's account or recommendations.

While the limited capacity of the Commission may be acknowledged, it is nonetheless surprising that Cabramatta, the 'heroin capital' of Australia, did not receive the detailed attention accorded to Kings Cross.[67] Our research in the area suggested that, during the Royal Commission's period, there were grounds for considerable concern about practices of police undertaking drug policing (Maher et al 1997, 1998). It also indicated that some unlawful policing practices must be related to relations between police and minority communities: racism is integral, not

---

65 Contrast the identification of institutionalised racism in English policing by the inquiry into the death of Stephen Lawrence (Macpherson 1998).

66 Similarly, see Delahunty's criticism (1998) of the Commission's failure to deal seriously with relations between police and young people.

67 The Report did not purport to be comprehensive, but only as presenting 'snapshots'. It noted that some inquiries were handed on to the Police Integrity Commission (Wood 1997a: 83). Marrickville was the subject of a particular study. The report noted that it has 'a multi-cultural population' (Wood 1997a: 182), but this did not appear as a significant feature in the analysis. The Commission includes a 'case study' of the North West Major Crime Squad which mentions in passing thefts by officers seconded to a task force 'set up to target the explosion of drug dealing in Cabramatta' (1997a: 175-81 at 178).

incidental, to such dealings (Dixon and Maher 1999b). Many young Indo-Chinese people in Cabramatta 'accept' malpractice either because they see no means of redress or because its cost (eg confiscation of drugs or money) is less than the cost of arrest and prosecution. Indeed, some police regarded such seizures and confiscations as a form of 'taxation' (Wood 1997a: 118). Significantly, this is the same term used by young heroin users in relation to the money taken from them by gang members. Not surprisingly, perhaps, some regard the police as a gang: 'they do things like gangs do – take money off people, they tax people, they charge you when they feel like it, don't charge you when they feel like it – they're a gang'.[68]

The Royal Commission's failure to take adequate account of such perceptions meant that its direct contribution to tackling problems between police and ethnic minorities was minimal. One result was that when serious problems between police and groups of young people in South West Sydney were thrown into the spotlight by the attack on Lakemba police station in November 1998 (see above), popular discourse was dominated by clichéd descriptions of the action as 'unAustralian'.[69] The fact that violence (albeit not in this extreme form) was a predictable and predicted (Dixon 1998) outcome of the aggressive street policing operations which preceded it was largely unrecognised (Dixon and Maher 1999b). The intimate relations between police activity, community relations, and disorder could usefully have been explained by the Royal Commission.

9.   The victims of corruption

It has become little more than a cliché to insist that criminal justice pays inadequate attention to the victims of crime. However, the victims of police corruption and misconduct were shadowy figures in the Commission's Report. Only police whistleblowers received direct attention (1997b: 397-421). This is particularly problematic as regards the victims of process corruption. Verballing, loading up, perjury, and related activities had tangible results in the conviction and punishment of innocent people. The Commission recognised this, yet devoted only five pages to discussion of remedying miscarriages of justice (1997b: 485-90). It recommended against the creation of an independent body to review questioned convictions, arguing that the available system was adequate (although needing to be supplemented by additional powers, legal aid,

---

68   Tram Nguyen, Channel 10 News, 10 December 1997.
69   '18 bullets that changed a city' *Daily Telegraph*, 2 November 1997.

and compensation). The Commission relied upon those who had been wrongly convicted to complain. This 'common sense' was simply unrealistic: such people often lack the ability (financial and otherwise) to complain; they lack the faith in the legal system to take their complaints seriously. In such circumstances, relying on complainants to step forward, rather than actively seeking them out, compounded their mistreatment (cf Anderson 1997).

Equally significantly was the symbolic import of the Commission's recommendation. As the Commission noted, the Government had already rejected consideration of a separate body to review miscarriages on the ground that 'there were insufficient cases to warrant that course being taken' (1997b: 488). But if malpractice was as widespread as the Commission reported, then miscarriages must be common and numerous. At play here (in both the Government's statement and the Commission's downbeat treatment) was a belief (connected to broader culture, discussed below) that miscarriages of justice are not a matter of much concern: their victims may not have been guilty of the crime for which they were convicted, but they were probably guilty of something. The absence of these victims in the Commission's Report is similar to their absence from the media.

Symptomatically, on the rare occasion that such victims attracted attention, the *Sydney Morning Herald*'s feature[70] focused on a particularly unattractive complainant, Kym Royall, whom the reporter introduced as 'your criminal from central casting'. This was reinforced by the accompanying photograph, of Royall in a Black Uhlans T-shirt, displaying his heavily tattooed arms. Here, for 'respectable' Sydney, was a nightmare incarnate. Royall's story was presumably attractive to the journalist in that it involved allegations that he had been subjected to verballing and an extortion attempt by police officers in Kings Cross whose notoriety had already been established by the Royal Commission. But as an example of a miscarriage of justice, it was an unfortunate choice. On his own account of the event which led to his imprisonment (the death of his girlfriend), he was, at least, morally responsible. Whatever the motivation of the journalist, the article was likely to confirm that Royall was, in his own words, 'just some crim they thought they could lock up and no-one would care'.[71] Of course, miscarriages of justice do

---

70   'In the frame' *Sydney Morning Herald*, 3 February 1996. The headline of another report – 'Criminals queue up to request retrials' (*Sydney Morning Herald*, 2 July 1997) – made clear its attitude towards those complaining that they were the victims of miscarriages. For a more positive piece, see 'The "framed" queue for freedom' *Sydney Morning Herald*, 21 October 1996.

71   'In the frame' *Sydney Morning Herald*, 3 February 1996.

not usually land on people who have had no previous contact with the law. But as an example which would raise public concern about miscarriages, Royall's was a singly unfortunate choice.

This treatment of the victims of corruption draws attention to the fact that 'the Commission was part of the enterprise, not an external force delivered to put it back on the rails' (Wells 1995: 12). Here, Celia Wells was commenting on the Royal Commission on Criminal Justice (in England and Wales). There are significant similarities between the Wood and the Runciman Commissions. Underlying them is a standpoint inside criminal justice. This conditions the failure to appreciate (far less remedy) the wrongs done to its victims. As Wells suggests, the lack of apology characterises this. So too does the brusque insistence on 'getting on with the job of fighting crime' which has been heard in both England and New South Wales. Some important lessons might be taken from the controversy over the 'stolen generation' of Aboriginal children about the need to say sorry (Krygier 1997).

10. Other players in the criminal justice process

There was an unease running through the Commission's reports about the responsibility of other individuals and institutions in the criminal justice process for the problems which were exposed. As Brown (1998) has demonstrated, on numerous occasions the involvement of other players became an issue; but on each occasion, the matter was not investigated in depth and the logical connection – that some police misconduct is facilitated and encouraged by structures and processes of criminal justice – was not made. While it could legitimately be argued that the Commission's terms of reference did not allow for an already weighty agenda to supplemented by such substantial matters, the failure to connect policing to the sectors of criminal justice which it supplies and services was a serious mistake.

On occasions, a more troubling account is given, in which police were blamed for the ignorance of their criminal justice partners: process corruption 'has escaped the attention of the Judiciary, and of those involved in the prosecution process, from whom the truth has been concealed' (Wood 1996b: 46). Elsewhere, Wood suggested that process corruption was not overlooked, but was 'compounded by . . . members of the judiciary apparently condoning it' (Wood 1997a: 36). If, Wood reported, 'the "police verbal" and "loading" of accused' became 'an art form within certain sections of the NSW Police Service' (1996b: 40), then considerable responsibility should have been sheeted home to those who were so quick to discount such allegations 'as the standard response of a guilty accused' (1996b: 40). The fact that it was not does little to instil confidence in the depth of the reform process. More worryingly, there was no questioning of the assumption that process corruption originates within the police: the possibility that judges, magistrates, lawyers and their professional associations might have responsibility for such corruption either directly or by omission was unexplored. As Brown suggests, 'the police are entitled to feel aggrieved when so much attention is devoted to the pernicious aspects of police culture(s) and at the same time other aspects of the network of legal cultures which connect and overlap with police cultures and practices are ignored or glossed over, the agency and responsibility of powerful players such as the judiciary, prosecutors and the legal profession minimised or denied' (Brown 1998: 237). Having rejected 'bad apple' analyses within the police, the Commission effectively reinstated them at an institutional level: the Police Service as the bad apple which threatens the wholesomeness of the criminal justice barrel. Such metaphors are unhelpful at any level.

There is room for just one example here (for others, see Brown 1998). An extremely important police activity – the investigation of offences between the arrest of suspects and laying charges against them – was substantially unregulated until 1998 (when the *Detention After Arrest Act* was implemented: see above) because policy-makers and legislators ignored the issue for many years despite a High Court decision and reports by the Australian and NSW Law Reform Commissions which made clear the imperative need for reform. Left in this vacuum, police managed by exploiting loopholes in the law and by relying on courts not to exclude evidence obtained from suspects during unlawful detention (Dixon 1997: ch 5; Wood 1997a: 36). The latter point indicates another realm of complicity: magistrates and judges encouraged the police to break, bend and avoid the law by not penalising them for doing so. Lawyers, too, share responsibility, whether it be prosecutors who encouraged police to evade the law or defence lawyers who did not challenge unlawfully obtained evidence and encouraged guilty pleas (notwithstanding Justice Wood's reference to the 'considerable concern within the Defence Bar' about process corruption in the period since 1970 (1997a: 79)).

In such a context, it is hardly surprising if some police officers are cynical about the legal system. When Manning and Redlinger (1977) referred to the 'invitational edges of corruption', they drew attention to the opportunities for and encouragement of corruption which are produced by unenforceable prohibitions of desired goods and services. But structuring a criminal justice process around confessions and guilty pleas, establishing expectations (convictions) without providing appropriate tools (post arrest detention powers) and failing to penalise unlawful conduct during investigations can also properly be regarded as invitations to corruption.[72] A justice process which tolerated or encouraged unlawful investigative detention must bear a substantial responsibility for other elements of 'process corruption'. Yet each time the Royal Commission's Report was taken, by the flow of evidence, to recognise responsibilities beyond the police (as in the case of detention after arrest: see 1997b: 36-7), the analysis was undeveloped, and the point was lost (Brown 1998). Indeed, it is clear that the widespread practice of verballing depended upon judicial credulity and a willingness to turn a blind eye to police malpractice (for reasons to be discussed below). In this respect, the Royal Commission's reports lacked a vital dimension. There must be concern that, if problems are not addressed, they will not go away. This cliché is of particular significance: if experience in England and Wales is any guide, then a change in judicial attitudes towards police practices is a vital precondition of success for any attempt to regulate police investigations (cf Dixon 1997: 169-77; 1999a).

What was seen as an unfair focus on the problems of policing contributed to negative and defensive police responses to the Royal Commission. Janet Chan's research on the socialisation of police recruits reports that almost half of the interviewed probationary constables in the study made negative comments about the Royal Commission, complaining that it led to low morale, that police felt inhibited in their work, that the public saw all police as corrupt, that the Royal Commission had ruined careers and lives, and that it engendered distrust. An inquiry which located the problems of policing in a wider investigation of criminal justice might have enabled a more positive response (Chan 1998).

11. Police culture or political culture?

The suggestion above that responsibility for misconduct must be spread beyond the police requires some analysis of the sources of the problem. The Commission's treatment of some 'external factors that have limited the disclosure of corruption' was brief and inadequate. For example, references to 'the ingrained political concern to contain embarrassment in any area of the public sector' (Wood 1997a: 203) barely touched real

---

72   The external structural pressures distinguish this from other cases where police simply argue for the legalisation of their own unlawful practices.

issues of how corruption is produced and sustained. The discussion of the relationship between 'politics and policing' (1997a 33-4) focused individualistically on corrupt relations between police officers and politicians, concluding that contemporary New South Wales is very different from pre-Fitzgerald Queensland. This implicitly justifies the failure of the Wood Commission to place policing in the context of local political cultures and structures which was a distinguishing feature of the Fitzgerald Report. (1989: ch 3). As Janet Chan's work makes clear, changing police culture requires changing 'the social, economic, legal and political sites in which policing takes place' (1997: 92) and that previous reform efforts have had limited success because their focus was too narrow (1997: 230-3).

While 'police culture' has become virtually a cliché in public discourse, it is necessary to acknowledge that significant elements of what is described as police culture are simply expressions of a wider social and political culture, not least the deep complacency and conservatism of so many criminal justice professionals. Crucial elements of this are a lay criminology which distinguishes between criminals and respectable people and a consequential mandate for the police to protect the latter from the former. If doing so involves cutting corners, so be it: police should not be subject to pettifogging legal constraints. Some argue that police reform is at the cost of crime control: 'when we weeded out the bent coppers, we threw out the baby with the bath water'.[73] So long as policing is directed at 'them' rather than 'us', corruption may be regarded as an acceptable price for efficiency.

This connects with a derisory attitude towards criminal justice politics. New South Wales politicians who misrepresent crime problems, exploit public fears and offer hopeless solutions indicate clearly that they do not – despite their expressions of commitment and concern – take crime and criminal justice seriously. It is treated not as an important and complex area of public administration, but one in which talk back radio is regarded as a more significant guide to policy than are research and official statistics, and in which simplistic slogans ('zero tolerance', 'tough on crime, tough on the causes of crime', et cetera ad nauseam) stand for policy in what Hogg and Brown castigate as 'the uncivil politics of law and order' (1998: ch 1).

---

73   Letter, *Sydney Morning Herald*, 5 November 1998. See also the suggestion that 'a squeaky-clean police force may also turn out to be a supremely ignorant one' in 'Crime gets lost in the big picture' *Sun-Herald*, 8 November 1998.

The Royal Commission attempted to challenge dominant accounts by firmly rejecting the view that process corruption is acceptable (1997b: 427) and in a well-informed critique of the myth that 'if police are given more resources, especially personnel, they will be able to protect communities against crime' (1997b: 247, cf 247-9). Unfortunately, this has been ignored in subsequent political debate, in which commitments to providing more police and diverting police resources into providing a quick response to calls for service have been taken as a litmus test of criminal justice policy.[74] Similarly simplistic conclusions are drawn from an increase in the rate of some recorded crimes. In a vulgar version of Anechiarico and Jacobs' critique of anti-corruption activity, it is suggested that the reform process has reduced the Police Service's efficiency in criminal investigation (Martin 1998). Commissioner Ryan commented that 'the Police Service had "taken its eye off the ball" while it cleaned up corruption within the force and that was the cause of the State's high crime rate'.[75]

> The arrest rates have gone down . . . that's why crime is going up. . . What I have to do is say to the cops: 'Never mind this reform business . . . this is what it will mean to you over time and we'll get there. But for now concentrate on . . . getting crime down'.[76]

Since the Commission reported, a new panacea for policing problems has come on the local market – zero tolerance. It is repeatedly argued that New South Wales should copy the New York Police Department's program which, it is claimed, is responsible for the dramatic fall in crime rates since the mid-1990s. There is room here not for adequate critique (see Dixon 1998, 1999b), but only for the skeleton of an argument. First, the responsibility of the NYPD for the decrease in crime is overstated. Second, the significance of 'zero tolerance' tactics within the NYPD's strategy is exaggerated. Third, the impact that zero tolerance policing has had in New York is unlikely to be replicable in New South Wales because of fundamental differences in law, the role of the state, criminal

---

74 See the response of the Minister of Police, Paul Whelan, to the Royal Commission Report, *Sydney Morning Herald*, 17 October 1997. It has long been established by police research that 'there is no evidence that reducing the time the police take to get to crime scenes increases the chances that criminals will be caught' (Bayley 1994: 6). Nonetheless, response times were the subject of the Audit Office's first study of policing, providing a good example of how audit-accountability is driven by what can be counted, rather than by what is important (cf Audit Office 1998; Power 1997).

75 'Stay out of politics Ryan told' *Daily Telegraph*, 25 September 1997; see also 'Crime is soaring says Ryan' *Sun-Herald*, 21 September 1997.

76 Quoted, 'Get back on the beat' *Sun-Herald*, 21 September 1997; see also Ryan 1997b.

populations and patterns of crime. Fourth, in considering any effect that zero tolerance policing could have, one must be aware of its potentially counterproductive cost. Research on policing operations in Cabramatta which were influenced by New York's experience shows that improving quality of life in the city centre was won at the cost of increasing serious risks to public health, making the drug market more organised and less amenable to control, and harming police-community relations (see Dixon and Maher 1998, 1999a; Maher et al 1998; Maher and Dixon 1999).

The 'New York miracle' has had two effects on discourse about policing in New South Wales which are connected but which need to be distinguished. First, 'zero tolerance' has become a highly effective slogan in law and order rhetoric. Condensing a range of unspecific commitments to harshness in criminal justice, it has been irresistible to politicians and media commentators alike. In this guise, the broader significance of the emergence of 'zero tolerance' is as a vehicle for bypassing the Royal Commission's concerns and agenda for change and reinstating other priorities. Law and order lobbyists resumed their familiar positions in response to a number of specific incidents (murders of police, attacks on elderly, reports of increasing crime rates) which were taken as evidence of crisis. Among these was an industrial dispute on the waterfront to which NSW Police responded with discretion and restraint. Similarly, the Commissioner refused to endorse some public meetings about crime, suggesting that they encouraged excessive fear of crime.[77] These incidents provided the opportunity for some Coalition politicians and sections of the media to end Peter Ryan's 'honeymoon' and to criticise his leadership.[78] There was also embarrassment and uncertainty caused by misunderstandings over police participation in the Gay and Lesbian Mardi Gras,[79] involvement of very senior officers in the PIC's investigation of police networks of influence and possible corruption in Olympics security contracts,[80] allegations of impropriety in the awarding of a major telecommunications equipment contract,[81] questioning of claims that police have reduced crime,[82] and doubts about Ryan's candour

---

77 'Ryan Says Crime Meetings Create Fear' *Sydney Morning Herald*, 13 May 1998.
78 Ibid and 'Not Such an Arresting Situation' *Sunday Telegraph*, 3 May 1998; '"Honeymoon Now Over" for Ryan: Collins' *Sun Herald*, 17 May 1998; 'Ryan under Fire as Crime Fear Grows' *Sydney Morning Herald*, 14 May 1998; 'Making Sense of Crime' *Daily Telegraph*, 18 April 1998; 'When Two for One is Not a Good Deal' *Daily Telegraph*, 2 June 1998.
79 'White Knights to White Ants' *Sydney Morning Herald*, 14 February 1998.
80 'Ryan Cuts Top Cop's Powers' *Sun-Herald*, 24 May 1998.
81 'Radio giant courted our police' *Sydney morning Herald*, 8 September 1999.
82 'Copping it Sweet' *Sydney Morning Herald*, 7 August 1999.

regarding his commitment to New South Wales.[83] It was argued above that the Commission's recommendations on accountability were weakened by excessive reliance on Peter Ryan. However, this should be distinguished from the sometimes virulent criticism of Ryan in the popular media which suggested that the reform process was misguided or counterproductive.[84]

Secondly, and perhaps more significantly, the NSW Police Service is developing a new crime control strategy which draws heavily on the New York experience. Research showed that conventional policing – random patrol and reactive investigation – cannot significantly reduce crime. The lesson taken from this by those who guided change in the NYPD is not that 'nothing works', but rather that policing can be effective if it is specific and adopts a risk management approach. Instead of random patrol and reactive investigation, police should focus their resources on proactive policing of risky people (repeat offenders and repeat victims); risky places; risky property; and risky times. They should do so by directive, involved management which uses computer technology allowing them to map crime patterns over time and place and to direct resources to places, people, and times of greatest risk. The NYPD's Compstat process has been adapted into the NSW Police Service's Operations and Crime Review in which the Commissioner and the Deputy Commissioners examine Local Area Commanders' performance in tackling crime. The OCR involves an admirably high level of managerial involvement and technical sophistication. However, there are grounds for concern about their focus. The very heavy reliance on arrest rates as a measure of officers' productivity undervalues policing which does not prioritise arrests, such as community policing and crime prevention strategies.[85] In England, HM Inspectorate of Constabulary has warned that an 'increasingly aggressive and demonstrable performance

---

83   Soon after expressing his commitment to NSW and negotiating a $110,000 pay rise, Ryan was interviewed for the post of Metropolitan Police Commissioner. The next day, he withdrew his candidacy. While he claimed that he and his wife had decided that 'our future is in Australia', cynics assumed that the decision was made when it became clear that Ryan was not a front-runner for the appointment. See 'Ryan Says No to Top London Job' *Daily Telegraph*, 21 July 1999; 'London Calling' and 'Ryan Has a Bob Each-Way' *Sydney Morning Herald*, 22 July 1999, 'Ryan Pulls Out of Running for Met Chief Post' *Police Review*, 30 July 1999, p 10.

84   For examples, see Martin (1998); cartoons by Warren, *Daily Telegraph*, 10 February and 30 April 1998; 'When Two for One is Not a Good Deal' *Daily Telegraph*, 2 June 1998.

85   NSW Police are clearly influenced by the use in England of auditing in criminal justice. Criticisms of the impact of the Audit Commission's work on policing policy and practice are relevant to developments in New South Wales: see Leishman et al eds 1996; Power 1997.

culture' may lead to 'lapses in integrity' and 'unethical practices' (HMIC 1999: 19). In NSW, officers are encouraged to engage in 'in your face policing'. The other current term, 'firm but fair policing' sounds less aggressive, but unfortunately echoes Richard Nixon's 1968 campaign rhetoric (Marlow and Pitts 1998: 1). It is acknowledged that this kind of policing is likely to lead to more complaints, but consideration of complaints has not yet been built into the OCR process. The Police Service still needs to take seriously the crucial lesson that legitimacy and efficiency are interdependent, that people's cooperation with criminal justice depends heavily upon their perception of the fairness of its processes (Dixon 1999b).

12. Conclusion: changing police?

These comments may be criticised by some for being carping and negative. Such a reaction would fit the dominant mood, in which support for police and a reform process controlled by the police is de rigueur. More generally, it is a further indication of the way that discourse about policing is double-tracked: on one, specific issues are discussed; on another, values and commitments are expressed. There is nothing original about this. However, it needs to be openly acknowledged so that, literally, we know what we are talking about. It may be politically necessary to present each reform process as original and to see corruption as a dragon to be slain. Unfortunately, the record of programs which employ such rhetoric has not been impressive. Perhaps a more modest and considered approach would be better: reform could be seen as a long-term, continuing project, and corruption could be seen as a normal condition (albeit one causing great harm which is to be minimised). However, such a discursive shift would require a much broader change in our politics of law and order at a time when the significant currents are running in the wrong direction. Among the useful functions of the Police Integrity Commission may be the maintenance of the Wood Commission's fine hearing room for use at the next Royal Commission into the NSW Police Service.

Bibliography

Allen, J (1984) 'The making of a prostitute proletariat in early twentieth century NSW', in Daniels, K (ed) *So Much Hard Work: Women and Prostitution in Australian History.* Fontana, Sydney.

Anderson, T (1997) 'Policing redefined', *Framed*, No 8, pp 10-11.

Anechiarico, F and Jacobs, JB (1996) *The Pursuit of Absolute Integrity: How Corruption Control Makes Government Ineffective.* University of Chicago Press, Chicago.

Anon (1991) 'Building integrity and reducing drug corruption' *The Police Chief* (January) pp 27-41.

Arantz, P (1993) *A Collusion of Powers.* Arantz, Dunedoo.

Argyris, C and Schon, D (1985) *Organizational Learning.* Addison-Wesley, Reading, Mass.

Ashworth, A (1994) *The Criminal Process.* Clarendon Press, Oxford.

Audit Commission (1993) *Helping with Enquiries: Tackling Crime Effectively.* HMSO, London.

Audit Office (1998) *Police Response to Calls for Assistance.* Audit Office, Sydney.

Australian Law Reform Commission (ALRC) (1992) *Multiculturalism and the Law.* Report No 57, AGPS, Canberra.

Avery, J (1981) *Police – Force or Service?* Butterworths, Sydney.

Avery, J (1989) 'Issues in police leadership', in Chappell, D and Wilson, P (eds) *Australian Policing.* Butterworths, Sydney.

Baker, H (1997) 'A lesson in transformational leadership', *Management.* May, pp 5-7.

Baldwin, R (1995) *Rules and Government.* Clarendon Press, Oxford.

Baldwin, R and Kinsey, R (1982) *Police Powers and Politics.* Quartet Books, London.

Baldwin, R and Kinsey, R (1985) 'Rules, realism and the police act' *Critical Social Policy*, Vol 12, pp 89-102.

Banton, M (1964) *The Policeman in the Community.* Basic Books, New York.

Barlow, VM and Proctor, C (1980) 'Professionalism and ethics' *Australian Police Journal*, Vol 34, pp 116-29.

Barrett, M (1993) 'Top quality management and whistleblowing', paper presented at Criminal Justice Commission conference on *Whistleblowers – Concerned Citizens or Disloyal Mates?*, November 1993.

Bayley, D (1991) 'Preface', in Goldsmith, AJ (ed) *Complaints Against Police: The Trend To External Review.* Clarendon Press, Oxford.

Bayley, D (1994) *Police for the Future.* Oxford University Press, New York.

Bayley, DH and Mendelsohn, H (1969) *Minorities and the Police: Confrontation in America.* The Free Press, New York.

Bersten, M (1990) 'Police and politics in Australia' *Criminal Law Journal*, Vol 14, pp 302-316.

Birkinshaw, P (1994) *Grievances, Remedies and the State.* 2nd edition, Sweet and Maxwell, London.

Bittner, E (1978) 'The functions of the police in modern society', in Manning, P and Van Maanen, J (eds) *Policing: A View from the Street.* Goodyear, Santa Monica, California.

Bittner, E (1990) *Aspects of Police Work.* Northeastern University Press, Boston.

Blackstone, W (1769) *Commentaries on the Laws of England: Book 4: Of Public Wrongs.* Clarendon Press, Oxford.

Blissett, R (1987) 'Vale CIB' *NSW Police News,* Vol 67, No 10, pp 15-17.

Bolen, J (1997) *Reform in Policing: Lessons from the Whitrod Era.* Hawkins Press, Sydney.

Bongiorno, B (1994) 'A DPP's approach: some problems in the prosecution of police officers', in Moore, D and Wettenhall, R (eds) *Keeping the Peace: Police Accountability and Oversight.* University of Canberra and The Royal Institute of Public Administration Australia, Canberra.

Bottomley, AK, Coleman, CA, Dixon, D, Gill, M and Wall, D (1991) *The Impact of PACE: Policing in a Northern Force.* Centre for Criminology & Criminal Justice, Hull.

Bourdieu, P (1990) *The Logic of Practice.* Stanford University Press, Stanford.

Bourdieu, P and Wacquant, LJD (1992) *An Invitation to Reflexive Sociology.* Polity Press, Cambridge.

Bradley, D (1992) 'Escaping Plato's cave: the possible future of police education', in Moir, P and Eijkman, H (eds) *Policing Australia.* Macmillan, Melbourne.

Bradley, D and Cioccarelli, P (1989) 'Chasing Vollmer's fancy: current developments in police education', in Chappell, D and Wilson, P (eds) *Australian Policing.* Butterworths, Sydney.

Bradley, D and Cioccarelli, P (1994) 'A new accountability: education and the liberation of policing', in Bryett, K and Lewis, C (eds) *Un-Peeling Tradition: Contemporary Policing.* Macmillan, South Melbourne

Bradley, D, Walker, N and Wilkie, R (1986) *Managing the Police.* Wheatsheaf, Brighton.

Braithwaite, J (1992) 'Good and bad police services and how to pick them', in Moir, P & Eijkman, H (eds) *Policing Australia.* Macmillan, South Melbourne.

Braunstein, S and Tyre, M (1992) 'Building a more ethical police department' *The Police Chief,* January, pp 30-34.

Brereton, D (1998) 'The investigative paradigm and the role of research: dealing with the problem of police misconduct', Paper presented to the *ANZ Society of Criminology Conference,* Gold Coast, July.

Brien, S (1996) *Serving the Force: 75 Years of the Police Association of NSW, 1921-1996.* Focus Publishing, Edgecliff NSW.

Brogden, M (1982) *The Police: Autonomy and Consent.* Academic Press, London.

Brogden, M and Shearing, C (1993) *Policing for a New South Africa.* Routledge, London and New York.

Brown, D (1997) *PACE Ten Years On: A Review of the Research.* Home Office, London.

Brown, DB (1997) 'Breaking the code of silence' *Alternative Law Journal*, Vol 22, No 5, pp 220-4.

Brown, DB (1998) 'The Royal Commission into the NSW Police Service: process corruption and the limits of judicial reflexivity' *Current Issues in Criminal Justice*, Vol 9, No 3, pp 228-40.

Brown, DB and Duffy, B (1991) 'Privatising police verbal: the growth industry in prison informants', in Carrington, K et al (eds) *Travesty.* Pluto, Leichhardt.

Brown, MT (1990) *Working Ethics: Strategies for Decision-making and Organizational Responsibility.* Jossey-Bass Publishers, San Francisco.

Cain, M (1973) *Society and the Policeman's Role.* Routledge and Kegan Paul, London.

Carrington, K et al (eds) (1991) *Travesty.* Pluto, Leichhardt.

Carter, DL and Stephens, DW (1991) 'Police ethics, integrity and off-duty behaviour', in Barker, T and Carter, D (eds) *Police Deviance.* Anderson Publishing, Cincinnati.

Cassidy, B (1998) 'Outstanding success of Operation Puccini' *Police Service Weekly*, Vol 10, No 22, pp 4-5.

Centre For Applied Research In Education, (1990) *The NSW Police Recruitment Education Programme: An Independent Evaluation.* Unpublished report, University of East Anglia.

Chan, J (1992) *Policing in a Multicultural Society: A Study of the NSW Police.* Final Report to the NSW Police Service.

Chan, J (1996) 'Changing police culture' *British Journal of Criminology*, Vol 36, No 1, pp 109-134.

Chan, J (1997) *Changing Police Culture: Policing in a Multicultural Society.* Cambridge University Press, Melbourne.

Chan, J (1998) 'Learning the culture: the effects of gender, age and ethnicity on the socialisation of police recruits', Paper to the American Society of Criminology Annual Meetings, November 1997, San Diego.

Chan, J (1999) 'Governing police practice: limits of the new accountability' *British Journal of Sociology*, Vol 50, No 2, pp 251-70.

Chappell, D and Wilson, PR (1969) *The Police and the Public in Australia and New Zealand.* University of Queensland Press, St Lucia.

Cioccarelli, P (1994) 'Moral dilemmas in policing', paper presented to the Australian & New Zealand Society of Criminology conference, Sydney, September 1994.

Clark, A, Wilkinson, M, Snow, D and Suich, M (1978) 'The politics of organised crime' *National Times* 16 September, 18-20.

Clark, G (1991) 'Codes of conduct in theory and practice', in Electoral and Administrative Review Commission, *Record of Proceedings: Public Seminar on Public Ethics, Public Trust – Codes of Conduct for Public Officials.* EARC, Brisbane.

Clarke, RV and Hough, M (eds) (1980) *The Effectiveness of Policing.* Farnborough, Gower.

Cohen, H (1983) 'Teaching police ethics' *Teaching Philosophy*, Vol 6, pp 231-43.

Cohen, HS and Feldberg, M (1991) *Power and Restraint: The Moral Dimension of Police Work*. Praeger, New York.

Cordner, GW (1989) 'Written rules and regulations: are they necessary?' *FBI Law Enforcement Bulletin*, Vol 58, No 7, pp 17-21.

Cossins, A (1999) 'A reply to the NSW Royal Commission inquiry into paedophilia' *Australian & New Zealand Journal of Criminology* Vol 32, pp 42-50.

Criminal Justice Commission (1991) *Report on SP Bookmaking and Related Criminal Activities in Queensland*. CJC, Brisbane.

Criminal Justice Commission (1997) *Integrity in the Queensland Police Service: Implementation and Impact of the Fitzgerald Inquiry Reforms*. CJC, Brisbane.

Cunneen, C and Robb, T (1987) *Criminal Justice in North-West NSW*. Bureau of Crime Statistics and Research, Sydney,

Czarniawska-Joerges, B (1992) *Exploring Complex Organizations: A Cultural Perspective*. Sage, Newbury Park, CA.

Dalglish, C (1991) 'Managing for ethical behaviour in the public sector', in Electoral and Administrative Review Commission, *Seminar Papers: Public Seminar on Public Ethics, Public Trust – Codes of Conduct for Public Officials*. EARC, Brisbane.

Darvall-Steven, R (1994) 'Police codes of ethics in Australia' *Criminology Australia*, Vol 6 No 2, pp 26-31.

Davidow, B and Williams, J (1993) 'Enhancing the ethical culture: the approach adopted by the Roads & Traffic Authority of NSW' *Australian Journal of Public Administration*, Vol 52, pp 376-82.

Davids, C and Hancock, L (1998) 'Policing, accountability and citizenship in the market state' *Australian and New Zealand Journal of Criminology*, Vol 31, pp 38-68.

Davis, KC (1975) *Police Discretion*. West Publishing, St Paul, Minn.

Davis, KC (1977) *Discretionary Justice*. University of Illinois Press, Urbana (1st edition 1971).

Davis, M (1991) 'Do cops really need a code of ethics? *Criminal Justice Ethics*, Vol 10, pp 14-28.

Davis, M (1995) 'Code of ethics', in WG Bailey, ed *The Encyclopaedia of Police Science*. 2nd edition, Garland, New York.

Delahunty, B (1998) 'Taking "Kiddie Cops" and "Care Bears" seriously' *Alternative Law Journal*, Vol 23, pp 13-18.

Delattre, EJ (1989) *Character and Cops*. American Enterprise Institute for Public Policy Research, Washington DC.

Dixon, D (1991) *From Prohibition to Regulation*. Clarendon Press, Oxford.

Dixon, D (1992) 'Legal regulation and policing practice' *Social and Legal Studies*, Vol 1, pp 515-41.

Dixon, D (1996a) 'Illegal betting in Britain and Australia: contrasts in control strategies and cultures', in McMillen, J (ed) *Gambling Cultures*. Routledge, London.

Dixon, D (1996b) 'Reform of policing by legal regulation: international experience in criminal investigation' *Current Issues in Criminal Justice*, Vol 7, pp 287-301.

Dixon, D (1997) *Law in Policing: Legal Regulation and Police Practices.* Clarendon Press, Oxford.

Dixon, D (1998) 'Broken windows, zero tolerance and the New York miracle' *Current Issues in Criminal Justice*, Vol 10, No 1, pp 96-106.

Dixon, D (1999a) 'Police investigative procedures: changing legal and political contexts of policing practices', in Walker, C and Starmer, K (eds) *Miscarriages of Justice.* Blackstone Press, London.

Dixon, D (1999b) 'Beyond zero tolerance', Paper presented to the Australian Institute of Criminology Conference, *Mapping the Boundaries of Australia's Criminal Justice System*, Canberra, 22-23 March.

Dixon D, Bottomley, AK, Coleman, CA, Gill, M and Wall, D (1989) 'Reality and rules in the construction and regulation of police suspicion' *International Journal of the Sociology of Law*, Vol 17, pp 185-206.

Dixon, D, Bottomley, AK, Coleman, C, Gill, M and Wall, D (1990) 'Safeguarding the rights of suspects in police custody' *Policing and Society*, Vol 1, pp 115-140.

Dixon, D and Maher, L (1998) 'The policing of drug offences', in Chan, J, Dixon, D, Maher, L and Stubbs, J *Policing in Cabramatta.* NSW Police Service, Unpublished report.

Dixon, D and Maher, L (1999a) 'Law Enforcement, Harm Minimisation and Risk Management in a Street-level Drug Market'. Paper presented to the Australasian Conference on Drugs Strategy, Adelaide, 27-29 April.

Dixon, D and Maher, L (1999b) 'Walls of silence', in Hage, G and Couch, R (eds) *The Future of Australian Multiculturalism.* Research Institute for Humanities and Social Sciences, Sydney.

Doig, JW (1997) 'Corruption control and its critics', *Criminal Justice Ethics.* Summer/Fall, pp 35-45.

Dovey, J (1954) *Report of the Royal Commission of Inquiry into Certain Matters relating to David Edward Studley-Ruxton.* Government Printer, Sydney,

Downes, D and Rock, P (1982) *Understanding Deviance.* Oxford University Press, Oxford.

Doyle, JF (1992) 'Empowering and restraining the police' *Criminal Justice Ethics*, Vol 11, pp 52-7.

Drew, KJ (1989) 'Criminal investigation: the police perspective' *Current Issues in Criminal Justice*, Vol 1, No 1, pp 46-63.

EARC (1990) *Protection of Whistleblowers*, Issues Paper No 10, Electoral and Administrative Review Commission, Brisbane.

EARC (1991) *Codes of Conduct for Public Officials*, Issues Paper No 15, Electoral and Administrative Review Commission, Brisbane.

EARC (1992) *Report on the Review of Codes of Conduct for Public Officials*, Electoral and Administrative Review Commission, Brisbane.

Egger, S and Findlay, M (1988) 'The politics of police discretion', in Findlay, M and Hogg, R (eds) *Understanding Crime and Criminal Justice.* Law Book Company, Sydney.

Elliston, F and Feldberg, M (eds) (1985) *Moral Issues in Police Work*. Rowan & Allanheld, Totowa.

Ericson, R (1981) *Making Crime: A Study of Detective Work*. Butterworths, Toronto.

Ericson, R (1982) *Reproducing Order: A Study of Police Patrol*, University of Toronto Press, Toronto.

Ericson, R, Baranek, P and Chan, J (1987) *Visualizing Deviance: A Study of News Organization*. University of Toronto Press, Toronto.

Ethics Interest Group (1991) 'Draft code of ethics for public servants ...' Submission to fellow members of RIPAA, unpublished.

Etter, B (1995) 'Mastering innovation and change in police agencies', in Etter, B and Palmer, M (eds) *Police Leadership in Australasia*. Federation Press, Sydney.

Ewin, RE (1990) 'Loyalty: the police' *Criminal Justice Ethics*, Vol 9, pp 3-15.

Felkenes, GT (1984) 'Attitudes of police officers toward their professional ethics' *Journal of Criminal Justice*, Vol 12, pp 211-20.

Fielding, N (1988) *Joining Forces: Police Training, Socialization, and Occupational Competence*. Routledge, London.

Findlay, M and Stewart, A (1991) 'Implementing corruption prevention strategies through codes of conduct' *Current Issues in Criminal Justice*, Vol 3, pp 250-64.

Findlay, M, Odgers, S and Yeo, S (1994) *Australian Criminal Justice*. Oxford University Press, Melbourne.

Finnane, M (1990a) 'Police corruption and police reform: the Fitzgerald Inquiry in Queensland, Australia' *Policing and Society*, Vol 1, pp 159-171.

Finnane, M (1990b) 'Governing the police', in Smith, F (ed) *Ireland, England and Australia: Essays in Honour of Oliver MacDonagh*. ANU and Cork University Press, Canberra and Cork.

Finnane, M (1994) *Police and Government: Histories of Policing in Australia*. Oxford University Press, Melbourne.

Finnane, M (ed) (1987) *Policing in Australia: Historical Perspectives*. UNSW Press, Kensington.

Fitzgerald, GE (1989) *Report of a Commission of Inquiry into Possible Illegal Activities and Associated Police Misconduct*. Government Printer, Brisbane.

Frank, MG, McConkey, KM, Huon, GF and Hesketh, BL (1995) *Individual Perspectives on Police Ethics*. National Police Research Unit, Payneham.

Freckelton, I (1991) 'Shooting the messenger: the trial and execution of the Victorian Police Complaints Authority', in Goldsmith, AJ (ed) *Complaints Against Police: The Trend To External Review*. Clarendon Press, Oxford.

Freckelton, I and Selby, H (1989) 'Piercing the blue veil: an assessment of external review of police', in Chappell, D and Wilson, P (eds) *Australian Policing*. Butterworths, Sydney.

Gardiner, S (1973) *The Commissioner Allan Story*. Tempo, Dee Why West.

Garfinkel, H (1967) *Studies in Ethnomethodology*. Prentice-Hall, Englewood Cliffs, NJ.

Giddens, A (1984) *The Constitution of Society*. Polity Press, Cambridge.

Golder, H and Allen, J (1979) 'Prostitution in NSW, 1870-1932', *Refractory Girl*, December.

Golder, H and Hogg, R (1987) 'Policing Sydney in the late nineteenth century', in Finnane, M (ed) *Policing in Australia*. UNSW Press, Kensington.

Goldsmith, AJ (1991a) 'Introduction', in Goldsmith, AJ (ed) *Complaints Against Police: The Trend To External Review*. Clarendon Press, Oxford.

Goldsmith, AJ (1991b) 'External review and self-regulation', in Goldsmith, AJ (ed) *Complaints Against Police: The Trend To External Review*. Clarendon Press, Oxford.

Goldsmith, AJ (1991c) 'Complaints against the police', in McKillop, S and Vernon, J (eds) *The Police and the Community in the 1990s*, Australian Institute of Criminology, Canberra.

Gorta, A (1998) *Minimising Corruption*. Independent Commission Against Corruption, Sydney.

Gouldner, AV (1954) *Patterns of Industrial Bureaucracy*. Free Press, New York.

Grabosky, P (ed) (1977) *Government Illegality*. Australian Institute of Criminology, Canberra.

Gramsci, A (1971) *Selections from the Prison Notebooks*. Lawrence & Wishart, London.

Greene, JR and Mastrofski, SD (eds) (1988) *Community Policing*. Praeger, New York.

Griffith, G and Simpson, R (1998) *Street Offences and Crime Prevention*. NSW Parliamentary Library Research Service, Sydney.

Grimshaw, R and Jefferson, T (1987) *Interpreting Policework*. Allen and Unwin, London.

Hailsham, L (1981) *Halsbury's Laws of England*. 4th edition, Vol 36, Butterworths, London.

Harding, R (1968) *Police Killings in Australia*. Penguin, Ringwood, Vic.

Harris Research Centre (1993) *Survey of Conflict Customers*. Report for Surrey Police.

Hart, HLA (1961) *The Concept of Law*. Oxford University Press, Oxford.

Hawkins, G (1963) 'The policeman's lot.' *The Bulletin*, 1 June, 15-18.

Heffernan, WC (1982) 'Two approaches to police ethics' *Criminal Justice Review*, Vol 7, pp 28-35.

Henry, V (1990a) *Patterns of Police Corruption and Reform: Comparing New York City and Queensland*. Centre for Australian Public Sector Management, Brisbane.

Henry, V (1990b) 'Lifting the "blue curtain": some controversial strategies to control police corruption' *National Police Research Unit Review*, Vol 6, pp 48-55.

Henry, V (1992) 'Variations in Levels of Cynicism Among Australian Police Recruits as a Function of a Revised Training Program', Unpublished paper.

Henry, V (1994) 'Police corruption: tradition and evolution', in Bryett, K and Lewis, C (eds) *Un-Peeling Tradition*. Macmillan, South Melbourne.

Hilliard, B (1988) 'High spirits in West Mids' *Police Review* 15 July 1988, p 1489.

HMIC (1999) *Police Integrity* London: Home Office and HM Inspectorate of Constabulary.

Hogg, R (1991) 'Identifying and reforming the problems of the justice system', in Carrington, K et al (eds) *Travesty*. Pluto, Leichhardt.

Hogg, R and Brown, D (1998) *Rethinking Law and Order*, Pluto Press, Annandale.

Hogg, R and Hawker, B (1983) 'The politics of police independence', *Legal Service Bulletin*, pp 161-5, 221-4.

Holdaway, S (1983) *Inside the British Police*. Basil Blackwell, Oxford.

Home Office Research and Statistics Branch (1994) 'Special edition: research undertaken for the Royal Commission on Criminal Justice', *Research Bulletin*, No 35.

Huon, GF, Hesketh, BL, Frank, MG, McConkey, K, and McGrath, GM (1995) *Perceptions of Ethical Dilemmas*. National Police Research Unit, Payneham.

Hyams, MT (1991) 'Communicating the ethical standard' *The Police Chief* (October) pp 127-33.

ICAC (1989) *Report on Investigation Relating to the Raid on Frank Hakim's Office*. Independent Commission Against Corruption, Sydney.

ICAC (1993) *Report on Investigation into the Use of Informers*. Independent Commission Against Corruption, Sydney.

ICAC (1994a) *Investigation into the Relationship between Police and Criminals: First Report*. Independent Commission Against Corruption, Sydney.

ICAC (1994b) *Investigation into the Relationship between Police and Criminals: Second Report*. Independent Commission Against Corruption, Sydney.

ICAC (1997) *Monitoring the Impact of the NSW Protected Disclosures Act 1994*. Independent Commission Against Corruption, Sydney.

ICAC/NSW Police (1993) *A High Risk Area: The Management of Criminal Investigations*. Independent Commission Against Corruption/NSW Police, Sydney.

Jackson, G (1988) 'Man or Board: the NSW experience', in Freckelton, I and Selby, H (eds) *Police in Our Society*. Butterworths, Sydney.

Jackson, G (1991) 'Reform of policing in NSW' *Anglo-American Law Review*, Vol 20, pp 15-26.

Jefferson, T and Grimshaw, R (1984) *Controlling the Constable*. Frederick Muller, London.

Johnston, L (1992) *The Rebirth of Private Policing*. Routledge, London.

Joint Select Committee Upon Police Administration (1993) *First Report: the Circumstances which Resulted in the Resignation of the Honourable EP Pickering MLC as Minister for Police and Emergency Services*. NSW Parliament.

Joint Select Committee Upon Police Administration (1993) *Second Report*. NSW Parliament, Sydney.

Jones, T and Newburn, T (1997) *Policing after the Act*. Policy Studies Institute, London.

Jones, T and Newburn, T (1998) *Private Security and Public Policing*. Clarendon Press, Oxford.

Jones, T, Newburn, T, and Smith, D (1994) *Democracy and Policing*. Policy Studies Institute, London.

Kappeler, VE, Sluder, RD and Alpert, GP (1998) *Forces of Deviance: Understanding the Dark Side of Policing*. 2nd edn, Waveland Press, Prospect Heights.

Keith, M (1993) *Race, Riots, and Policing*. UCL Press, London.

Kernaghan, K (1975) *Ethical Conduct*. Institute for Public Administration of Canada, Toronto.

Kernaghan, K (1980) 'Codes of ethics and public administration' *Public Administration*, Vol 58, pp 207-23.

Kleinig, J (1990) 'Teaching and learning police ethics' *Journal of Criminal Justice*, Vol 18, pp 1-18.

Kleinig, J (1993) *Professional Law Enforcement Codes*. Greenwood Press, Westport, Conn.

Kleinig, J (1996) *The Ethics of Policing*. Cambridge University Press, Cambridge.

Kleinig, J ed (1993) 'Loyalty: a symposium' *Criminal Justice Ethics*, Vol 12, pp 56-78.

Krygier, M (1997) *Between Fear and Hope*. ABC Books, Sydney.

Lauer, AR (1994) 'Policing in the 90s: its role and accountability', in Moore, D and Wettenhall, R (eds) *Keeping the Peace*. RIPAA, Canberra.

Lauer, T (1995) 'Nurturing innovative patrol strategies', in Etter, B and Palmer, M (eds) *Police Leadership in Australasia*. Federation Press, Sydney.

LeClere, M (1982) 'Police ethics and conduct' *International Criminal Police Review*, No 358, pp 122-31.

Lee, A (1992) 'Do we need a code of ethics?' *Policing*, Vol 8, pp 172-84.

Lee, J (1981) 'Some structural aspects of police deviance in relations with minority groups', in Shearing, C (ed) *Organizational Police Deviance*. Butterworths, Toronto.

Lee, JA (1990) *Report of the Royal Commission of Inquiry into the Arrest, Charging and Withdrawal of Charges Against Harold James Blackburn and Matters Associated Therewith*. NSW Government, Sydney.

Leishman, F, Loveday, B and Savage, SP (eds) (1996) *Core Issues in Policing*. Longman, London.

Leo, RA and Thomas, GC (eds) (1998) *The Miranda Debate: Law, Justice. and Policing*. Northeastern University Press, Boston.

Lewis, C (1994) 'Independent external civilian review of police conduct', in Bryett, K and Lewis, C (eds) *Un-Peeling Tradition: Contemporary Policing*. Macmillan, South Melbourne.

Lusher, EA (1977) *Report on the Inquiry into the Legalising of Gambling Casinos in NSW*. Government Printer, Sydney.

Lusher, EA (1981) *Report of the Commission to Inquire into NSW Police Administration*. Government Printer, Sydney.

Lustgarten, L (1986) *The Governance of Police*. Sweet and Maxwell, London.

McConkey, KM, Huon, GF, and Frank, MG (1996) *Practical Ethics in the Police Service*. National Police Research Unit, Payneham.

McConville, M (1989) 'Weaknesses in the British justice system', *Times Higher Education Supplement*. 3 November.

McConville, M, Sanders, A and Leng, R (1991) *The Case for the Prosecution*. Routledge, London.

McCormack, RJ (1987) 'Confronting police corruption: organizational initiatives for internal control', in Ward, RH and McCormack, R *Managing Police Corruption*. Office of International Criminal Justice, Chicago.

MacCormaic, S (1988) 'The formative years', *NSW Police News*, January, pp 28-30.

McCoy, AW (1980) *Drug Traffic: Narcotics and Organized Crime in Australia*. Harper and Row, Sydney.

McNee, D (1983) *McNee's Law*. Collins, London.

Macpherson, W (1998) *Report of the Stephen Lawrence Inquiry*, Cm 4262, HMSO, London.

Maguire, M and Norris, C (1992) *The Conduct and Supervision of Criminal Investigations*. Royal Commission on Criminal Justice Research Study No 5, HMSO, London.

Maguire, M, Noaks, N, Hobbs, R and Brearley, N (1991) *Assessing Investigative Performance*. Unpublished report to the Home Office.

Maher, L and Dixon, D (1999) 'Policing and public health: law enforcement and harm minimization in a street-level drug market' *British Journal of Criminology*, Vol 39, No 4, pp 488-512.

Maher, L, Dixon, D, Lynskey, M and Hall, W (1998) *Running the Risks: Heroin, Health and Harm in South-West Sydney*. National Drug and Alcohol Research Centre Monograph, NDARC, Sydney.

Maher, L, Dixon, D, Swift, W and Nguyen, T (1997) *Anh Hai: Young Asian Background People's Perceptions and Experiences of Policing*. UNSW Faculty of Law Research Monograph, Kensington.

Mangan, TJ (1992) 'Organizational integrity critical to law enforcement success' *The Police Chief* (March) pp 47-9.

Manning, P (1977) *Police Work*. MIT Press, Cambridge, Mass.

Manning, P (1978a) 'The police: mandate, strategies, and appearances', in Manning, P and Van Maanen, J (eds) *Policing: A View from the Street*. Goodyear, Santa Monica, California.

Manning, P (1978b) 'Lying, secrecy and social control', in Manning, P and Van Maanen, J (eds) *Policing: A View from the Street*. Goodyear, Santa Monica, California.

Manning, P (1978c) 'Rules, colleagues, and situationally justified actions', in Manning, P and Van Maanen, J (eds) *Policing: A View from the Street*. Goodyear, Santa Monica, California.

Manning, P (1989) 'Occupational culture', in Bailey, WG (ed) *The Encyclopedia of Police Science*. Garland, New York and London.

Manning, P (1993) 'Toward a Theory of Police Organization Polarities and Change', Paper to the *International Conference on Social Change in Policing*, 3-5 August 1993, Taipei.

Manning, P (1997) *Police Work*. Second edition. Waveland Press, Prospect Heights.

Manning, P and Redlinger, LJ (1977) 'Invitational edges of corruption: some consequences of narcotics law enforcement', in Rock PE (ed) *Drugs and Politics*. Transaction, Rutgers, NJ.

Manning, P and Van Maanen, J (eds) (1978) *Policing: A View from the Street*. Goodyear, Santa Monica, California.

Marin, RJ (1991) 'Professionalism and ethics in policing' *Canadian Police College Journal*, Vol 15, pp 291-309.

Mark, R (1978) *In the Office of Constable*. Collins, London.

Marlow, A and Pitts, J (1998) 'Law and order, crime control and community safety', in Marlow, A and Pitts, J (eds) *Planning Safer Communities*. Russell House, Lyme Regis.

Marr, D (1976) 'Reformer Wran's delicate task' *The Bulletin*, Vol 98, No 5031 (6 November) pp 23-25.

Martin, B (1998) 'Ryan's blues' *The Bulletin*, 14 July, pp 36-8.

Massey, D (1993) 'Why us and why? Some reflections on teaching ethics to police' *Police Studies*, Vol 16, pp 77-83.

Mastrofski, SD and Uchida, C (1993) 'Transforming the police' *Journal of Research in Crime and Delinquency*, Vol 30, pp 330-58.

Maxwell, J (1954) *Report of the Royal Commission on Liquor Laws in NSW*. Government Printer, Sydney.

Metropolitan Police (1985) *The Principles of Policing and Guidance for Professional Behaviour*. Metropolitan Police, London.

Metropolitan Police (1989) *The Plus Programme*. Metropolitan Police, London.

Miller, S, Blackler, J and Alexandra, A (1997) *Police Ethics*. Allen & Unwin, Sydney.

Milner, NA (1974) 'Supreme Court effectiveness and the police organisation', in Westart, JC (ed) *Police Practices*. Oceana, Dobbs Ferry.

Model Criminal Code Officers' Committee (1997) *Serious Drug Offences*. MCCOG, Canberra.

Moffitt, A (1974) *Report of the Royal Commission into Organised Crime in Clubs in NSW*. Government Printer, Sydney.

Mollen, M (1994) *Report of the Commission to Investigate Allegations of Police Corruption and the Anti-Corruption Procedures of the Police Department*. Mollen Commission, New York.

Moore, DB (1991) 'Origins of the police mandate: the Australian case reconsidered' *Police Studies*, Vol 4, p 107-20.

Moore, E (1991) 'Codes of conduct in theory and practice', in Electoral and Administrative Review Commission, *Record of Proceedings: Public Seminar on Public Ethics, Public Trust – Codes of Conduct for Public Officials*. EARC, Brisbane.

Moore, MH (1992) 'Problem-solving and community policing', in Tonry M and Morris N (eds) *Modern Policing*. Chicago UP, Chicago.

Moore, MH and Stephens, DW (1991) *Beyond Command and Control*. Police Executive Research Forum, Washington DC.

Morgan, G (1986) *Images of Organization*. Sage, Newbury Park, CA.

Morgan, R and Newburn, T (1997) *The Future of Policing*. Clarendon Press, Oxford.

Morin Commission (1976) *Gambling in America: Final Report of the Commission on the Review of the National Policy Towards Gambling*. US Government Printing Office, Washington DC.

Morris, N and Hawkins, G (1970) *The Honest Politician's Guide to Crime Control*. University of Chicago Press, Chicago.

Morton, J (1993) *Bent Coppers: A Survey of Police Corruption*. Warner, London.

Moss, I (1998) 'Using complaints to improve policing', Paper for the Sydney Institute of Criminology seminar on *Police Powers and Practices*, August.

Mugford, S (1992) 'Policing euphoria', in Moir, P and Eijkman, H (eds) *Policing Australia*. Macmillan, South Melbourne.

Muir, WK (1977) *Police: Streetcorner Politicians*. University of Chicago Press, Chicago.

Nadelmann, EA (1992) 'Thinking seriously about alternatives to drug prohibition', *Daedalus*, No 121, pp 85-132.

National Crime Faculty (1998) *A Practical Guide to Investigative Interviewing*. NCF, Bramshill.

Newburn, T (1999) *Understanding and Preventing Police Corruption*. Home Office, London.

Newnham, N (1992) 'Reform of the police', in Hede, A, Prasser, S and Neylan, M (eds) *Keeping Them Honest*. Queensland University Press, St Lucia.

Newton, T (1995) 'The place of ethics in investigative interviewing by police officers', paper presented to the British Criminology Conference, Loughborough University.

Niederhoffer, A (1967) *Behind the Shield*. Doubleday, Garden City, New York.

Norman, RG (1988) 'Creating a basic value statement' *The Police Chief* (October), Vol 15, pp 66-7.

Northumbria Police (1994) *Report of an Enquiry into the Practices and Procedures adopted by Police Officers during Interviews with George Robert Thomas Heron following the Murder of Nikki Davie Allan*. Northumbria Police, Ponteland.

Norton, J (1991) 'Code of conduct: some implications for administration', in Electoral and Administrative Review Commission, *Seminar Papers: Public Seminar on Public Ethics, Public Trust – Codes of Conduct for Public Officials*. EARC, Brisbane.

NSW LRC (1990) *Criminal Procedure: Police Powers of Detention and Investigation after Arrest*. Report 66. NSW Law Reform Commission, Sydney.

NSW Ombudsman (1993) *Inquiry into the Circumstances Surrounding the Injuries Suffered by Angus Rigg*. NSW Ombudsman, Sydney.

NSW Ombudsman (1998a) *Police Adversely Mentioned at the Police Royal Commission*. NSW Ombudsman, Sydney.

NSW Ombudsman (1998b) *Annual Report 1997-1998*. NSW Ombudsman, Sydney.

NSW Ombudsman (1998c) *Risk Assessment of Police Officers.* NSW Ombudsman, Sydney.

NSW Police (1988) *NSW Police Service 1984 to 1988 to...* NSW Police Service, Sydney.

NSW Police (1994) *Australian Quality Award Application.* NSW Police Service, Sydney.

NSW Police (1995) *Comprehensive Review of Criminal Investigation.* NSW Police Service, Sydney.

NSW Police Department, *Annual Report,* 1960, 1964, 1969, 1970, 1971, 1975, 1980.

O'Hara, J (1988) *A Mug's Game: A History of Gaming and Betting in Australia.* NSW University Press, Kensington.

Odgers, S (1990) 'Police interrogation: a decade of legal development' *Criminal Law Journal,* Vol 14, pp 220-48.

Offer, C (1994) 'Do the police need a code of ethics?' *Royal Canadian Mounted Police Gazette,* Vol 56, pp 1-7.

Ouchi, WG and Wilkins, AL (1985) 'Organizational culture' *Annual Review of Sociology,* Vol 11, pp 457-83.

Page, R and Swanton, B (1983) 'Complaints against police in NSW' *Australian Journal of Public Administration,* Vol 42, No 4, pp 503-28.

Pike, MS (1985) *The Principles of Policing.* Macmillan, London.

Plehwe, R (1973) 'Some aspects of the constitutional status of Australian police forces' *Public Administration,* Vol 3, pp 32-44.

Plehwe, R and Wettenhall, R (1979) 'Reflections on the Salisbury affair: police-government relations in Australia' *Australian Quarterly,* Vol 51, pp 75-89.

Police Integrity Commission (1997) *Annual Report 1996-1997.* PIC, Sydney.

Police Integrity Commission (1998) *Report to Parliament: Operation Jade.* PIC, Sydney.

Pollock-Byrne, JM (1988) 'Teaching criminal justice ethics' *The Justice Professional,* Vol 3, pp 283-97.

Powell, WW and DiMaggio, PJ (ed) (1991) *The New Institutionalism in Organizational Analysis.* University of Chicago Press, Chicago.

Power, M (1997) *The Audit Society.* Clarendon Press, Oxford.

Prenzler, T (1997) 'The decay of reform: police and politics in post-Fitzgerald Queensland' *Queensland Review,* Vol 4, No 2, pp 13-25.

Prenzler, T, Harrison, A, and Ede, A (1996) 'The Royal Commission into the NSW Police Service' *Police News,* November, pp 47-53.

Preston, N (1992) 'Can virtue be regulated? An examination of the EARC proposals for a code of conduct for public officials in Queensland' *Australian Journal of Public Administration,* Vol 51, pp 410-15.

Preston, N (1995) 'Queensland legislates for a new code of ethics' *Directions in Government,* (February) 17-18, 25.

Punch, M (1985) *Conduct Unbecoming: The Social Construction of Police Deviance and Control.* Tavistock, London.

RCPPP (1929) *Report of the Royal Commission on Police Powers and Procedure.* Cmd.3297, HMSO, London.

Reiner, R (1992) *The Politics of the Police*. Second edition Harvester Wheatsheaf, Hemel Hempstead.

Reuss-Ianni, E and Ianni, F (1983) 'Street cops and management cops: the two cultures of policing', in Punch, M (ed) *Control in the Police Organisation*. MIT Press, Cambridge, Mass.

Robinette, HM (1991) 'Police ethics' *The Police Chief* (January) 42-7.

Rogan, P (1986) *Report of the Select Committee of the Legislative Assembly upon Prostitution*. Parliament of NSW, Sydney.

Rohr, JA (1989) *Ethics for Bureaucrats*. 2nd edition, Marcel Dekker, New York.

Ryan, P (1996) *Reform of the NSW Police Service – Phase 1* Parliament of NSW, 2nd session, 1996-97, PP 199.

Ryan, P (1997a) 'Address to Law Week Seminar', Sydney, May.

Ryan, P (1997b) 'Crime, property and society' *The Sydney Papers* Vol 7 No 4, pp 100-103.

Sackmann, S (1991) *Cultural Knowledge in Organizations*. Sage, Newbury Park, CA.

Sacks, H (1978) 'Notes on police assessment of moral character', in Manning P and Van Maanen J (eds) *Policing: A View from the Street*. Goodyear, Santa Monica, California.

Sampford, C (1992) 'Maintaining an ethical and responsible government sector: legal regulation, ethical standard setting and institutional design', paper presented to CJC conference on *Corruption Prevention and Fraud Risk Assessment in the Public Sector*, Brisbane, 26 May 1992.

Scarman, L (1981) *The Brixton Disorders*. HMSO, London.

Schein, EH (1985) *Organizational Culture and Leadership*. Jossey-Bass, San Francisco.

Scott, WR (1966) 'Professionals in bureaucracies – areas of conflict', in Vollmer, HM and Mills, DL (eds) *Professionalization*. Prentice Hall, Englewood Cliffs, NJ.

Seggie, K (1988) 'Aspects of the Role of the Police Force in NSW and its Relation to the Government, 1900-1930', PhD thesis, Macquarie University.

Shearing, C (1981) 'Deviance and conformity in the reproduction of order', in Shearing, C (ed) *Organisational Police Deviance*. Butterworths, Toronto.

Shearing, CD and Ericson, RV (1991) 'Culture as figurative action' *British Journal of Sociology*, Vol 42, pp 481-506.

Shepherd, E (1991) 'Ethical interviewing' *Policing*, Vol 7, pp 42-60.

Sherman, LJ (1982) 'Learning police ethics' *Criminal Justice Ethics* Vol 1, pp 10-19.

Sherman, LJ (1987) *Controlling Police Corruption*. National Institute of Law Enforcement and Criminal Justice, Washington DC.

Sherman, LW (1974a) 'Towards a sociological theory of police corruption', in Sherman, LW (ed) *Police Corruption: A Sociological Perspective*. Anchor Books, New York.

Sherman, LW (1974b) 'Explanation and policy recommendations', in Sherman, LW (ed) *Police Corruption: A Sociological Perspective*. Anchor Books, New York.

Sherman, LW (1978) *Scandal and Reform*. University of California Press, Berkeley.

Sherman, LW (ed) (1974) *Police Corruption: A Sociological Perspective*. Anchor Books, New York.

Shernock, SK (1990) 'The effects of patrol officers' defensiveness towards the outside world on their ethical orientations', *Criminal Justice Ethics*, Vol 9, pp 24-42.

Simpson, R (1998) *Initial Responses to the Wood Royal Commission Report on Paedophilia*. NSW Parliamentary Library Research Service Briefing Paper 8/98, Sydney.

Skolnick, J (1966) *Justice Without Trial*. John Wiley and Sons, New York.

Skolnick, J (1972 and 1992) 'Changing conceptions of the police', *Great Ideas Today*. Encyclopaedia Britannica, Chicago.

Skolnick, J and Fyfe, J (1993) *Above the Law: Police and the Excessive Use of Force*. The Free Press, New York.

Smith, D (1994) 'The political and social constraints to reform', in Bryett, K and Lewis, C (eds) *Un-Peeling Tradition: Contemporary Policing* Macmillan, Melbourne.

Smith, DJ (1986) 'The framework of law and policing practice', in Benyon, J and Bourn, C (eds) *The Police*. Pergamon, Oxford.

Sparrow, MK, Moore, MH and Kennedy, DM (1990) *Beyond 911: A New Era for Policing*. Basic Books, New York.

Stewart, J (1983) *Report of the Royal Commission of Inquiry into Drug Trafficking*. AGPS, Canberra.

Swanton, B and Hoban, L (1990) 'Frederick John Hanson, CBE, QPM, 11th Commissioner of NSW Police' *NSW Police News*, Vol 70, No 12, pp 29-33.

Taylor, L (1997) 'Interview with Mr Justice Wood' *NSW Police News*, July, pp 15, 17, 19-21, 23.

Tendler, S (1988) 'Nothing you want to know about everything', *Police Review* 15 July 1988, p 1488.

Van Maanen, J (1974) 'Working the street: a developmental view of police behaviour', in Jacobs, J (ed) *The Potential for Reform of Criminal Justice*. Sage, Beverley Hills, Cal.

Van Maanen, J (1978a) 'Kinsmen in repose: occupational perspectives of patrolmen', in Manning P and Van Maanen, J (eds) *Policing: A View from the Street*. Goodyear, Santa Monica, California.

Van Maanen, J (1978b) 'The asshole' in Manning, P and Van Maanen, J (eds) *Policing: A View from the Street*. Goodyear, Santa Monica, California.

Van Maanen, J (1983) 'The Boss: first-line supervision in an American police agency', in Punch, M (ed) *Control in the Police Organization*. MIT Press, Cambridge, Mass.

Victoria Police (1988) *Ethics and Professional Standards*. Victoria Police, Melbourne.

von Hirsch, A and Ashworth, A (eds) (1998) *Principled Sentencing*. Hart Publishing, Oxford.

Wakefield, S (1976) 'Ethics and the public service' *Public Administration Review*, Vol 36, pp 661-8.

Walker, R (1984) 'The NSW Police Force, 1862-1900' *Journal of Australian Studies*, Vol 15, pp 25-39.

Walker, R (1986) 'Violence in industrial conflicts in NSW in the late nineteenth century' *Historical Studies*, Vol 22, pp 54-70.

Walker, S (1993) *Taming the System: The Control of Discretion in Criminal Justice.* Oxford University Press, New York.

Ward, RH and McCormack, R (1987) 'An anti-corruption manual for administrators in law enforcement', in Ward, RH and McCormack, R *Managing Police Corruption.* Office of International Criminal Justice, Chicago.

Weick, K (1969) *The Social Psychology of Organising.* Addison-Wesley, Reading, Mass.

Wells, C (1995) 'What Runciman didn't say', in Attwooll, A and Goldberg, D (eds) *Criminal Justice.* Franz Steiner Verlag, Stuttgart.

Westley, W (1970) *Violence and the Police.* MIT Press, Cambridge, Mass.

Whyte, WF (1943) *Street Corner Society.* University of Chicago Press, Chicago.

Wilkinson, M (1979) 'Police corruption: what the secret dossier says', *National Times*, 10-16 June, p 10.

Willingham, M and Tucker, ML (1988) 'Ethics and values training: a multifaceted approach', *The Police Chief* (November) 70-1.

Wilson, JQ (1968) *Varieties of Police Behaviour.* Harvard University Press, Cambridge, Mass.

Wilson, JQ (1978) 'The police and crime', in Manning, P and Van Maanen, J (eds) *Policing: A View from the Street.* Goodyear, Santa Monica, California.

Wood, JRT (1996a) *Interim Report of the Royal Commission into the NSW Police Service.* RCNSWPS, Sydney.

Wood, JRT (1996b) *Interim Report of the Royal Commission into the NSW Police Service: Immediate Measures for the Reform of the Police Service of NSW.* RCNSWPS, Sydney.

Wood, JRT (1997a) *Final Report of the Royal Commission into the NSW Police Service: Volume 1: Corruption.* RCNSWPS, Sydney.

Wood, JRT (1997b) *Final Report of the Royal Commission into the NSW Police Service: Volume 2: Reform.* RCNSWPS, Sydney.

Wood, JRT (1997c) *Final Report of the Royal Commission into the NSW Police Service: Volume 3: Appendices.* RCNSWPS, Sydney.

Wood, JRT (1997d) *Final Report of the Royal Commission into the NSW Police Service: Volume 4: The Paedophile Inquiry.* RCNSWPS, Sydney.

Wood, JRT (1999) 'Issues impacting upon corruption investigation in the Australian environment.' Paper presented to 8th Annual Internal Investigations Conference, 2 September 1999, Sydney.

Woodward, J (1979) *Report of the Royal Commission into Drug Trafficking.* Government Printer, Sydney.

Wootten, JH (1991) *Report of the Inquiry into the Death of David John Gundy.* Royal Commission into Aboriginal Deaths in Custody, Canberra.

Wortley, R (1993) 'The Limits of Police Education', Paper presented at the Conference, *Police Education in Australia: The Way Ahead.* 6-7 April 1993, Brisbane.

Wortley, R (1995) 'Police prejudice as a function of training and outgroup contact: a longitudinal investigation' *Law and Human Behavior*, Vol 19, No 3, pp 305-317.

Wotherspoon, G (1989) ' "The greatest menace facing Australia": homosexuality and the state in NSW during the cold war' *Labour History*, Vol 56, pp 15-28.

Wren, TE (1985) 'Whistleblowing and loyalty to one's friends', in Heffernan, WC et al (eds) *Police Ethics: Hard Choices in Law Enforcement.* John Jay Press, New York.

Index

Aboriginal Deaths in Custody Royal Commission, 43

Aborigines, 27, 34, 172

Allan, Norman, 10, 13-17

Allen, Bill, 25

Anderson, Tim, 47-48

'Appendix 31', 148

Arantz, Phillip, 14-15

Askin, Robert, 15, 18-19

Avery, John, 2, 11, 24-26, 70

Canada, 116, 155

Carr, Bob, 154, 166

***Children (Protection and Parental Responsibility) Act* 1997 (NSW)**, 163

Codes of ethics, 70-73, 82-84
    codes of practice, 75-77
    drafting, 79-81
    enforcement of, 77-79
    "professionalism", and, 85-87
    uniqueness of police, 73-75

Community relations, 24, 87
    community consultation, 155-57
    police service, need for, 24-28
    "social contract", 88

Corruption, 64-68
    deviance or normality, as, 167-68
    drugs, and, 65-66, 158-61
    gambling, and, 62-64
    "good cause" and "process", attitudes to, 44-46
    public inquiries, and, *see* Inquiries
    victims of, 170-72
    see also New South Wales Police Service; Police accountability;
        Wood Royal Commission

***Crimes Amendment (Detention after Arrest) Act* 1997 (NSW)**, 161-63

Criminal Justice Commission, 32

***Criminal Justice and Public Order Act* 1994 (NSW)**, 166

Criminal justice system, 122, 172-74
    cynicism towards, 89
    internal organisation, 123-26
    police, active role of, 126-28
    police powers, and, 165-66
    see also Community relations; Corruption

***Crimes Legislation Amendment (Police and Public Safety) Act* 1998 (NSW)**, 163-64, 166

Delaney, Commissioner, 11-13, 17

Drug markets, 61-62, 158-61, 176-77

***Drug Misuse and Trafficking Amendment (Ongoing Dealing) Act* 1998 (NSW)**, 160-61

England, 40, 44, 49, 62, 90, 94-96, 145-46, 155-56, 178

External oversight bodies, 2, 130

Fitzgerald Report, 103, 119, 144

Hanson, Fred, 19

Hatton, John, 1-2

Her Majesty's Inspectorate of Constabulary, 178

Homosexuality, 11-12

Independent Commission Against Corruption (ICAC), 130, 144

Inquiries, 29
        Blackburn inquiry, 44, 46-47
        ICAC's Milloo inquiry, 32
        Lusher inquiry, 20-24, 31
        Moffitt Commission, 30
        Select Committee on Prostitution, 30-31
        Stewart Commission, 30
        Wood Commission *see* Wood Royal Commission

Investigative practices, 67-68
        "case theory" strategy, 46-48
        informants, use of, 51
        reforming, 50-51
        see also Legal regulation

Lauer, Tony, 2-3, 91

Legal regulation
        attitudes to, 43-44
        illegal markets, of, 61-67, 121
        investigative detention, of, 39-43
        policing practice, of, 49-50, 96-97
        see also Investigative practices; Police accountability; Police reform; Rules and regulations

MacKay, WJ, 9-11

McKell, WJ, 9

Managerialism, 148-52

Markell, Judge, 9

Media, 139-40

Minorities, 141, 168-70

Miscarriages of justice, 170-72

Moffitt, Justice, 18

New South Wales Crime Commission, 144

New South Wales Law Reform Commission, 162

New South Wales Police Service
    attitudes to law, 37-39
    closed archives, 6
    corporate identity, 11
    corruption and reform, 28-35
    Labor government, and, 26
    1960s, 13, 17
    1970s, 14-24, 33
    1980s, 1, 24-27
    1990s, 27-28
    pre-1960s, 7-13
    specialisation of functions, 10
    see also Police Board; Police reform

New York, 65, 140, 146, 176-78

Ombudsman, 2, 18, 33, 130, 144
    enhanced powers, 25

Police accountability, 52-55
    complaints procedures, 55-61
    Mollen Commission, 57-59
    parliamentary accountability, 152-55

Police administration
    complacency, 19
    police functions, regionalisation of, 26
    standards of, 15
    see also Police Board; Police reform; Rules and regulations; Wood
        Royal Commission

Police Association, 18-19, 34, 139

Police Board, 2, 23-25, 153

Police Boys Club, 11

***Police and Criminal Evidence Act* 1984 (England and Wales)**, 49-50, 94-97

Police culture, 10, 81, 135-37
    assumptions about, 100-01
    characteristics of, 99
    cultural change, prospects for, 129-31
    definition, 98
    Fitzgerald Report, 103
    Mollen Report, 104-05, 125-26, 145
    multiple cultures, existence of, 115-17
    organisational culture, and, 101-03
    police practice, affect on, 105, 117-18
    police cultural knowledge, 106-11
    political context, 119-21, 174-79
    transmission of culture, 111-15
    see also Police reform; Professional policing

Police education, 42, 82-83, 154

Police Integrity Commission, 56, 140-41, 144, 179

Police powers, 55, 160-66
> 1920s statutory reform, 8-9
> abuse of, 15, 88
> criminal justice, in, 165-66
> discretions, 102
> police service, need for, 24-28
> significance of, 88-89
> *see also* Investigations; Police culture; Police reform

***Police Powers (Vehicles) Act* 1998 (NSW)**, 166

***Police and Public Safety Act* 1998 (NSW)**, 157

Police reform, 139, 147-48
> community consultation, 155-57
> managing policing, 148-52
> parliamentary accountability, 152-55
> Police Integrity Commission, 144
> Wood Royal Commission, ignoring, 141
> *see also* ICAC; Ombudsman; Wood Royal Commission

***Police Regulation Amendment Act* 1964 (NSW)**, 64

***Police Service Act* 1990 (NSW)**, 27, 36, 69, 71, 73

Police training, 2, 24, 82, 112-13

Police unions, 8-9

Professional policing, 85-87, 131-35

Promotion
> merit, by, 104
> seniority, by, 9, 24

***Protected Disclosures Act* 1994 (NSW)**, 74

***Public Sector Ethics Act* 1994 (Qld)**, 69

Queensland, 29, 57, 70, 112, 128, 140

Rules and regulations, 89-91
> discretion, and, 92-94
> professionalism, and, 92

Ryan, Peter, 153, 156, 167-68, 177-78

United States of America, 65, 72-73, 82, 90, 104, 116, 125-26, 130, 140, 145, 176-78

Urquhart, Hon PD, 2

Victims of corruption, 170-72

Victorian Police Complaints Authority, 56

Wood, Hon JRT, 2, 5, 139, 141

Wood, Mervyn, 19-20

Wood Royal Commission, 2, 28, 34, 138-42, 145-48
> community consultation, 155-57
> managing policing, 148-52
> parliamentary accountability, 152-55

Wran, Neville, 18-20